W9-ASF-678

WITHDRAWN

# A STAR-WHEELED SKY

JAN 1 8 2019

**BAEN BOOKS by
BRAD R. TORGERSEN**

*The Chaplain's War*
*A Star-Wheeled Sky*

# A STAR-WHEELED SKY

# BRAD R. TORGERSEN

WITHDRAWN

WHITCHURCH-STOUFFVILLE PUBLIC LIBRARY

A STAR-WHEELED SKY

This is a work of fiction. All the characters and events portrayed in this book are fictional, and any resemblance to real people or incidents is purely coincidental.

Copyright © 2018 by Brad R. Torgersen

All rights reserved, including the right to reproduce this book or portions thereof in any form.

A Baen Books Original

Baen Publishing Enterprises
P.O. Box 1403
Riverdale, NY 10471
www.baen.com

ISBN: 978-1-4814-8362-9

Cover art by Alan Pollack

First Baen printing, December 2018

Distributed by Simon & Schuster
1230 Avenue of the Americas
New York, NY 10020

10  9  8  7  6  5  4  3  2  1

Pages by Joy Freeman (www.pagesbyjoy.com)
Printed in the United States of America

To Toni Weisskopf and Tony Daniel, of Baen Books—
both of whom were more patient with me than I deserved.


And to Dr. Stanley Schmidt, who edited my first
readers' choice award-winning story at *Analog* magazine.
Stan played a large part in not only my genesis as a Hard
Science Fiction author, but me becoming a Baen man too.

# A STAR-WHEELED SKY

# PROLOGUE

THE MONITOR *DAFFODIL* WAS FAIRLY STANDARD FOR HER CLASS: just thirty-seven crew, all packed into tight living conditions, with most of the ship's space given over to mammoth tanks for both fuel and reaction mass. She hung in space well outside her Waypoint's transit radius, far beyond the flotilla of security ships which patrolled the Waypoint's perimeter.

Unlike the rest of the watch fleet, *Daffodil* possessed minimal weaponry. In the event that a hostile force emerged from the Waypoint, *Daffodil* had exactly one job: leave the flotilla to do the fighting, and hie to the planets of the inner system. If she were to be jammed or intercepted, *Daffodil* possessed a dozen high-gee launches which could sprint ahead of the mothercraft. All it took was for one launch to come within broadcast range of the command force, thus sounding the alarm.

*Daffodil* herself—and all of her crew—were deemed expendable.

The Constellar office of Deep Space Operations and Defense ensured that all of *Daffodil*'s crew were accorded commensurate hazard pay.

Moreover, to do the job right, *Daffodil* had that rarest and most expensive piece of equipment: a Key. The Key was the only way to alert the attendant security flotilla that their Waypoint was in use—gaining precious seconds of time which might make the difference between victory and defeat.

Presently, *Daffodil*'s on-shift Waypoint pilot was tucked into his gee chair. The half-meter-sized spherical Key itself was mounted

1

in the center of a control console over the Waypoint pilot's knees. Unlike the people actually flying *Daffodil*, the Waypoint pilot was oblivious to his ship's relative attitude and velocity in relation to the orbital plane of the system's primary sun. His mind was focused purely on the Waypoint itself, as well as the other Waypoints he could sense through *Daffodil*'s single Key.

His eyes were closed, and his hands moved across the Key's impossibly smooth, alien surface. It was mentally exhausting work. Waypoint pilots took triple downtime as a result. Without sufficient sleep and recovery, constant use of a Key would drive most men mad. Likewise, the aptitude tests—for Key training—had a steep failure rate. Perhaps one individual in a hundred showed any ability for the vocation. Something to do with the Keys not being originally built to interface with human minds. Or so the schoolmasters said.

*Daffodil*'s on-shift Waypoint pilot was nearing the end of his day. As always at that hour, he had a headache, and his steel-blue one-piece spaceflight uniform was moist with perspiration. Pushing these discomforts out of his conscious awareness, the pilot concentrated on the skein of the Waywork proper—hanging like a spider's web in his mind's eye. If he took both hands off the Key's surface, this mental picture of the Waywork blurred and disappeared. Keeping at least one hand on the Key at all times ensured that his perception of the Waywork remained clear. Like any properly schooled Waypoint pilot, he knew the Waywork intimately: fifty-six stars, spread across an irregularly shaped lump of interstellar space, each star joined to the whole by the filaments of the web.

The majority of that territory belonged to Starstate Constellar's sworn enemy: Starstate Nautilan. Some of it also belonged to the other Starstates: Yamato, Sultari, and Amethyne. Only a few systems remained friendly: Constellar's home territory—the last bastion of freedom in human space.

The extent of the Waywork had never changed. Not in the many centuries since people had initially stumbled across the first known Keys, during humanity's long, desperate, slower-than-light exodus from Earth.

*Earth,* the Waypoint pilot thought, *now there is a name straight from legend!*

Where exactly the cradle of humankind could be found—in the vastness of the Milky Way—was unknown. No records had survived the migration, nor the battles which had ensued thereafter.

Human space was defined by the Waywork, and the Waywork defined human space. Earth was somewhere outside. Perhaps far outside? Lost, orbiting one of the countless number of other suns, all burning silently across the galaxy—systems humanity could not hope to reach without a prohibitively monumental investment in time, blood, and treasure.

As if on cue, a new Waypoint suddenly manifested in the pilot's mental map.

Audibly gasping, he yanked his hands off the Key, and rubbed at his eyes with balled fists—the throbbing in his head becoming especially pronounced.

"You okay, Herreta?" asked a nearby voice. The *Daffodil*'s lone surgeon spent the bulk of her time in the ship's command module, keeping an eye on the Waypoint pilots during duty hours. Like himself, the surgeon wore a standard one-piece space duty uniform, only her shoulders were decorated with the insignia of a medical officer.

"Affirmative," he replied, still rubbing at his face with his hands, then wiping the sweat and oil on his thighs.

"Twenty more minutes, then you're done for forty-eight hours," the surgeon said reassuringly.

"I'll be okay," Herreta said, more to bolster his own confidence than to reassure the medical officer presently peering at him over the back of her gee chair. Hallucinations were a known sign that a Key user was about to tip over the edge. But Herreta was young. Too young, yet, to file his medical papers. Besides which, Constellar was still at war—and needed every able-bodied trooper it could get.

The Waypoint pilot gently put his hands back onto the surface of the Key. When his mental map of the Waywork steadied, Herreta quickly counted up the Waypoints . . . and held his breath. The fifty-seventh Waypoint hung apart from the familiar, ageless shape of the Waywork proper.

Exhaling slowly, then taking several deep breaths, Herreta opened his eyes, stretched his neck from one side to the other, cracked his knuckles, then reapplied his hands to the Key's surface . . . and again counted fifty-seven Waypoints.

"Do you need someone to jump in early?" the surgeon asked.

"Maybe," Herreta replied. "But get the captain over here first."

In a command module so small, with so few crew, the skipper

of the *Daffodil* heard every word the Waypoint pilot said, and was out of his gee chair almost instantly—floating over to the Waypoint pilot's station.

The light from multiple displays and holograms glowed across the air-circulation ductwork which composed the command module's ceiling. There was precious little direct illumination. It would have interfered with the readouts. And was superfluous, when every switch, touchpad, knob, dial, and lever was backlit.

"Incoming?" the captain said, his voice grim. "We'd better alert Commodore Iakar, aboard the *Comet.*"

"Nossir," Herreta said. "Something else. Something I thought I'd never see—not in my whole life."

Now the entire population of the command module were turned in their gee chairs, staring quietly at the Waypoint pilot.

"Go on," ordered the captain.

"It's a new coordinate on the Waywork map, sir."

"I beg your pardon?" the captain blurted.

"A new Waypoint, sir."

"But... that's not possible."

"Yessir. Nevertheless, it's there. Plain as day."

"Get the other Waypoint pilots down here," the captain ordered firmly. "We need confirmation."

"But they're sleeping—" the surgeon began to protest.

"Do it," the captain barked. "*Now.*"

In short order, the entire ship's compliment of Waypoint pilots were clustered around the gee chair where the Key was integrated into *Daffodil*'s architecture. One by one, they took turns in the seat, each of them applying his or her hands to the Key's surface. And one by one, each of them repeated what Herreta had said.

"What do we do now?" Herreta asked, swallowing hard. He still couldn't believe it.

"Put Commodore Iakar on my chair's secure channel," the captain ordered his communications officer. "Then sound the ship-wide underway alarm. We're breaking station as soon as the reactor is ready."

"What for?" the surgeon asked. "We're not under attack!"

"If our Waypoint pilots can see it," the captain said loudly, returning to his seat, "that means every other Waypoint pilot in the Waywork can see it too. Including those of Starstate Nautilan. We dare not let them reach the new Waypoint first!"

# PART ONE

PART ONE

# CHAPTER 1

ZURI MIKTON'S RESIGNATION LETTER WAS SHORT, AND BLUNT. Perhaps a bit too blunt? She was friends with a few people who would be highly disappointed in her for quitting. Given the present state of Constellar's affairs, the nation needed experienced officers. But in Zuri's case, she knew she wasn't doing anybody any favors by hanging around—taking up space at a desk assignment, with precisely zero chance for advancement. Better to put her soldiering days behind her, and get on with the business of life. Let somebody much younger, and with far fewer blotches on his record, take the job.

Yet, Admiral Mikton hadn't been able to push the SEND icon. For weeks, she'd brought the letter up every morning. Rereading its terse few sentences. Changing a word here, and a word there. Once the letter was received and acknowledged, there would be no going back. Zuri would be done. The Constellar Deep Space Operations and Defense personnel office would process her for retirement, and she'd find herself shipping back home—or anywhere else across Constellar—in civilian clothes.

What would it be like, to be a sixty-year-old military dropout, albeit with a significant military pension?

Zuri didn't really have an answer to that question. Which is why she kept committing the letter to her DRAFTS folder at the end of every evening.

"Ma'am," said one of the three young ensigns who worked the communications desk of Admiral Mikton's Interplanetary

7

Command Center, "there's an encrypted message coming in from the Waypoint monitor, *Daffodil*."

Like everyone else in the ICC, the ensign wore a pressed two-piece DSOD duty suit, with sharp creases in both the steel-blue pants—an officer's black stripe down the exterior of each leg—and the mustard-yellow topcoat. His subdued silver rank was pinned to the topcoat's largish oxford-style collar, but he didn't have maroon battle stripes below the elbow, like some of the older veterans—both commissioned and noncommissioned alike. His boots were brown simulated leather, low top, fashioned spacer style, with a high shine. And what little was visible of his undershirt, at the neck, was aluminum gray. A communications branch insignia—black, to match the stripe on his pants—decorated each of his shoulders.

Zuri sat up in her chair, snapping her attention away from her mail to the main hologram suspended in the air over the heads of the ICC's duty personnel.

"If the Waypoint security force is under attack, why didn't our alarm system trip over?" Zuri demanded.

The ensign's fingers flew across his keyboard. "It's not that kind of message, ma'am," he said. "Commodore Iakar's code has been attached—so we know he's authenticating it...whatever it is. The decryption warning says this is for your eyes, and your eyes alone."

Zuri slowly leaned back in her chair. How odd.

"Send it to my workstation," she ordered.

The ICC was shaped like a small amphitheater, with Admiral Mikton's seat and computer console being positioned at the highest level, toward the very rear. From that vantage point she could survey the entire room, and every piece of the Interplanetary Command puzzle. But her specific seat had no one behind it—no eyes to watch over Zuri's shoulder. She received the encrypted message from the *Daffodil*, using her workstation's battle traffic interface, then pressed her hand to the workstation's reader. A tiny stripe of blue light swept over her palm, then the battle traffic interface glowed green, and Zuri was able to read the full text of the message which had been transmitted.

Like her resignation letter, the message from the *Daffodil*'s captain was short, and to the point. She reread the message three times, to be sure she was understanding the situation correctly, then Zuri double-checked Commodore Iakar's attached code. Yup. Authenticity confirmed. It was not a joke.

Zuri sat silently for a few moments, her fist at her mouth while she gently gnawed on the knuckle of her thumb. Of all the things she might have expected when she dressed for work that morning, *this* particular bit of news was at the very bottom of Zuri's list.

"Watch commander," Zuri called out, "put us on class-three alert."

Several heads swiveled around, eyes staring up at the admiral as she looked out into the air—at the holographic representation of the star system over which she had presided, as top-most DSOD officer, for the past few years. A class-three alert was unusual. Most of the staff in the room who'd not gone on a fleet exercise had never even heard a class three being called—outside of mock drills.

"Class-three alert, is that correct, ma'am?" asked the lieutenant who was sitting at the watch commander's station. Like the younger ensign before him, the lieutenant too lacked maroon battle stripes below his elbows.

"You heard me," Zuri said firmly, "and transmit to Commodore Iakar that the encrypted message has been received, and understood. Since he's short one monitor now, he's going to have to be extra diligent about watching the Waypoint—in the monitor's absence. We don't want our excitement over the discovery to leave us with our pants down, should anyone try a sneak attack on this system."

"Begging your pardon, ma'am," the watch commander said, "But what 'discovery' are you talking about?"

"First things first," Zuri said. "Bring us up to proper alert status, please."

The watch commander dipped his chin to his chest—in acknowledgment of the order—then turned around and began typing rapidly at his keyboard. Within moments, the man's voice was carrying throughout the ICC, as well as being broadcast to every DSOD-coded receiver in the entire system.

"THIS IS A class-three ALERT, AS ORDERED BY THE INTERPLANETARY COMMAND CENTER. REPEAT, THIS IS A class-three ALERT. ALL DOWNTRACE PERSONNEL AND FACILITIES ARE TO REPORT READINESS AND AWAIT FURTHER INSTRUCTIONS. THIS IS NOT A DRILL. REPEAT AGAIN, class-three ALERT. class-three ALERT."

Suddenly the ICC was alive with commotion. One of the huge flatscreen status boards on the far wall flickered to life, and displayed the throbbing orange symbol for live-action alert. The hologram of the system itself—suspended in the air directly over the amphitheater, where all eyes could see it, and Zuri especially had a clear view—sparkled, as each of the DSOD's different assets began to acknowledge the class three. Little icons closest to the ICC went from brown, to yellow, to green, very quickly. Other locations much farther away—light-minutes distant—would take longer.

Meanwhile, Admiral Mikton knew she had several jobs to do at once.

"I want to talk to the First Family representative," she said, locking eyes with the same ensign who'd originally taken the encrypted message from the *Daffodil*. "Then I want somebody to give me a quick count on every spacecraft in this system that is Key equipped. Military, civilian, it doesn't matter. If it's interstellar, I want to know what it is, who owns it, and how to get in touch with them."

# CHAPTER 2

WYODRETH ANTAGEAN WAS SITTING AT HIS FATHER'S DESK WHEN the blue-legged-and-mustard-coated DSOD people strode through his executive office door. There were five of them, three male and two female. Having done an obligatory stint with the DSOD right out of prep school, Wyodreth knew their type, and didn't need to be told their ranks. He himself still held a reserve commission, though it had been a long time since Wyodreth had set foot onboard an active-duty warship. These days he was up to his neck in the family business—a task he found more challenging than anything the military had ever thrown at him.

As the five DSOD folk took up positions around the office, sidearms prominently displayed in pistol-belted, cross-draw holsters, Wyodreth had the distinct impression that his day would shortly be taking a turn for the worse.

He cleared his throat. "If you're here to renegotiate military bulk-cargo rates—"

The oldest DSOD officer cut Wyodreth off. "Can this office be fully secured?"

Wyodreth eyed the man who had addressed him. "Yes. Why?"

"Do it," the officer ordered, as one of the junior DSOD people went to activate the electronic lock on the door. Outside, Wyodreth's administrative assistant kept glancing sidelong through the wall of glass—no doubt wondering why the military had taken a sudden interest in her boss.

Wyodreth gave his assistant a smile and a nod, then tapped

11

the small control panel on the desk, which opaqued the glass and activated a localized sonic distorter to neutralize listening devices.

"This had better be good," Wyodreth said testily. "I'm a very busy man. Since my father took ill, much of his day-to-day work has fallen into *my* lap. What can Antagean Starlines do for Constellar's office of Deep Space Operations and Defense?"

The oldest officer removed a thin hardcopy folder from his impact-proof valise, and dropped the folder onto Wyodreth's desk.

"Antagean has three Slipway-capable ships currently in dock," the man said. "As of now, their itineraries are to be scrubbed. They're being called up, per Article Nineteen of the First Families Compact. DSOD compensation terms are standard, and generous— with bonuses included. It's all in the paperwork."

Wyodreth stared at the officer for several seconds, then picked up the folder and opened it. Inside were sheets with the Deep Space Operations and Defense seal at the top, and the grand coat of arms of Starstate Constellar watermarked into each page. Scanning the verbiage, Wyodreth could see that the officer's estimation was accurate: the terms were generous indeed.

But there was a second group of papers in the folder, also with a DSOD seal at the top.

Wyodreth dropped the folder to his desk.

"My ships aren't the only things being called up," he said, exasperated. "Do you have any idea how horrible your timing is?"

"Couldn't be helped, sir," the officer said. "Your orders come from the desk of Admiral Mikton herself. If you look at the bottom, sir, you'll also see that they include a brevet promotion for the duration of the mission."

"Mission?" Wyodreth said, shoving the folder away from him. "My 'mission' is to keep the company running until my father's latest battery of treatments is complete. I can't just disengage from corporate oversight at the drop of a hat. What's this all about, anyway? Why does DSOD need my ships so suddenly that you can't bring in your own craft from one of the other systems?"

The DSOD people all eyed each other, then the oldest officer pointed to the holographic control unit on the office wall.

"May I?"

Wyodreth waved his hand at them, and reclined in his father's leather chair—Wyo's chin and mouth obscured by a clenched fist.

*Of all the stupid, silly, harebrained . . .*

But Wyodreth kept his composure, and allowed the officer to slide a data card into the holographic control unit's slot. Hitting a few of the glowing buttons on the control unit's surface—his fingers moving deftly—the officer then stepped back, and suddenly the center of the office was glowing with a life-sized recording of a trim, gray-haired DSOD woman wearing the clusters of a flag officer on her collar.

"Mister Antagean," the visage spoke, "you must forgive the abrupt nature of this communication, and these two sets of orders. One of our DSOD monitors in this system became aware of a situation which required immediate action, and we need not only your available starliners, but yourself as well. Ordinarily, if the DSOD presses civilian ships into the fleet, we crew them with DSOD personnel. But since we don't have time for that, I believe it's best if we put an Antagean corporate man in charge of those ships. Somebody the civilian crews will take orders from, and who can seamlessly interface with DSOD chain of command as well.

"Your reserve commission is hereby upgraded to the active rank of lieutenant *commander,* effective immediately. You are to report for duty at once.

"Don't bother heading home to pack. Your file says you have no dependents. A message can be sent to your sister's office, letting her know that you're detached for the duration. Since she's been helping you run Antagean Starlines in your father's stead, I am sure she has a contingency plan in place—in case you're unavailable for normal work."

"What the hell's so urgent that I can't even—!"

But the recording continued, oblivious to Wyodreth's outburst.

"These men and women standing in your office are under my personal orders to escort you to DSOD reception. Everything you need, including travel kit and uniforms, has already been prepared for you. As for the question foremost in your mind—what's it all about?—pay close attention."

The image of Admiral Mikton dissolved, and was replaced with the familiar lines of human space. Antagean made its money on those lines. It was one of the few civilian space operators in Starstate Constellar with authority from the First Families to own and operate Keys. Wyodreth himself had spent a fair amount of his youth moving along those lines. His father had thought it necessary that Wyodreth learn the job from the ground up. Just as Wyograd Antagean himself had done at the company's inception.

Wyodreth stared at the blinking Waypoint which stood apart from the rest of the Waywork, roughly on the border between Starstate Nautilan and Starstate Constellar—if the border extended that far, which it never had.

"By the Exodus..." Wyodreth breathed, instantly recognizing the significance of that blinking light.

"Something's happened which hasn't ever happened before," Admiral Mikton said. "There's a new Waypoint on Constellar's flank. Uncharted territory. Our system—though not a strategic focus in the war until now—is the closest known Constellar Waypoint within striking distance of the new Waypoint. There is a Nautilan system within reach as well, but just barely. A DSOD monitor ship went ahead, on its own initiative. To reconnoiter. Now we're moving every available Slipway-capable ship, as quickly as it can be moved. This means your starliners. We intend to put down the Constellar flag on whatever real estate we might find at the new location. Planet-finder telescopes give us a general idea of what to expect. But as you know, nobody has visited a truly unexplored system since the initial settling of the Waywork. Opportunities like this do not come even within the span of a dozen lifetimes. That's all I can tell you for now, Lieutenant Commander Antagean. I look forward to meeting you at the spaceport in one hour."

The holographic map of the Waywork faded out. And the office lights automatically came back up.

Wyodreth sat, stunned—staring into the air where the map had previously been.

"Sir?" the DSOD officer said. "We should get moving."

"Right," Wyodreth said, puffing his cheeks as he exhaled. "Everybody *out,* and leave me be—for five minutes. I've got to alert my father, my sister, and the company board."

"Yessir," the officer said, nodding his chin to his chest—a sign of obeisance, since Wyodreth now officially outranked him.

Then the officer was waving both himself and his people out of the room.

Wyodreth sat in silence, staring at the computer built into his father's desk. Then he reluctantly reached for the keyboard, and started to punch in company communication codes.

# CHAPTER 3

THE PLANET OSWIGHT WAS LIKE SO MANY OTHER TERRESTRIAL worlds in the Waywork: a barren sphere of rock and sand, which may have once had liquid water running across its surface, but was now a desiccated, lifeless ball, with negligible atmosphere. Of the many hundreds of known planets spread throughout the Starstates, only five of them were Earthlike. Or, at least, comparable to the version of Earth which had come down to the present time, in stories and myth. Each of those five sat at the relative center of a different Starstate—clement capitals, from which their respective governments ruled.

Oswight, by comparison, was average: thin air, and terrain sparsely populated between underground settlements and the few bubble cities erected on its surface. The planet itself might have been ignored altogether, except for the fact that its three asteroid moons were each rich with industrial ores, making them ideal for shipyards and shipbuilding. Dome farms on Oswight's surface kept the workers in orbit properly fed, while also providing them with a convenient place to relax and experience a touch of clement luxury.

Oswight's main spaceport was also average: the atmosphere could not support spaceplane operation, so the port's landing field was studded with gantries for ground-to-orbit-and-back clipper craft—the sort of tried-and-tested wedge-shaped vehicles which had served across the Waywork for well over a thousand years.

Garsina Oswight—of the First Family Oswight—watched

through the curved safety glass of a spaceport observation tower as one such clipper craft blasted its way into the sky on a shaft of fire. There were at least a score of others, each waiting for liftoff. All being hurriedly packed with soldiers, ships' crew, consumables, weapons, surveying equipment, and other necessities—the hastily assembled components of a hastily planned adventure.

Which Garsina herself intended to participate in, whether her father liked it or not.

"No," Bremen Oswight said for the second time, slamming the heel of his knee-length black boot onto the metal of the observation deck.

"It makes sense," Garsina said emphatically, not bothering to face her father's angry glare. "I've devoted my schooling to study of the Waymakers, and this may be a once-in-a-millennium chance to unlock some of their secrets!"

The youngest heir to the Oswight Family title was not dressed in her usual finery. She had instead donned a snuggly formfitting charcoal-gray zipsuit more appropriate for trips outside the airlock than conducting matters of state. The zipsuit had impact and abrasion-resistant armor at the shoulders, knees, elbows, and hips, as well as limited meteoroid and radiation shielding. Armadillo pleating allowed flexibility throughout. If need be, an environment helmet could be attached at the collar, with a separate streamlined backpack for atmosphere generation and filtration. The zipsuit's calf-high boots had thick tread and medium heels. As opposed to the sensible flats she ordinarily wore when participating in Oswight Family business away from home.

"If the expedition didn't stand a good chance of meeting Nautilan gunboats on the other side, I might say yes," Bremen said, his deep voice practically growling with disapproval. "But the truth is, we have no idea what's waiting for Admiral Mikton's armada once she gets there. The trip's too dangerous, Garsina. I can't allow it."

"Three civilian starliners, two military long-range scouts, one oversized frigate, and the Oswight Family interstellar yacht hardly compose an armada, Father."

"All the more reason for you to not go!" Bremen thundered. "There are other Waymaker experts to perform this work. *Military* experts. I need you here, since your brothers are away at the Constellar Council."

"And what is there for me to *do* on this world?" Garsina said bitterly. "The mindless administration of our Family estate? Entertaining official visitors at the Family hall? Correspondence with bureaucrats, each seeking our Family's favor?"

"Any one of those things is vitally important to the Oswight interest," Bremen said reproachfully. "Neither of your brothers ever shirked his duty when dispatched to perform important but mundane chores of state. My daughter, please understand. To be a member of a First Family is to endure certain burdens. Do you think I had any choice when I was your age? I wanted to stay in the DSOD. I could have risen to Admiral Mikton's rank. Partaken in great battles! But your grandmother had other plans for me. She sent your aunt and uncle to fight. Neither of whom returned home, I might add. Their remains are still out there, drifting in space. Eventually, I came to realize that *I* had been the lucky one. You should feel lucky too."

Now Garsina did turn to face her father—her eyes welling up with hot tears.

"You have four dozen different functionaries, all of whom are desperate to assume more important roles within the Family bureaucracy. Loyal men and women who have served you ably, and will continue to serve you ably. Let *them* manage our holdings. Have them participate in the local System Quorum. They already do most of these jobs anyway. I'm just a figurehead."

"And if something happens to you?" Bremen said, his own eyes suddenly brimming with hot tears. "How could I bear it? With your mother already gone? The Family Oswight lost one matriarch. It cannot afford to lose another."

Garsina considered. She'd seen that look on her father's face before. His officious patina had melted, revealing the pain underneath. Her mother's death was a blow from which Bremen Oswight had not entirely recovered. He was desperate to not have to endure such loss again.

For much of her own life, Garsina had tended to think of herself as just one of three: she and her twin brothers. Take away one, and there would be two left. All of them worthy heirs. The Family would proudly continue. Except now, with the ghost of Garsilva Oswight invoked, Garsina realized—not for the first time—that she was the only woman left in her house. That made her an especially precious commodity.

But the stars also beckoned. So much potential and possibility. Forever out of reach, if Garsina devoted herself solely to staid matters of Oswight obligation.

Another clipper's engines roared to life, pushing the craft up into the black sky. Garsina watched it fly, taking her heart aloft with it.

"You can command me not to go," she said coldly, "and I will obey your order. But know this, Father. I will hate you for it, for the rest of my life. Because others will go to the new system, and others will make the discoveries that *I* could have made. Who knows what awaits humanity on the other side of the new Waypoint? It might change everything! Including the course of the war! The Oswight legacy is already secure, Father. You have Brekor and Bretan for that. They are married. Soon, they will give you a score of grandchildren."

"But—" he began to retort, and she talked right over the top of him. She'd seen her late mother do it more than once. Garsina was an apt pupil.

"I have devoted my adult life to understanding the Waymakers, their relics, and what little we know of their species, from fossils and scraps of technology. The Keys. Father, what if what's discovered on the other side helps us to finally understand the inner workings of the Keys? The Waywork is our home, and our prison too. That's the whole damned reason we're at war in the first place. There is nowhere else for humans to *go*. There has *been* nowhere else, since the beginning. Our lives are like those tiny spacecraft you build in bottles. We're closed in. We cannot get out. Not until now, at least. I *must* be part of this expedition. The university research group wants me to go too. I'm their best, and they know it. 'Enough lecturing! Time for doing!' That's what they said. Please, Father, don't deny me this. What good is our Family name, if all we do is carefully tend our little fiefdom, while our enemies in Nautilan threaten to destroy Constellar utterly?"

Garsina could tell that her father desperately wanted to invent a reason to say no. But her words had given him pause. She could see him working it all out in his mind. He might have been stubborn, but he was not a fool. He knew what had to be done.

She took three steps and grabbed up one of his large, shaking hands in both of hers.

"Please?" she said, squeezing his fingers tightly. "Destiny doesn't knock at every door. When it knocks at ours, we must answer."

His eyes slowly closed, and he brought the skin of her wrist up to his damp face.

"Promise me you'll be careful," he said through a clenched throat. "Don't take any stupid risks."

"I promise," she said, feeling tears escape from the corner of each eye.

"May God and your mother forgive me," he said. "Go. Go! Do us proud, Garsina. Do us all proud."

# CHAPTER 4

MANY LIGHT-YEARS DISTANT FROM PLANET OSWIGHT, AN ALTOGETHER different test of wills was taking place. Golsubril Vex—kosmarch of Nautilan—was unused to getting so much pushback from her system's general officers. Ordinarily, the men and women at the top of Starstate Nautilan's military chain were selected for their obedience, even more than their ability. A willingness to execute orders—without hesitation, without question—was one of the main reasons why Nautilan had been ascendant within the Waywork for as long as Golsubril Vex could remember. It would only be a matter of time before every system in the Waywork was united beneath Nautilan's blood-red flag.

But first, there was the matter of the mysterious Waypoint which had appeared near Nautilan's border with Starstate Constellar. A Waypoint which now lay within Vex's exclusive reach.

"We must wait, Madam Kosmarch," grumbled General Ekk, running his spotted hand over his bald head. "Assemble an overwhelming number of ships. Then proceed unchallenged."

"Unchallenged?" Vex said, her eyebrow arching. "For all we know, Starstate Constellar has already moved many ships across the Slipway. Give them too much time to dig in, and Nautilan's fleet and army may both pay a very high price for such a delay. Perhaps too high a price?"

"Better than rushing in, Madam Kosmarch," said General Ticonner, who served as Ekk's deputy. "For generations, our standing strategy has always paid off. There is no war trickery which can gain Constellar any advantage over us now. One by one, we have pruned away their outer systems. Just as we have pruned away systems from the other Starstates too. We can produce and maintain more ships than they can. We have more people than they do. Even if we waited months—to assemble an expeditionary battle fleet—Constellar's admirals, in their Deep Space Operations and Defense chain of command, cannot divert sufficient strength to cover this newly discovered Waypoint. Not without leaving themselves fatally vulnerable in other areas."

Vex's marble-and-column audience chamber glowed with the light from a supersized map of the Waywork. Fifty-seven stars, all linked by tendrils of laser light: each representing one of the Slipways over which interstellar travel was achieved. It was a wholly artificial construct—left over from the era of the Way-makers. Who had vanished from this portion of the galaxy half a million years before.

Until a few hours ago, the structure of the Waywork had been static. And was assumed to always remain thus. Using the alien Keys, humanity could access the Waywork. But no Slipways beyond the confines of the Waywork had ever been created. Nobody knew how to even go about trying. The Keys were as inscrutable as they were indestructible. They permitted access to the Waywork. But not expansion.

Unless something fundamental had suddenly changed.

"I agree that our strategy has worked well, so far," Vex said, using a trackball on her chair's arm to slowly spin the Waywork in the air—the way a child might spin a star wheel, looking for the different constellations each culture saw in each planet's sky. "But we're assuming all conditions will remain constant. Clearly, the appearance of a fifty-seventh Waypoint outside of the Waywork is a sign that we can no longer make such an assumption. And though we in our system do not have the resources to deploy a fleet with truly superior capability, we can at least send a probe force. The results of this probe will tell us whether or not additional military resources have to be applied to the problem."

The shoulders of both Ekk and Ticonner sagged.

*I know what they're thinking,* Vex thought to herself. *This isn't the way they've been taught to do it according to war doctrine. Ignoring or flouting the rules is a good way to ruin one's career. Or worse. Oh, gentlemen. You have so little faith. You've been bred too well. Trust me to do what I have been bred for, and we shall have victory. With the potential for so much more!*

"Worry not," Vex soothed, her low, melodic voice echoing around the audience chamber. "I am taking full responsibility for this decision."

"Then who shall lead the probe, Madam Kosmarch?" General Ekk asked hesitantly.

"I will, of course," she said calmly, a slight smile curling up the corners of her full lips.

"You?" both generals said in unison, practically stuttering the word.

"Why not?" she asked.

"It's just that . . . well, Madam Kosmarch, you see . . . we cannot guarantee your safety!"

*Here again,* Vex thought. *A pedant's attention to tradition and duty. It's unheard of for any kosmarch to participate in a military venture, beyond the rechristening of newly conquered and pacified worlds. And if this were a mere frontier system being carved out of the hide of a rival Starstate, I might be content to fulfill an obligatory role. But my senses tell me this time there is a great deal more at stake. Involving the fate of not just this new system on our back doorstep, but Nautilan as a whole. Perhaps even the Waywork in its entirety?*

"My decision is final," Vex announced, rising from her chair—her kosmarch's official olive-drab robe swirling slightly.

The two generals—their own olive-drab uniforms neat and crisp—turned to look at each other, then they looked back to their mistress.

"I want to leave in less than a day's time," she commanded them.

"We hear, and we obey," they said, snapping their heels together, then bowing at the waist. When they straightened, they turned as a unit, and marched swiftly out of the audience chamber, letting the chamber's automatic doors slip quietly shut behind them.

Golsubril Vex continued to play with the trackball on the arm of her chair, caressing it with carefully manicured fingertips. The Waywork gradually rotated end over end, like a collection of jewels joined with pencil lines of fire. Her eyes kept drifting back to the single new jewel which stuck out of the side of the Waywork—its light throbbing intensely.

"This might be the fulcrum," Vex said quietly, to no one but herself. "All my life, I've been waiting for an opportunity to change the game."

*And put the whole of human space under my thumb!*

# CHAPTER 5

ZURI MIKTON TRIED TO BE A WOMAN WITH PROPER PERSPECTIVE. During a career spanning decades of service to both Constellar and the First Families, she had learned to leaven her enthusiasm for fresh opportunities with a healthy dose of realistic expectation. Timetables were a guideline, not an absolute. Someone or something was always early, as well as always late. You would seldom have everything you wanted, but you could usually get what you needed—with a little creative fudging around the edges. And, most important of all, the requirements of the mission at the outset would never match the requirements of the mission at the conclusion.

That last axiom had bitten Admiral Mikton in the ass on more than one occasion. Most famously during the DSOD's rout at the hands of a Nautilan invasion fleet, during the battle for the planet Cartarrus. It had been the one and only time then-Commodore Mikton found herself personally leading the defense, after the destruction of Fleet Admiral Hichel's flagship. For a full week, Mikton had leveraged less than ten Constellar warships against twenty frontline Nautilan vessels. For her trouble, Commodore Mikton cost herself more than half her force—along with almost a thousand lives—while inflicting an impressive eight kills. And *still* she lost the system, eventually retreating through the Waypoint in her damaged prototype battlecruiser.

Just one more star crossed off the Constellar map. Another piece of free soil annexed during Nautilan's bloated, monolithic march toward total Waywork domination.

25

Too many of the DSOD's battles had gone like that during Zuri's lifetime. The giant wall of names attached to the war memorial at Constellar's capital spoke of numerous friends lost to the never-ending fight. And while Zuri's remaining peers might have understandingly forgiven her for the defeat at Cartarrus, the Constellar Council's ever-enduring War Directorate did not.

Thus Commodore Mikton found herself quietly promoted out of her extant command, and placed in charge of the DSOD forces watching over Planet Oswight, and the Oswight Family holdings in their system.

It was an auxiliary role, supporting the main effort to hold the line against more Nautilan incursions. Oswight didn't have a lot of people, but its moons could build ships. Those ships were vital to bolstering Constellar's combat assets in other systems. Presumably, Nautilan had its eye on Oswight. But there were other, more strategically important targets to be handled first. Thus Admiral Mikton had spent the last five years of her life as a planet-bound administrator. Making sure her Waypoint was effectively ready for an attack that never came. Knowing her days as a tactician—leading potential assaults which might liberate conquered worlds—were over.

Now?

The dice were suddenly being rolled again.

Admiral Mikton would not be present to learn about the strategic shifts DSOD would make, to deal with the unheard of manifestation of a new Waypoint in a new system. She would be on the other side. For better or for worse, this was her chance to once again *do* something. Put Constellar back on the advance. Take fresh ground. Hold it. Erase her failure at Cartarrus.

Not that her flimsy expeditionary force to the new system would match up against even half the number of Nautilan ships which had hit Cartarrus. There were new ships being brought online from Oswight's yards every year, but they lacked both Keys and trained crews. Besides which, every day Admiral Mikton delayed acting was a day Nautilan might use to move people and equipment across their own Slipway to the new star.

It was a now or never proposition.

So, Zuri made do with the ships she had to work with, as well as the people attached to those ships. Many of them were gathered before her now. It was a quickly assembled briefing, just prior to departing for orbit.

The Antagean fellow seemed solid enough. He was a fish out of water in his ill-fitted uniform—one size too large, it turned out—but his eyes were sharp, and he spoke both intelligently and with the experience of a man who had done time traversing the Waywork in the service of his father's company. She'd have taken him, on account of his authority over his father's three starliners, even without Antagean's reserve credentials. That he had DSOD military training was just a bonus. It meant he knew how to follow orders, and could also think within the DSOD's operational framework. Would he be cool under fire?

The scion of Family Oswight was younger. But seemed able. She would double as the mission's Waymaker expert. Lady Garsina did not travel in the resplendent gowns of a tourist. She wore clothing better suited to xenoarcheology, and had a tough-looking majordomo always at her side. The older man's silver-streaked beard and mustache were trimmed military neat, and he was built like a rocket stack. He had the ceremonial sword of his Lady's house strapped to one hip, and an outsized sidearm—with use-worn handle—riding on the other. Like his charge, the majordomo's clothing was suited for austerity, though his shoulders had epaulets bearing the colorful crest of Family Oswight. Other handlers and servants obeyed the majordomo without question.

Best of all, the entire entourage brought with them Family Oswight's interstellar yacht. Which would nicely compliment the other civilian ships Admiral Mikton commanded. If the far side of the new Waypoint could be secured, the yacht was small enough to fit into the bays of some of the larger ships in Commodore Iakar's flotilla. Thus allowing Mikton to begin shuttling Iakar's assets across the Slipway, one at a time, while auxiliary ships from beyond could be brought in to reinforce the Oswight side.

A process which would have been much faster and easier, if Mikton had had more Keys to work with. But she didn't. Ships—and commands—along the frontier with Nautilan took priority. So Mikton would have to do it the hard way. At least until the DSOD could mobilize at the strategic level. *If* they mobilized. A decision which would only be made once Mikton had returned a proper survey report.

To that end, Antagean's starliners were going to be kept busy. Lacking armament, they would be used for two things: making detailed charting runs on the new system's planets, and carrying

DSOD troops and equipment—for an initial outpost—across the Slipway. As with the Family Oswight yacht, the Antagean starliners could eventually be used for piggybacking additional warships to the new system. But first came the chore of figuring out which of the new system's worlds—if any—would be worth fighting to keep.

Everyone assembled seemed anxious to get moving.

Zuri climbed up on an interstellar modular freight crate, and cleared her throat.

"I'll make it quick," Mikton said loudly, so that the scrum of personnel occupying the small spaceport holding bay could hear her. "Once we reach orbit, my flag transfers to the frigate *Catapult*. All directives for this Task Group will be issued from there. You will take orders from me, or from my deputy, Commodore Urrl. If need be, the Task Group can also look to the *Catapult*'s captain as acting group leader. Many of you may be unused to taking commands from people in uniform. Try to remember that what we do, we do out of utmost need. You've all been previously briefed about the specifics of the Task Group's mission. I'm here now to tell you that there's far more to this expedition than simply laying claim to a piece of territory.

"For as long as any of us can remember, Starstate Constellar has been under threat from its largest neighbor. We've tried peace treaties, as well as alliances with the other Starstates, and none of it's held back Starstate Nautilan's relentless quest to consume our nation.

"We—the people in this room—cannot allow Nautilan to advance one light-year farther. There's no clue, yet, to tell us what we'll find on the other side of the new Waypoint. We'll know more when we can rendezvous with the monitor *Daffodil*, which serves as our vanguard. Suffice it to say that we're claiming the new system, not just for the Constellar Council, but for the future of liberty in the Waywork as a whole. The freedom of your children, and your children's children, may depend on what we each do—in these next few days, or weeks, or even months.

"I therefore call on each of you to do your duty to the last. Not just as employees. Nor merely as paid soldiers of the state. But as *patriots*. Men and women who know what it means to serve a cause higher than themselves. If you believe you can't do that—if you can't look me in the eye and follow me over the Slipway—now is the time to raise your hand, and back out."

Every head in the bay swiveled back and forth, waiting.

There were no takers.

"Very well then," Admiral Mikton said. "Get to your clippers. Have a safe launch. And, *may God favor the bold and the free!*"

"VICTORY WITH HONOR, HURRAH, HURRAH!" every DSOD member thundered back at her, completing the time-honored Constellar military motto.

Some of the civilians shouted too, including the Lady Oswight's majordomo—who hollered loudest of all.

The scrum immediately broke, with people going this way and that, all rushing to get to their respective concourses. Admiral Mikton's deputy, along with their small cluster of staff officers, proceeded through the southeastern pressure hatch, which led into a long subterranean tube stretching out underneath the spaceport's kilometers of tarmac. The tube flooring was a moveable beltway, split down the middle by a safety railing, with one half going out to the launch gantries, and the other half going back to the terminals. One by one, each of the staff stepped on and were whisked away, serenaded by the sound of humming machinery.

Outside of her small security valise, Admiral Mikton carried nothing. She'd previously packed all of her duffels, and sent them ahead to be stowed with the bulk cargo. It had been a long time since she'd been to space. As the motorized beltway carried her closer and closer to the clipper which would take her into orbit, Zuri felt a small thrill of excitement.

"Quite a thing to be witnessing fulfillment of the Word," said the officer standing on the beltway directly behind the admiral.

Zuri turned and looked at the short man, who wore a DSOD uniform similar to her own, but with the frocking of a priest draped around his neck. Chaplain Ortteo wasn't considered mission-essential for this expedition, but DSOD policy said flag officers conducting field operations had to carry at least one. So Ortteo was it.

In truth, Zuri didn't have much use for men of the cloth. She'd been a skeptic of organized faith most of her adult life, and didn't believe in the literal truth of the Word—though the Word was invoked numerous times in both Constellar law and DSOD doctrine. As to the specific part of the Word which Chaplain Ortteo was citing, Zuri could not guess.

"You'll forgive me if I am not up on scripture," she said.

"Eighteenth Prophecy," Chaplain Ortteo said with a smile. "The fifth passage reads, 'When men have dwelled long enough in darkness, God shall open a doorway through the loneliest wall of heaven.' Later in the same Prophecy, the thirteenth passage says, 'Going forward on ships of fire, the wicked and the righteous will each claim dominion over hallowed soil. And the bones of the dead shall rise and speak, passing judgment.' There's a lot more in the Eighteenth, but you get the idea."

"Do you believe that's what's happening now?" Zuri asked.

"I think it's a distinct possibility," Ortteo said enthusiastically.

"The Prophecies have all been interpreted and reinterpreted to mean many sorts of things," Zuri reminded him. "A lot of the time, whether the specific interpretation is correct or not depends purely on how willing the listener is to subjectively ignore the parts in the passages which don't fit our present reality."

"Quite true, Admiral," Ortteo said. "But I remain an optimist. After all, we *are* participating in something historic, are we not? A doorway *has* been opened, yes? I can't ignore the similarities and still call myself faithful to the Word. On some level, it *all* has to be true somehow. Regardless of whether or not our interpretation is correct."

"So," Zuri said, "does that make us the 'righteous' from that story, or do we get to be the other guys?"

Chaplain Ortteo laughed heartily.

"I am hoping God is charitable with Starstate Constellar."

"Let's *both* hope that," Zuri said, and patted the religious officer on his shoulder.

Arriving at the beltway's end, Admiral Mikton led the way to the third of five different lifts, each ascending up a separate clipper gantry. The lift car was vacuum-proofed, its double doors opening with a slight hiss—as the pressure in the car equalized with the pressure at the gantry's base. The lot of them could squeeze into the car, but just barely. When the doors shut, Admiral Mikton felt her stomach jolt, as the lift car shot upward. Her stomach jolted again when the car quickly stopped, and then she was exiting through the double doors into the pressurized gangway leading across to the hatch of the clipper itself.

A space-suited orderly was waiting for them, and saluted as the admiral approached.

"We're fully fueled and ready to fly, ma'am," he said.

"Any problems with the clippers which have taken off so far?" Admiral Mikton asked.

"Not so far as I know, ma'am. We're coming up on our window for launch, so if you'll allow me to show you to your seats, we'll be on our way."

Like almost every spacecraft in existence, both large and small, the clipper was constructed in the manner of a building—its decks stacked perpendicular to the engines, like the floors of a skyscraper. When under thrust, the ship and its crew would experience a comfortable facsimile of gravity. For launch, however, both crew and passengers would be restricted to gee chairs. In the case of passengers specifically, those gee chairs were equipped with quick-deploy shrouds, so that no one catching a lift to orbit need bother with a clumsy suit. If the clipper depressurized, the shrouds would deploy and maintain individual atmosphere for every occupant until help arrived, or the crew—who *were* in suits—could get the clipper to a safe harbor.

Admiral Mikton took her seat with the rest of her staff, buckling herself in tightly. Each gee chair was angled forty-five degrees to the plane of the deck, ensuring that when the engines kicked off, blood would not rush dangerously from any heads. Small lap tables, with attached display screens and keyboards, could be deployed from the sides, swinging around to rest over a passenger's knees. Zuri used hers to call up a real-time chart showing the number of clippers which had already departed, and those yet to go. Inquiries from the ships in orbital dock had already begun to funnel into the Task Group command team message queue. While the rest of the passengers got settled, and the countdown to liftoff wound down, Admiral Mikton flagged those items she needed to attend to personally, and deferred the rest to her deputy, who would answer as he was able.

For the first few minutes of flight, there wouldn't be much to do except hang on tight.

Just before the flight deck signaled the all clear to light the engines, Zuri switched her screen to show a perpendicular view out the side of the clipper's nose. She could see the other clippers being readied in their gantries, and the smooth surface of the tarmac terminating in the far distance, against a backdrop of jumbled rock, further backed by jagged hills. The sky over those hills was beige, fading to rust red, which faded to black—with

Planet Oswight's main sun casting stark shadows to one side of the irregular mountains. For a brief moment, Zuri wondered if she would ever return to see that barren landscape again.

Then the clipper was shaking and roaring—its cluster of fusion-rocket motors blasting a mechanized dragon's breath down into the ducted baffles beneath the clipper's launch stand. An audible *thunk-a-thunk* announced that the clipper's gantry had cut loose, and the clipper began to rise. Slowly, but only for the first few seconds. Then, with increasing vigor—the acceleration pressing everyone aboard into the ample cushioning of their gee chairs.

In her officer candidate days, Zuri would have given a whoop and a holler. Now, she simply smiled to herself. Enjoying the muscular, robust feeling of the clipper defying Planet Oswight's gravity, as the ship climbed faster and faster for orbit. The view on her screen gradually revolved and tipped over, until the landscape was gone altogether. Just the stars showed—bright and perfect.

Zuri had experienced such launches countless times, but she never ceased to wonder how it must have been for the first human beings—far back in the mists of a different age—who'd gone into space. Had they been terrified? Exhilarated? A combination of both? How had the gravity of ancient, lost Earth compared to the worlds people now inhabited? The modern clipper used a hydrogen-fusion powerplant design which had not changed in hundreds of years. What had the very first spacecraft used? Chemical rockets? Solid fuel? Had the first spacefaring human beings, cocooned within the earliest spacecraft designs, been confident that their vessels would survive launch, and return?

So much about that era was eternally buried behind the wall of ignorance known as the Exodus. The home world of all humans, their star, and the other planets which surrounded it, were phantoms of legend—sources of endless speculation, some of which ran wild. Had the people of Earth been supremely long-lived and intelligent, possessing unfathomable wisdom and technology?

Or had they been more like the humans of the Waywork?

The fact that the Exodus had happened at all seemed to be ample evidence for the latter scenario. The war which had driven humanity from its birthplace must have been terrible indeed. Though very few details of that war remained. The survivors had escaped in slower-than-light arks—mammoth vessels more akin to mobile asteroids than the spacecraft used in the Way-work today. With no Keys nor any Waywork to utilize, the arks crept through interstellar space at a snail's pace. For generations. Desperately seeking clement shores, on which to build new lives, and new civilizations.

All the arks which had eventually reached the Waywork had been subsequently cannibalized or destroyed. Like Earth, they lived now only in legend. As did the other arks which had presumably gone wide of the Waywork. Stranded forever in the vastness of interstellar night? Settling isolated colonies forever cut off from the rest of those who survived? Perishing—voiceless—amidst the timeless immensity of the galaxy itself?

The new system, waiting for Zuri's Task Group, would hopefully answer some of these questions.

# CHAPTER 6

WYODRETH ANTAGEAN SUPPRESSED THE FEELING OF FLIGHTINESS that dominated his senses. The experience of perpetually falling was a shock to his system after months spent living in Planet Oswight's comfortable gravity. Now that he was crossing the clipper gangway to one of the three Antagean starliners which had been drafted into Constellar military service, Wyodreth left himself a mental note to get out and see the company's orbital operations more often. It wasn't good to get soft.

"Sir," said the Antagean-uniformed civilian flight officer on the other side of the ship's hatch.

"Everything's still 'go,' Miss Wef?" Wyodreth asked.

"We've had three other clippers dock, transferring personnel and cargo," the flight officer replied. "Yours is the last of the day."

"Any problem interfacing with the Task Group ship-to-ship network that Admiral Mikton is running?"

"Once the military installed their special encrypt-decrypt units in our communication module, things got better."

"Good. How's Captain Loper, and the rest of the team?"

"Other than being fantastically annoyed at seeing his vacation cut short? Fine. The rest of us are just happy to hear about the nice bonuses."

"You oughta be," Wyodreth said, smiling. "Even I was impressed with the DSOD's offer. Hopefully none of you will have to be earning that money the hard way."

Wyodreth patted the flight officer on her shoulder, and began

to pull himself past her. He was anxious to get to the command
module, where he'd be able to get onto the Antagean intranet
and talk to the other two ships he was shepherding for this trip.

"Sir?" she said.

"Yes, Miss Wef?" Wyodreth said, pausing his movement.

"Do you really think it's going to be dangerous?"

"I honestly can't say," he admitted. "It's not like any of us
have ever done this before. Not even the DSOD. It's a chance to
literally go where nobody has ever gone. What that entails for
us, in terms of risk, is difficult to gauge. I certainly hope that
Captain Loper—and the other captains—put out my message
to all three crews. Anybody who's not up for this can say so. I
won't fault anybody for staying behind. Though, you'd be fools
to pass on the cash."

"Oh, we love the kick in the paycheck!" Miss Wef exclaimed,
smiling. "It's just that . . . well, having all these military people
around—they were putting lockers full of weapons into one of
the cargo modules—sorta makes me nervous."

"Don't sweat it," Wyodreth said to her. "Having military
people around makes *me* nervous too."

He tugged at the hem of his one-size-too-big DSOD mustard-
yellow topcoat, for emphasis.

Wef, along with several nearby Antagean employees, all broke
out in laughter.

"Come on," Wyodreth said to them all, "let's get our visitors strapped down and taken care of, right? We've still got my
father's reputation to uphold. We may be under Admiral Mikton's
command for now, but Antagean delivers first-rate service, before
anything else. No matter who our passengers are."

The crew chorused their understanding, and began to politely
herd the people coming in behind Wyodreth, to their respective
seats.

Like the clippers which had come up from Planet Oswight,
each of the Antagean ships was built more or less like a high-rise,
with thrust delivered via nuclear-fusion motors on the ground
floor. Unlike the clippers, the starliners each had huge storage
tanks for the slush hydrogen which was used as both reactor
fuel and reaction mass—a necessary encumbrance, considering
the vast distances each starliner needed to cover in a very short
span of time.

Not that crossing over the Slipway would require a great deal of fuel. The Key consumed the equivalent of a strategic hydrogen bomb during the instantaneous interstellar voyage. Which ate up just a fraction of the total hydrogen stored aboard.

No, the bulk of the mass would be eaten up pushing each ship out to the distant Waypoint, and back again.

Which reminded Wyodreth of a problem nobody had yet properly addressed. How were any of them supposed to tank up once they reached the other side of the mystery Waypoint? The standard starship facilities used to store and transfer slush hydrogen had been in existence throughout the Waywork for many centuries. Every significant outpost had them, along with the attendant manufacturing industry.

The Task Group's destination—presumably—had no such amenities. And while there were ways to distill the necessary slush hydrogen from raw materials at the destination, such a process would be messy, and protracted.

With full tanks, each of the Antagean ships had enough fuel and reaction mass aboard to make a couple of full transits of a given system's planetary plane—end to end. But no more. If suitable natural reserves could not be easily found or accessed, the entire Task Group might find itself stranded.

"Figure it out as we go," Wyodreth muttered under his breath, as he packed into a lift car that ran up and down a tube at the spine of the ship. He waited patiently while various civilian and military personnel got off at different levels—the civilians doing most of the directing, and the military people obediently going where they were told—then he was stepping off at the lift alcove within the command module proper.

Captain Loper was there to greet his boss.

"Another thirty minutes," the captain said, his graying hair forming a half wreath around his shining, bald head. "Then I think we can button up, and join the formation that's already taking shape a few thousand kilometers out from dock."

"Any problems with the cargo Admiral Mikton's ordered aboard?"

"We gave them precise specifications," Loper said, "but they still sent up too much. Their own quartermaster officers have had to work it out, deciding which crates and lockers to keep, and which to send back with the clippers. I gather they didn't get a lot of prep time themselves. DSOD is usually pretty good about not overdoing it, or underdoing it for that matter. But on this job? Nope."

"Well, if anyone had told me this morning, that I'd be doing *any* of this by dinner," Wyodreth said, then let the thought hang in the air between them.

Captain Loper merely grunted. A lifetime civilian pilot, he was nevertheless one of the most experienced men on the Antagean payroll. He'd been one of Wyograd's first hires upon founding the company—before Wyodreth himself had been born. When Wyodreth had been a young man, sent to space to learn the ropes, Captain Loper had been a patient teacher. He'd since become one of the few people Wyodreth actually considered to be a friend.

The two men trusted each other.

"Congratulations," Loper said, pointing at the new pin on Wyodreth's collar.

"Thanks," Wyodreth said. "Temporary."

"Betcha you keep it, if we get back in one piece."

"You're that optimistic, eh?"

"Your dad hired me for my sunny side."

"And a good thing too. Look…Captain, I meant what I said. Nobody is under any company expectation to participate in the mission. Not even you."

"Are you kidding? By the Waymakers' Ghosts, I wouldn't miss this. We're about to create history. I can tell my grandchildren all about it. Or, at least, *somebody* can tell them."

"Yeah. Well, before we go writing our collective epitaph, let's ensure that we keep the Antagean end up. Some of these lifer DSOD people don't take too well to being passengers only. Be courteous, but be firm. If anybody gets out of line, and won't take no for an answer, you let me know, and *I* will make them take no for an answer. We're being paid, sure, but we're not getting enough to be treated badly."

"You think there will be fighting on the other side of the Waypoint?"

"I think we'd be foolish to assume that Starstate Nautilan is not sending its own expeditionary force over their Slipway. Admiral Mikton, and that delegation from Family Oswight, are sure to bring some diplomatic clout to the table. But if the Nauties decide to shoot first and ask questions later, we might wind up caught in a nasty situation out of which there is no clean escape route."

"Speaking of the delegation," Loper said, after clearing his throat uncomfortably.

"Yes?" Wyodreth asked.

"There was a bit of a switch-up during travel to orbit. Lady Oswight is currently making herself comfortable in the ship's executive suite. Her, and that old bruiser who's along to keep an eye on her."

"You're joking."

"No."

"Why, by the Exodus, are they *here*? They've got their own ship for this voyage!"

"Something about the Lady Oswight demanding to be part of the crew that's going to be exploring the planets orbiting the target star, versus riding back and forth across the Slipway while they bring over fighting spacecraft from the security flotilla."

"What about her helpers and other staff?"

"They went to the Family ship. Just the Lady Oswight and her bodyguard are with us. Oh, and one other unexpected guest too. He was on the clipper that docked right before yours did."

"Who?"

"You ever hear of Zoam Kalbi?"

"No . . . wait, yes. Yes. God, he's that infotainer. Right? What is *he* doing onboard?"

"Last-minute addition," Loper said. "He cited Article Thirty-six."

"I didn't even know he was in this system," Wyodreth admitted.

"Apparently, he was already here, doing some freelance work on an entirely different story, when he got word about the new Waypoint."

"So much for DSOD confidentiality!"

"Inevitable," Loper said. "Every Waypoint pilot—civilian or military—can see the new system on their charts now. Across the whole of the Waywork. There was no way this wasn't going to become a very big deal, very, very fast. We're just the ones who happen to be closest. The other Starstates will be chewing down Constellar's front door, begging for an opportunity to cross Constellar space and see the new system."

Wyodreth massaged his forehead with a meaty palm, then slowly slid that palm down over his face, his fingers scraping the stubble which had accumulated on his cheeks during the day.

"Dealing with a royal pain in the ass from a First Family is bad enough," he said. "But carting along an infotainer too? I am amazed Admiral Mikton permitted it."

"Article Thirty-six is fairly broad," Captain Loper said, then smiled wickedly. "You're DSOD. You know that infotainers have been present and accounted for during every Constellar engagement going all the way back to the beginning of the war. Plus, the discovery of a new system is just the kind of story that could make any infotainer drool."

Wyodreth stared at nothing, his head tilted forward. The Antageans had no love for infotainers, nor the First Families for that matter. Dealing with both had been a necessary evil since the birth of the family business. But that didn't mean Wyograd, nor his son after him, had to like it. In Wyodreth's experience, infotainers and Family folk alike tended to have an overinflated opinion of their own importance. So far as Wyodreth was concerned, the fact that the former had the ears and eyes of the public, while the latter had the money and the traditional social standing, didn't immunize either party against being complete pains in the collective Antagean ass.

"You want to move to another ship?" Captain Loper asked, only half joking.

"No," Wyodreth said, groaning the word. "What would be the point? Dad always used to say to me, 'Keep your friends close, and your enemies closer.' I'd rather have Lady Oswight and Zoam Kalbi somewhere I can keep an eye on them. If they're here, I'd better damned well be here too. For the sake of corporate public relations, if nothing else."

Captain Loper nodded his understanding, then turned and pushed off with his toes, expertly gliding through the hatch into the command module proper. Wyodreth followed suit, and soon found himself sitting at one of the free workstations, using a keyboard and headset to talk to the captains of the other two ships under his control. Unlike the ships of the DSOD, none of Antagean's ships carried names. The family owned close to two dozen of them, with operational hubs in three different systems, including the current one. To Wyograd Antagean, a ship was simply a means to an end. He did not romanticize the starliner life. He merely stated—for Wyodreth's sake—the necessity of knowing all the bits and pieces. How each ship moved from star to star, and port to port. Maintenance schedules. Spare parts. Creating and maintaining separate depots across Constellar space, which would warehouse and service the various modules forever being grafted onto, and then pulled off, the spines of the starliners themselves.

Because a ship in the modern sense was not a whole thing. It was actually bunches of little, practically self-contained things— each and every item riding on the backbone of the ship, to be swapped out, serviced, and replaced at various intervals. There were modules on the present starliner which were older than Wyograd Antagean himself, as well as modules which had only come into service within the past two years. By the time a given starliner had seen two decades or more of service, easily seventy percent of itself had been turned over in the constant process of replacement and refurbishment.

So, the three starliners joining Admiral Mikton's fleet had Constellar commercial registry numbers. Nothing more.

It took the better part of an hour to confirm that all three ships had finally taken on the last of their cargo and passengers, and could now be released from their docks. There was no fanfare for such an event. No wharf filled with spectators, all waving goodbye. The ships merely withdrew from their cradles—noses coming unclamped from the standardized hardpoints built into the surface of the asteroid moon, which doubled as a space station. Negligible gravity meant that each starliner could maneuver easily on reaction thrusters alone. They wouldn't start up the main motors until they were well clear of the dockyard's minimum safety radius. And, then, only for as much thrust as was needed to nudge each of the three ships into their assigned places within the Task Group formation.

Along the way, Wyodreth fielded calls from his own people and DSOD personnel alike. On several occasions, he found himself directly speaking with Commodore Urrl, aboard the *Catapult*, who seemed to be the main orchestrator of things. As always when in uniform, Wyodreth found himself lapsing into the familiar tones and wording of explicitly military dialogue.

"They've sweated it into you," Wyograd Antagean had said one day, after overhearing his son discuss a matter of company logistics—while unconsciously using DSOD jargon.

"What do you mean?" Wyodreth had asked.

"Like a piece of shopworn leather," Wyograd had continued. "You keep the shape they want, even when you're not in use."

Wyodreth had never been entirely comfortable with that assessment. But now, as he prepared to lead his father's ships across many light-years to an unknown system of worlds circling an unknown star, Wyodreth had to admit his father had been correct. The DSOD's officer training program had left its mark. Wyodreth—who preferred being a civilian—couldn't help but notice in his behavior, and in the sound of his voice, the quality which his father had first noticed years earlier.

For the voyage out to the Waypoint, the three Antagean ships formed a flat-plane triangle. To the left and to the right were the two DSOD scouts—the *Gouger* and the *Tarinock*—with Mikton's flagship *Catapult* riding herd above, and the Oswight yacht *Hallibrand* passing below. As a Task Group, they synchronized their reactor ignitions and throttling so that this formation was kept coherent within a cubic space no larger than five kilometers to a side. There were no checks out portholes, nor sightings performed from any masts. Everything the pilots of each spacecraft needed to know was collected by the labyrinthine nest of gadgets and electronics which made up each ship's sensor module.

The scouts, of course, had more than one sensor module, and each of those was much more robust than anything Antagean Starlines had ever placed on any of its ships.

When they reached the far side of the Waypoint, those scouts—along with the monitor, *Daffodil*—would be the long-range eyes and ears of the Task Group.

Until then, however, there was little to do but wait. It would be many days before they reached the transit radius of the Waypoint. Time enough for Wyodreth and the other visitors to settle into their various cabins and dormitory compartments, take care of whatever sorting and tidying hadn't been handled on the ground, and get better acquainted with each other—as well as the plan for the mission ahead.

Satisfied that all three of his father's ships were performing normally, Wyodreth finally took off his headset and—with his old compatriot, Captain Loper—retired to the section of the galley module which had been cordoned off for distinguished guests, as well as ranking civilian and military personnel. There were no set meal times aboard the liner. Merely people getting on and off shift, taking breaks, or stealing a moment to find a snack. The galley module itself was overflowing with a variety of foodstuffs and prepackaged meals, all preserved against both decay and potential vacuum decompression.

People took what they wanted from the dial-to-order dispensers, making cold and hot portions available at all hours.

It wasn't gourmet. But then, it wasn't slop, either. A fact which Wyodreth had come to appreciate during his "sea legs" period, as a young man. And at many points afterward.

His only specific regret in the moment was having to muster the courage to face the two people onboard whom he least wanted to face—and present himself as having a good time while doing it.

# CHAPTER 7

ELVIN AXABRAST WAS UNHAPPY. OF THAT, THERE COULD BE NO question. Garsina Oswight had known that he would not approve of her self-reassignment—ship to ship—during the flight from Planet Oswight's surface. The old jack-of-all-trades body servant had been in Family Oswight's employ since before Garsina herself had been born. Stubborn. Overly cautious. He'd been the one piece of freight Garsina knew she couldn't throw off the moment she was out of her father's sight. And now that they were finally speeding toward the distant Waypoint, massaging Elvin's ruffled feathers was going to be a major chore.

"It's been a long time since you went to space," Garsina said to the old servant, across the small galley table where they sat. The civilian ship was thrusting at a comfortable half gee, giving everyone aboard the luxury of things sticking where you put them. Including plates and containers filled with food, drinking bottles, and disposable utensils.

"Aye," Elvin said monosyllabically before sporking another hunk of meat and vegetable cake into his mouth.

"I would think even you might get excited for the change of pace," Garsina continued, hoping to get the man talking—versus merely glowering.

"Excitement is fine," he said, "when there's no one around to look out for."

"You could have just gone home, Elvin. If I'd ordered you

45

to remain aboard the clipper, after it undocked, would you have obeyed me?"

"Not a chance! Your father would have boiled me in oil."

"My father still thinks I'm fourteen years old."

"You *are* fourteen years old. At least in his eyes."

"How would you know? You've never been a father."

Elvin's eyes suddenly looked pained, and he went back to putting bites of his meal into his face.

"Sorry," Garsina said. "I didn't mean it to come out like that. I know your wife died with the baby who was never born."

"Yourself and your two brothers were all the children I ever needed."

"And your overwatch has been most appreciated, Elvin. I don't want to seem ungrateful. My brothers and I . . . we love you, as much as anyone can love someone not by blood. But there comes a time when you have to let us go. *All* of us. You didn't seem to have a problem with my brothers being sent abroad."

"Going to the capital on Family business is not the same thing as shipping out for hostile territory," the old man said, finally putting his spork down, and lacing his thick fingers together under his bearded chin. "You have to remember what I saw during my days in the war. Terrible stuff, aye. Blood, and death. That's nothing I'd want you to have to experience, ma'am. No matter how eager you are to strike out on your own, and make your mark."

Suddenly, there was a third person standing at the galley table's edge. He was shorter than most men, with a slight chin, and a hint of moustache and goatee on his face. His clothing was designer brand. Expensive. While his manner seemed extraordinarily nonchalant for someone interrupting the private conversation of a First Family member.

"I am so terribly sorry to intrude, Lady Oswight," the man said, his voice a bit on the high and nasal side. "But I've been looking for a chance to talk to you, ever since I came aboard."

"You want I should make him piss off?" Elvin growled.

"No," Garsina said. "This isn't the Family yacht. We need to be mannerly. Don't you recognize who this is? He's the infotainer who came to do an extensive exposé on Planet Oswight's orbital manufacturing facilities. Mister . . . Kalbi, isn't it?"

"You've read me," the man said, performing a small bow at the shoulders.

"Seen you," Garsina corrected, but with a smile. "I wasn't aware that the DSOD had granted permission for informational-ists to accompany this mission."

"I consider it an act of providence that I happened to be visiting your world at the precise period when the new Waypoint appeared in Constellar's skies. There will be many infotainers eager to claim their piece of fame regarding this system we're going to explore. But only one person gets to write the history of the first expedition."

Elvin grunted unhappily. Garsina reached out a hand and put it over the old man's fist, as it clenched on the table's surface.

"You'll have to forgive Mister Axabrast. His job is to ensure that I am kept happy and safe. Not every infotainer in Constellar has been kind to the First Families. Especially Family Oswight."

"An adversarial attitude comes with the territory in my profes-sion, Lady Oswight. Where the First Families are concerned, the concentration of so much wealth and influence into so few hands has always been cause for extraordinary scrutiny. Nevertheless, I am not here to pester you about your Family's dirty laundry. I only have eyes for the adventure ahead. And I'd rather we participate on friendly terms, since I'll be covering you—indeed, everyone who is part of this mission—until our return to Constellar space."

"I think that's a very professional attitude," Garsina said.

Elvin still didn't seem convinced.

"Thank you, Lady Oswight," Zoam said, doing another small bow at the shoulders.

A man somewhat older than Zoam, but much younger than Elvin—and wearing a slightly-too-big DSOD blue-and-yellow uniform—appeared at the opposite side of the table. He was tall, with a face that featured both a strong chin and intelligent eyes—surrounded by premature wrinkles. Those eyes quickly surveyed the three of them before the officer spoke.

"Lady," the man said, imitating Zoam's shoulder-level bow. "I wanted to make sure that you're satisfied with your accommoda-tions up to this point."

The officer's voice had a practiced quality to it, at a pleasantly low, masculine register. Very different from Zoam's.

"Yes indeed," Garsina said, spying the rank pin on the DSOD man's collar. "It was very generous of the ship's captain to offer us the executive suite. Myself and Mister Axabrast would have been satisfied with business-class cabins, just to make you aware. So the added luxury has not gone unnoticed."

"Excellent," the man—lieutenant commander?—said smoothly. "If there is anything I or any other Antagean crewmember can do to make your journey more comfortable, please let me know."

Garsina's brow knit, but only for a moment. Then she snapped her fingers and exclaimed, "You're the son of Wyograd Antagean! I saw you briefly before we boarded our clippers."

"Wyodreth Antagean," Zoam said, his tone polite, but with just a bit edge on his words. "You were the other person I specifically wanted to introduce myself to."

"At your service," Wyodreth said formally.

"As this expedition's informationalist," Zoam said, "I am hoping to have access to your ship's crew."

"For what purpose?" Wyodreth asked.

"I intend to live-document our expedition as thoroughly as possible. Including the thoughts and feelings of the civilians who have been...ah, how best to put it? Commandeered, for the voyage. Members of the military—yourself included—have an expectation upon them, regarding duty. But your crew? Today they find themselves compulsory participants in an adventure which might prove to be extremely dangerous. I'd like to see how they feel about that."

"You're welcome to talk to anyone you wish," Wyodreth said, keeping his tone professional, "provided you do it *off* the clock. They've got enough adjustments to make, adapting to a heightened readiness status. Without having an infotainer poking around in their work while they're on-shift."

"That sounds perfectly reasonable," Zoam replied, his eyes never blinking.

*Those eyes,* Garsina thought to herself. There was something about them she couldn't quite put her finger on. If there had been tension on account of Elvin's generally crusty demeanor, the flavor of the air had changed again with Antagean's arrival. He clearly had no love for Zoam Kalbi. But why? The infotainer's demeanor had been perfectly reasonable so far. Yet, he seemed to be setting something off, for both Axabrast and Antagean alike. Could it simply be a male thing? Garsina was experienced enough to know that some men simply didn't mix well, regardless of the circumstances.

After a few seconds of silence had passed, Kalbi gave Garsina another bow, and excused himself from the conversation. Wyodreth's gaze followed the man for a few moments, then the lieutenant commander returned his attention to Garsina herself.

"I'm afraid we're going to be seeing a lot of him on this trip," he said.

"Not necessarily a bad thing, I think. *Somebody* is going to have to tell this story, when it's all over."

"Let the infotainers tell their bloody stories," Elvin groused, "and let the soldiers fight the bloody battles."

"You seem to be a man who knows more than a little about the second part," Wyodreth said.

"Please, have a seat," Garsina said.

Antagean formally sat, his back erect and his attention focused.

"Mister Axabrast has been retained by the Family Oswight since my grandfather's time," she said. "Please forgive his coarseness. He was a decorated sergeant at the Battle of Faltarion."

"*Colour* Sergeant," Elvin corrected her, his voice warm in the way a father's voice is warm when he's talking to a favored child. "And the Lady does me too much credit. I was at Faltarion. And also Syberestad before that. But I just did my duty. No better nor worse than anybody else who fought. The best men and women...they're *still* there. Buried. Or floating as freeze-dried husks in space."

"If the tattoo on the back of your hand means anything," Wyodreth said, pointing to the faded mark on the older man's flesh, "it seems a bit more complicated. You're one of the Dissenters—the people who refused First Family rule, when this was a virgin system. And the Dissenters got crushed for their trouble."

"I see the lad knows his history," Elvin said, his eyes wary. "What of it?"

"Well, I mean, I'm just a little surprised," Wyodreth said. "I know there are many descendants of the original Dissenters who are presently working the Oswight shipyards and factories. But I'd never have expected to see a Dissenter in service to the Family Oswight proper."

"Not good enough for yah, am I, lad?" Elvin barked. "You've got a lot of nerve sitting at the Lady's table, and passing judgment."

Wyodreth held up his hands, taken aback by the sudden

outburst. Garsina could feel many pairs of eyes suddenly turned their way. A flush rose into her face.

"Elvin, I'm sure that's not what the lieutenant commander meant," Garsina said.

"Doesn't matter what he bloody meant," the older man said sternly. "He's got no business here. This may be his ship, but while you're aboard, he owes you his deference. Now, I suggest the lad picks up and goes, double quick, before I *really* lose my temper. I was fightin' the damned Nauties with my bare fists before he was even a twinkle in his sire's eye."

With that, Garsina could tell that Antagean had been dismissed from Axabrast's attention. The majordomo plowed back into his meal, sporking bites into his mouth without looking up.

Wyodreth's cheeks had also become flushed. He suddenly stood.

"Very well. I'd wanted to forge a friendly relationship with our resident First Family party for this voyage. But I now see it's going to be a strictly business affair. Fine. Lady Oswight, your comfort and safety are my top priority. Please inform any of the ship's crew of your needs and requirements at any time, and those needs shall be met. If they are not met, please inform me directly, using your priority code on the ship's internal network, and I will *ensure* that they are met."

The lieutenant commander's bow was much more pronounced than it needed to be—almost to the point of seeming mocking—and he disappeared from the space.

"God's gift to the officer corps," Elvin muttered through a mouthful.

"You don't have to remind *me* how you feel about officers," Garsina said, sighing, and shaking her head. If she'd felt offended by Antagean's abrupt departure, that feeling was small compared to her discouragement over the fact that things were already getting off to a bad start. Elvin was her shield against the world, sure. But sometimes the man seemed to assume that the best defense was a good offense. And while he'd ostensibly acted in her name, she sometimes felt like he went overboard—speaking as if it were her honor at stake, when in reality, it was Elvin's own status being questioned.

"You don't have to prove anything to these people," she said quietly, as she poked her spork at her own meal.

The old man swallowed slowly, then put his spork down.

"There's *always* something to prove, Lady. Did you see the way that Antagean chap behaved? He's got no respect for the First Families. I could see it in his eyes. You have to know these business types. It's all about their bottom line. No doubt the DSOD is paying a fortune for Antagean's ships, with Antagean's crews. He ought to be happy with that, and show you some proper manners. Instead, he thinks you're a nuisance. If I were a younger man, I'd give him a shiner to remind him of his place."

# CHAPTER 8

GOLSUBRIL VEX WATCHED THROUGH THE HARDENED, TRANSPARENT dome of her transport's executive cabin. Thrust from the transport's engines occasionally pushed her into her gee chair, but for the most part, she was working to overcome the physical discomfort of microgravity. Keeping her eyes on the ships moving in space around the transport helped distract her from the fact that her stomach was attempting to force itself up into her esophagus.

When had she last been in space? She couldn't really be sure. Probably the last time she'd attended a Great Chamber of kosmarchs—which occurred every five years to discuss the future of Starstate Nautilan and its eventual encompassing of the Waywork.

Though, to be fair, calling it a discussion was euphemistic. The truth was, the Great Chamber merely provided rubber-stamping for the plans being made and handed down by the Chamber's ruling committee. And the ruling committee was a force even Vex knew better than to openly question. So, like every other good kosmarch, she applauded that which demanded applause, and voiced her approval for that which ought to be approved, and made her own plans within her own means—apart from the influence of minds which, while technically more powerful, were also more limited in vision.

Because the contest wasn't just for control the Waywork. That was simply a first step. The contest was about who would lead humanity *after* the Waywork ceased to be an issue. Vex knew

53

none of the members of the Great Chamber occupied themselves with this question. They'd all lived so long with the reality of the Waywork that they'd grown used to looking at a limited horizon.

Except for Vex herself. The appearance of the new Waypoint on Vex's back door merely seemed like serendipitous confirmation of her destiny—to be the kind of Nautilan leader who, like the original leaders of long ago, didn't settle for the safe path.

Because what was power for, if it couldn't actually be used?

Which was why Vex was willing to risk placing herself at the tip of the spear for the expedition to the new star system. Many of the other kosmarchs were like the members of the ruling committee: too comfortable with their seats of luxury and control to want to put themselves in a position to lose either. At the last Great Chamber, Vex had worked hard to control her disdain as she'd listened to her peers obsessively talk about consolidation. Entrenching. The petty politics of ensuring lower-downs were kept in their places, and that proper attention had been paid to reinforcing the same allegiances which had delivered those kosmarchs to their lofty perches in the first place.

At one point Vex had stalked back to her private suite, and shouted curses into the pillow on her bed. Because she was surrounded by brilliant dolts. Having taught themselves to play the game as excellently as any kosmarch could hope to play it, Vex's peers were complacent. Satisfied. Unseeing.

Now... events were unfolding in ways which none had anticipated. And Golsubril Vex trusted absolutely in the idea that the flow of circumstances worked for the benefit of those who moved swiftly, and decisively. Convention be damned.

"Madam Kosmarch," said a voice through the speakers on either side of Vex's head, "we're coming into position now. General Ekk says we'll be able to dock within the next ten minutes. Do you have any orders for Ekk and his crew?"

"No," Golsubril said. "Not at this time. Please expedite docking, and inform me when my things have been taken aboard."

"Understood," said the voice. And the speakers clicked off.

Done by the book, the expedition Vex had assembled would be at least three times its current size. Both General Ekk and General Ticonner had complained—as much as their positions permitted—about the fact that Vex was ordering action well before either of the generals felt it was prudent. They were moving into uncharted interplanetary space without any heavy capital ships, and also without any logistics line. Just nine small warships, all destroyers. Each of them equipped with a Key, and each of them capable of jumping back and forth across the Waypoint as the need required. But no more.

It was of no consequence, though. Everything hinged on seizing the initiative. Whoever could force the universe to react to her decisions would maintain the upper hand. This was as true of Starstate Nautilan's internal affairs as it was of Waywork politics itself.

Several bright flashes in the blackness of interplanetary space indicated other ships carefully thrusting into formation with Ekk's flag vessel. Each of them looked like a jumbled building twenty to thirty stories high, with a huge radiation-shielding dish at the bottom—just above the nozzles for the main thrusters—and a sloped mushroom bow, for absorbing and deflecting interplanetary debris.

As objects of raw technology, starships had never especially fascinated Golsubril Vex. They were simply tools. A means to an end. Very large, very expensive, but not particularly special.

If she was impressed by anything, it was the fact that the Waymakers—having apparently constructed the web of the Waywork proper—essentially abandoned it. Leaving very little of themselves behind for humanity to find, and use. Almost as if the Waywork had been an afterthought.

Now *there* were minds worthy of study. A race capable of building technology which could bypass the laws of the universe itself—and then they threw it away!

What had *their* society looked like? What kinds of decisions had *their* kosmarchs grappled with?

Golsubril Vex believed—no, felt deep inside herself—that the answers were waiting for her. She just had to follow her path. Ekk, Ticonner, the people under their command...they were merely components in the vehicle. A less ambitious kosmarch would have shrunk from the task. But Vex embraced it. Allowed the audacity of the thing to crackle across the inside of her brain. Filling her with a kind of contained, yet highly potent energy. As if Vex herself were an instrument in a far grander, much larger universal motion—occurring on a level outside of ordinary human perception.

# CHAPTER 9

"THAT'S THE KOSMARCH'S TRANSPORT?" ASKED THE SHORT, PLUMP officer who floated next to General Ekk, in the receiving lounge of Ekk's destroyer. The transparent wall before them showed the blackness of space, followed by the huge sphere of the planet Jaalit—with Jaalit's yellow-white sun illuminating a crescent along half of Jaalit's circumference. A small, cone-shaped ship, recently launched from Jaalit's surface, was carefully maneuvering upward, so as to mate with the destroyer's docking assembly.

"Yes it is," Ekk said.

"Allowing her to come on this mission is a mistake," the plump man said.

Ekk's laughter was harsh. "Do you think I had a choice? If you'd bothered to complete flag school, you'd realize what kind of suicide it would be for me to openly defy the wishes of the kosmarch. Mistake or no, she's going with us. And we're just going to have to suffer through it. You especially, Colonel Jun."

The short, rotund man's face—already scowling—dropped into an even deeper expression of disapproval. "I have no stomach for the rhetorical knife fights at the flag level," Colonel Jun said. "Besides, the Waymakers are much more interesting. When I had the chance to get off the line of command, and convert my commission to academics, I jumped at it."

"Still happy with your decision?" Ekk said. "It didn't save you, ultimately. Because the kosmarch is going to be yours to deal with. On the other side."

"True, old friend. But I have an advantage you don't: I'm already dying."

To punctuate his point, the plump officer pulled a cloth from his pants pocket, and coughed into it several times.

Ekk's expression softened, and he turned his face away.

"I'm sorry that the cancer is getting worse."

"It is what it is," Jun said. "I'm just going to meet the black unknown a lot sooner than the rest of you. Which means there's nothing our beloved kosmarch can threaten me with."

"Or so you think," Ekk cautioned.

Jun merely coughed a few more times into the cloth, then slipped it—folded neat—back into his pocket.

"My parents are gone. My sister is gone. I have very few friends whom I acknowledge openly. Who could she hope to use against me, as leverage? I do not fear death. I embrace it. Also, Golsubril Vex aside, I never in my lifetime imagined I'd have this chance. To go beyond the Waywork. To see something new."

"How do we know there's anything worth finding over the Slipway?"

"Oh, there'll be something worth finding, all right. I don't believe in random coincidences, Ekk. You know that. Something or someone *made* this happen. Now. At this specific moment. All that remains is to go, and find out who. And what. And why. The knowledge of an unknown and still largely unexplored universe, potentially at my fingertips. The chance to obtain answers. Perhaps even make contact!"

"Contact with *what*, Colonel?"

"Who knows? The Waymakers, maybe. Does it really matter? Sitting around resifting the sands of Waywork worlds ... certainly wasn't getting us anywhere. We've already found everything that's worth finding, and it hasn't told us much. We have the Keys. We have bits and pieces of inert Waymaker technology. Some archeological digs on a few worlds, showing us very, very little. And absolutely *nothing* to tell us why the Waywork was originally built, or what it's for, or why the Waymakers let it go five thousand centuries ago."

"Why do such questions fascinate you?"

"Because ... it all has to *mean* something. Somehow. There must be a bigger context."

"Would this 'bigger context' cure your lungs?"

"No, but I might die believing there's more to the universe than the random assembling of molecules—that there is a power greater than ourselves, to make sense of it all."

"Careful, Colonel. The commissars frown on that kind of talk. We aren't primitives like Starstate Constellar."

"Primitives!" Jun spat, and laughed harshly. "We tell ourselves we're better than they are, yet they have stubbornly resisted us, while possessing barely a quarter of the resources. We chip away at their nation with chisels and hammers, splitting off a system here, and a system there. Oh, we'll own it all, eventually. But in the process, I think we may lose a great deal. There's a quality to those people which we, in our great regard for ourselves, sorely lack."

"Now you're talking heresy," Ekk remonstrated his smaller colleague. "Cancer or no, if we had any junior officers present, I'd have you escorted out of here and locked up until you've come to your senses—and recanted your opinion."

"I promise to keep my rantings to myself, for the duration," Jun said.

"You'd better, because it will be *me* taking the fall. I vouched for you with the kosmarch, after all."

The cone-shaped transport had gotten significantly closer. Small flashes from the holes on its nose and flanks indicated the pilot's careful use of reaction control thrusters as he maneuvered the surface-to-orbit ship for final docking. In short order, the mechanical sounds of ship-to-ship mating filled the air, and both Ekk and Jun grasped handles over their heads—to keep from being tossed around the receiving lounge. Even small amounts of energy could produce big effects in the weightlessness of space. Anything not explicitly secured to a bulkhead could become a potential missile.

A hatch at the other end of the lounge unsealed, and several space-suited figures appeared. They visually inspected the hatch seal, then used the grip surfaces on the bottoms of their boots to attach themselves to what more or less passed for a floor. Coming to rigid attention, they waited silently as the kosmarch appeared.

Colonel Jun had never met the woman. She reminded him of a cat as she slipped through the hatch and greeted General Ekk with a simple nod of her head.

"Madam Kosmarch," Ekk said formally. "Welcome aboard the

*Alliance.* Once your transport has undocked, we can begin final preparations for departure to the Waypoint."

"How long to the estimated Waypoint transit radius?" the kosmarch asked.

"If we achieve a nominal balance of thrust to fuel and fluid use, I estimate we can reach the coordinates within two weeks."

"Too long," she said. "I want us there in no more than ten days."

Colonel Jun watched Ekk wince slightly.

"Is there a problem?" she asked.

"The ship can do it," Ekk said hesitantly. "In fact, all of our vessels can. It's just that . . . well, we'd be thrusting at a significant percentage above normal gee, at the same time we'd be using up fuel and working fluid which we may not be able to easily replace once we've crossed over. There won't be any resupply ships coming in our wake. And there will be no friendly docks anticipating our arrival. Thrusting beyond normal gee can be uncomfortable, even for an experienced crew. I doubt you'd want to have to endure that kind of thing for very long, Madam Kosmarch. Besides which, our intelligence already indicates that there's nothing the nearest Constellar system could move ahead of us which would pose a serious threat to our squadron. Whether they arrive first or we arrive first, we'll outgun them by a very significant margin."

Jun watched the woman evaluating Ekk's report. She was strikingly beautiful. No surprise, that. All kosmarchs were drawn from a class of people genetically designed for leadership. This included looks, as well as brains. Her eyes were brightly intelligent, though also somewhat cold. They glanced from Ekk, to Jun, and back again, as if the kosmarch were trying to decide which of the two officers to punish first.

Then . . . she inhaled deeply, exhaled once, and relaxed.

"Very well, General. I will accede to your superior knowledge on these matters. When we get to the other side, we need to be prepared to fight. If taking more time to reach our Waypoint on this side will increase our chance of success on the other, that's reasonable. Can I assume that your companion is the man you've been telling me about?"

"Yes, Madam Kosmarch," Ekk said, visibly relieved. "Colonel Jun is the foremost scholar on Waymaker relics and science to which we have quick access."

"Madam Kosmarch," Jun said, dipping his chin to his chest. "I am at your service."

"Yes you are," she said matter-of-factly. "Since we have such a long time to wait, before making the actual crossing, I expect an in-depth briefing on everything you know about Waymaker technology, as well as what we might expect to find on the other side."

"Madam," Jun said, being sure to make sure his voice was clear, but not forceful, "I can tell you what I know. But I'm hesitant to speculate."

"Then what good are you, as a Waymaker expert?" she asked.

A fair question, Jun had to admit. Though he got the impression that if he didn't quickly provide her with a logical answer, she'd be showing him to the nearest airlock.

"There's still so much about them that we don't understand, Madam Kosmarch. We've never found any cities, nor any surviving records. Not even fossilized remains. We guess what their basic anatomy may have been like, based on some of the tools recovered. Tools which don't always appear to have an obvious purpose, I might add. I have a great many personal theories, but I don't want them to be the sole informers of your decisionmaking—regardless of which side of the Slipway we're on."

"Prudent thinking," she said. "But I still want to hear what you've got to say. Include whatever materials you consider relevant, and necessary. I want something new for each evening meal with the other officers aboard. Is that clear?"

"Yes, Madam Kosmarch," Jun said, and touched his chin to his chest one more time.

With that, Golsubril Vex maneuvered herself out of the receiving lounge, followed by a small platoon of guards, servants, and other hangers-on who all saw to the kosmarch's comfort, safety, and needs. Once they had departed, the space-suited crew of the transport visibly relaxed, and one of them used a handrail to pull herself over to where General Ekk waited.

"With your permission, sir, we'll be departing now. Unless there's anything else?"

The general waved the woman off, and nodded his head. She took her crew back through the hatch, which sealed tightly behind them. Followed by the mechanical sound of the transport uncoupling itself from the *Alliance*'s dock.

# CHAPTER 10

*CATAPULT* WAS TYPICAL FOR HER CLASS. SHIP-TO-SHIP WEAPONRY consisted of a honeycombed cluster of silos, filled with missiles all mounting nuclear-fusion warheads of various destructive yields. Those same missiles could also be used against ground targets if need be. To protect herself, *Catapult* had a second honeycombed cluster of antimissile silos, each designed to home on, intercept, and destroy incoming nukes. This system was backed by a point-defense network utilizing automated railguns which—while not sufficiently powerful in singular form to critically damage another large warship in space—could knock out incoming projectiles up to the size of something capable of carrying a bomb, or simply perforate the hull of an enemy ship when operated in concert.

As a last resort, the ship could aim its aft end in the direction of the enemy, and ignite the fusion thrusters—creating a stream of hydrogen plasma focused enough to cripple any vessel foolishly crossing *Catapult*'s wake within a few kilometers.

Unlike her larger cousins, *Catapult* didn't carry much in the way of actual armor. Her chief asset was maneuverability. Being light meant having less mass, which in turn meant need-ing less thrust and fuel to perform essential ship-to-ship combat maneuvers. And while it would only take one direct hit from a substantial nuke to break *Catapult*'s spine, she could effectively strafe larger vessels and escape to safe distance before worrying about counterattacks.

Or at least, that was what modern Constellar interplanetary

space war theory held to be true. Based on a combination of actual combat action and cleverly extrapolated astrophysics.

Zuri Mikton had never taken such a small ship into a fight. She wasn't quite sure the frigate would be up to the job of handling Nautilan ships larger than some of the enemy's outsized corvettes. And with over half her force being unarmed, there wasn't going to be any leeway. *Catapult* would be—along with the two long-range scouts—the only armed Constellar ship on the other side of the Waypoint capable of putting up sufficient resistance. Should there be any enemy vessels present upon arrival—*Daffodil* notwithstanding.

So, what did the new system offer?

"It's unremarkable," Commodore Urrl said, pointing his finger at the two-dimensional cross section on the main wall screen of *Catapult*'s small briefing room, adjacent to the command module. "This system has been in the planet-finder catalog for hundreds of years. Six gas worlds ranging in size from point-six jovian standard, to one-point-five jovian standard. All but one of those is on the perimeter, with the largest being very close to the home star—which is a yellow dwarf somewhat larger and brighter than Oswight's sun. I'd almost count the system as a binary, except indications are that the big jovian never underwent internal fusion.

"The central planets are harder to pinpoint. Guessing at least five terrestrials, ranging in mass from point-two terrestrial standard, to one-point-three terrestrial standard. There's some water there. As well as nitrogen. Perhaps a hint of oxygen? None of the planet-finder missions ever devoted extensive study time to this system, so we don't have much else to look at, besides the basic dossier."

"Oort and Kuiper formations?" Zuri asked her executive officer.

"We're guessing standard on both, though there does seem to be some evidence of two separate asteroid belts. One sandwiched between the jovians on the outside, and one between the big jovian on the inside and the next nearest terrestrial."

"Any word on the status of the *Daffodil*?"

"Negative," Urrl said. "I've been in touch with Iakar on an hourly basis, and *Daffodil* never came back over the Waypoint. We'll have to continue to assume she's keeping station in the new system, waiting for reinforcements to arrive."

"Copy," Zuri said, resting her chin on a knuckle. "What's your gut telling you?"

"Damned if I know, boss," Urrl said, slapping a hand down on the small table between them. "I've got very little in the way of hunches. I have to assume that everybody will want a piece of this, but they'll have to connect through Waypoints in Nautilan and Constellar space first. So . . . we've really only got one competitor to worry about. Unfortunately, it's the worst opponent we could ask for. When they start moving ships, they're going to move them in massive quantities. But that takes time. Which means the *Daffodil* might have given us the advantage—assuming there even *is* an advantage to getting there first. We're not even sure what it is we expect to find. You get some information off that Oswight woman who's over on Antagean's lead ship?"

"She spent thirty minutes giving me a lot of ideas," Zuri said. "But until we actually have some tangible reconnaissance to work with, I don't dare plan for specific scenarios. We're just going to have to chew our fingernails off until we hit the Waypoint, and hope that when we reach the other side there isn't a Nautilan battle group waiting for us."

Commodore Urrl drummed his fingers on his thighs, then reached for his microgravity coffee mug.

"Nothing from nothing means nothing," he muttered.

"Or everything," Zuri said. "It doesn't take a genius to hope that whatever we find over there, it helps us in the war."

"Some form of Waymaker weapon?" Urrl said, an eyebrow raised.

"Or maybe a piece of technology they never used as a weapon, but which might work to our advantage anyway. Imagine if all of the different Waypoints could somehow be forced to connect to each other at once?"

"Now *there's* a frightening thought," Urrl said. "The entirety of the Nautilan military could systematically pop into our space at any system they chose."

"Well, maybe. But what if it was something only we could use, and we used it first?"

"Hmmm, that's a much more attractive idea. Put together a strike fleet. Start hitting the Nauties anywhere, anytime we wanted. Make it random, so that they'd never be sure when we might spring up in their back yard—guns blazing. Yes, I like your imagination much more than I like my imagination. Mine is filled with too many dreary wargaming outcomes, all of which are bad for us."

"They've pretty much *been* bad for us, as long as either you or I have been in the service."

"Yeah," Urrl said glumly, while frowning.

"There's got to be some way we can work this discovery to Constellar advantage," Zuri said, standing up. She started to pace back and forth in front of the wall screen, her eyes focused on the air roughly one meter in front of her.

"Even if there's nothing worth having in the new system, it's bound to draw at least *some* of Nautilan's interest. Enough for them to risk thinning out their forces in other areas?"

"And then we hit back?" Urrl asked. "Regain some of what's been lost?"

"Yes," Zuri said.

"This assumes *your* bosses are even thinking offensively. And we both know they're not. Face it. Constellar is on a near-permanent defensive footing. We've been beaten so many times, we can't see straight. And there's nobody at the top level who is crazy enough to suggest that we try to turn the tables on our enemies—whether a realistic opportunity to do so presents itself, or not."

Zuri sat down again, and knotted her fingers into her close-cropped silver hair.

"Something's got to give," she said quietly. "Either we've got to break out, or we're going to break down. That's Nautilan's whole strategy, and has been for two centuries of almost continual hostilities. They push us, we react—and lose—then they push us again, and so on, and so forth. Just once in my life, I'd like to push *them* for a change. Make *them* have to think about it. Cost *them* a little blood and soil."

"Preaching to the converted," Urrl said, allowing himself a small smile. "And I really hope you're right, boss. Truly. I do. Nobody would be happier than me if we found something on the other side of the Waypoint—some way to flip the situation around. Put the Nauties on the defensive. Make them eat a little bit of their pride. That's something every single Constellar officer dreams about. But are we just imposing a lot of wishful thinking on what could turn out to be an entirely random, empty event? I'll happily go wherever you point me. You know that. But I have to admit, this mission has so many variables attached, I just can't do meaningful analysis. We literally don't *know* anything. And the only good part about it is that we can fairly bet on the idea that the Nauties aren't in any better shape. They're sitting around wondering the same things we are. Or, at least, similar things."

"I wish to hell we had comms with *Daffodil* right now," Zuri muttered. "That ship's got the goods—assuming they've survived, and can tell the tale. By the time we cross, *Daffodil* will have had many days to do a first-run survey. I want to hope that the information they can give us will help us make the right decisions, quickly enough, to gain or keep an upper hand."

Urrl's mouth buttoned up into a small frown.

"What's your sense about Antagean, and his crews?" he asked.

"You tell me," Zuri replied.

"I guess if I have to ask, I've already answered my own question," he muttered.

"I'm not thrilled bringing three boats filled with civilians on this trip, either." Zuri said.

"The lieutenant commander himself," Commodore Urrl said, "that's who really worries me. He's just a civilian playacting like he's one of us. I can tell the type. *All* of the Reserve is like that. Happier being out of the ranks than in them. You mark my words. When the pain comes, he's liable to fold. He hasn't fought the way you and I have both fought."

"There has to be a first time for everything," Zuri said.

"If he didn't fight when he was young," Urrl groused, "he's not much good to us now, at his age and rank. You learn those skills early, or you don't earn them at all."

"Maybe," Zuri said, then allowed herself a slow, exasperated exhale. "But it's not like we had better options. We're going to have to hope that Antagean doesn't crack once the rockets start flying. *If* they start flying. And if he does crack...I can always relieve him. Whether his crews like it, or not. They belong to us for the duration of the trip. The onus is on the lieutenant commander to prove he deserves his rank."

# CHAPTER 11

WYODRETH ANTAGEAN STEPPED INTO THE DIM LIGHT OF THE small starboard observation bubble—wearing a DSOD spaceflight coverall, versus the more formal two-piece uniform he'd worn at the Planet Oswight spaceport—and allowed himself to sink into one of the seven plush gee chairs which faced outward into the void. In the days since departing dock, the sun had diminished almost imperceptibly to the point that its light was now being challenged by some of the brighter stars set against the inky, permanent blackness of interstellar space.

All of which had seemed eternally out of mankind's reach for the entirety of Wyo's life. He'd spent his twenties and thirties becoming intimately familiar with Constellar's systems, and even a few of the systems in Starstates Yamato and Sultari on those rare occasions when Antagean liners had been tasked with handling international passengers and cargo. Now he'd be crossing the Slipway into virgin territory. It was a prospect as exciting as it was unnerving, precisely because everyone expected Starstate Nautilan to be doing the same. And Wyo dreaded the idea that one or more of his ships might fall before Nautilan missiles.

Running his father's business was challenging enough, even on the good days. He'd stepped into Dad's shoes not out of desire, but out of necessity. And while Seinar Antagean, his sister, was a capable number cruncher who ably kept the books, she was liable to get overwhelmed by the personnel aspect. Which was

69

where Wyo himself tended to do best—provided none of those personnel were getting killed.

A visitor quietly stepped into the observation bubble, and sat down one chair away from Wyo's own. He turned—the dim light making silhouettes of them both—and thought he recognized the Lady Oswight. She still wore the same type of zipsuit he'd seen her wearing on day one. Almost as if she didn't dare wear anything else. Wyo had occasionally seen spacephobes travel like that. Terrified that the ship might crack open at any moment, leaking all of the atmosphere into space. So they never set foot outside a pressure garment.

"Ma'am," Wyo said, reluctantly getting to his feet.

"Please, sit," the Lady said softly.

Wyo looked behind them, expecting the former colour sergeant to appear. When Axabrast did not emerge from the open pressure hatchway, Wyo slowly bent his knees, and returned to brooding in his gee chair.

"It's breathtaking," Garsina said. "I can see what the appeal is, for people who make their lives in space."

"There is a certain romance to it," Wyo admitted. "When I was younger, my father made sure I cut my teeth out here."

"What do you mean?" Garsina asked.

"I may have been the boss's son, but Dad made sure I started at the bottom of the food chain. I spent years learning just about every job there is to learn aboard a commercial starliner. No chore was too menial, nor too messy."

"Sounds like you didn't enjoy it," Garsina said.

"I didn't. I can look back on it, now, and see Dad's point. But at the time? I just kind of went around being angry a lot. Captain Loper can tell you some stories about that, if ever you get a chance to talk to him."

"Back home," Garsina said, "I had to beg my father, to let me do *any* kind of work."

"Your minder, Mister Axabrast, kept you from getting your hands dirty?"

"He's not my minder," Garsina snapped. Then she seemed to think better of herself—her expression transforming in the wan light—and said, "But he is my protector, when father wishes it."

"How did you manage to evade Axabrast's watchfulness at this hour?" Wyo asked.

"I left him talking to your engineers down in the reactor module. In addition to having a fascination for First Family etiquette, as it pertains to his longstanding assignment within the Oswight house, Mister Axabrast also enjoys spacecraft. It's a hobby of his, going back to when he was newly enlisted with Deep Space Operations and Defense. His first time out, as a young private, he fell in love with the ships. These huge, complex machines which carry us from world to world. He won't say so to me openly, but he's concerned that your civilian starliners aren't up to the challenge of this mission we've embarked upon."

Wyo made a scoffing sound.

"Just because we're not bristling with rockets doesn't mean these ships are weak. My father doesn't own many ships, but the spaceframes he *does* operate are the most robust variety available from any civilian shipyard anywhere in Constellar space. We've got the best reactors my father can buy, and we run our maintenance and module rotation schedule at twice the pace recommended by various manufacturers. For precisely the reason that Antagean can't afford to have a reputation for cheapness. We're too small, and we don't enjoy the favor of any particular First Family who can intercede on our behalf, in case something goes wrong. Our operational record, since the inception, is the best of any commercial line in the Starstate."

"I didn't mean to question you—or your father's—competence," Garsina said tersely. "Just informing you of Mister Axabrast's opinion."

"Well," Wyo said, "you can tell the *colour* sergeant for me that if he doesn't trust these ships—or the men and women running them—he's welcome to transport back to your family's yacht."

"Oh, he'd like that very much," Garsina said bitterly. "With me being pulled by the wrist!"

"So would I," Wyo muttered, and then realized the almost dead silence of the observation module made even under-the-breath speech sound very loud in his ears.

Garsina stood up stiffly, almost hopping out of her seat in the half-gee thrust.

"You think we're pests?"

"I didn't say—" Wyo blurted, but then realized it was too late.

"Typical businessman's son," Garsina said, almost spitting the words. "You happily take First Family money when it suits your corporate interests, but then you bad-mouth us behind our backs, and fight us tooth and nail in the Constellar Council! Is it any wonder that the Council is practically gridlocked every session? My brothers have spent years dueling rhetorically with commercial representatives forever trying to *counterbalance* the First Families, when it comes to legislation. Forgetting that none of you would be able to make a single coin without our support and oversight!"

Suddenly, Wyo saw red. He'd spent the past six months trying to navigate Oswight regional regulations, in regards to fee schedules, and what types and kinds of cargo were considered restricted at Oswight spaceports. Every system had its annoying local rules, true enough, but Oswight's were unusually costly, and sometimes even contradictory. He'd practically had to bribe several Oswight officials—without coming right out and calling it a bribe. And all for the sake of First Family insistence that they each maintain a microgovernment within their respective territories. At the expense of men—like Antagean—who simply had a job needing to be done.

"*Oversight*?" Wyo almost barked the word. "That's what you call it? As if the war isn't bad enough, you all chisel and chip away at the hard work done by honest people who aren't *good* enough for you, simply on account of being born common. If ever there was a time when Starstate Constellar *did* need the First Families, I think that time has long since passed. And every businessman and businesswoman in the Starstate will say the same thing—provided they're not keeping their mouths shut to avoid being slapped with phantom penalties and punitive taxation on account of having *offended* one of you!"

Part of Wyo's brain knew he was committing a serious error. If his father were present, doubtless Wyograd would be trying desperately to shut his son up, while apologizing to the Lady Oswight in the same breath. But Wyo didn't have his father's patience where politics was concerned. And after being yanked away from work, and plunged into the present predicament against his will, Wyo's nerves weren't up to the task of placating the Lady and her opinions of businessmen.

The heat radiating off Garsina's face—partially illuminated, and almost pink with anger—was palpable.

She made a noise of disgust, and stormed out of the observation bubble.

Wyo put a hand over his eyes, and sank lower into the gee chair.

"Way to go, Mister Company Man," he said softly, self-mocking. *When we get back,* he thought, *look for Antagean to get its corporate ass booted completely out of Oswight territory. Seinar is going to chew me out hard when that happens. We need the facilities orbiting Planet Oswight. If Family Oswight simply chooses to make those facilities too expensive for us... what recourse do we have?*

And then Wyo went back to being angry about the First Families all over again. It was absurd that any man should have to worry about being on the good side of those people, simply to keep a storefront open. Didn't Constellar make a lot of patriotic noise regarding freedom? Where was the freedom in a society which still afforded the First Families so much arbitrary power? Especially when so many of them had done nothing to earn it?

"Classy," said a familiar voice.

"Captain," Wyo said, recognizing his old friend and former mentor. He suddenly sat up, and absently rubbed a thumb under his nose. "How much of that noise did you hear?"

"Enough," Loper said.

"Where did she go?"

"Not a clue. She went past me like a clipper burning at one hundred and ten percent, and I knew better than to open my mouth. Wish you could say the same, sir."

"It's an impossible task," Wyo grunted, as Captain Loper descended into a gee chair opposite to where the Lady Oswight had most recently been sitting.

"Your father knew that when he started the business," said the older man. "But he always had a head for the political side of the job. The First Families are a pain in the ass, to be sure. But they're also part and parcel of our national fabric. They need us, and we need them, though we don't often like to admit it. And certainly not at the Constellar Council, where the long war between people who make money—and people who are born with money—continues."

"See, this is why I never wanted to sit in Dad's chair," Wyo admitted. "I knew I wasn't going to be very good at playing the game, in this regard. I think dad knows it too, though he's certainly tried over the years to help me see the value in it. I'm too much like my mom. And she didn't think much of the First Families either."

"No she didn't," Loper said, and chuckled quietly.

Silence descended for several minutes, then Wyo asked, "But if I'm not sitting in Dad's chair, what happens to you and everybody else who's depending on us—the Antageans—to keep the company running? Dad built the company because he loved the sport of it all. He loved working on starliners when he was young, and got it into his head that someday he'd run his own fleet of them. And that his fleet would be the best. Not the biggest. Not the most favored among his competitors. Just the fleet known for quality and competence, above all. It was the thing he staked the family reputation on. And both me and Seinar have done our damnedest to try to live up to that. But I am not sure it's enough."

"You talk like Wyograd's death is a foregone conclusion," Captain Loper said.

"Each time he gets sick," Wyo said gravely, "we find out it's worse than the last time. Treatments can bring him back to full health, for a while. But each new low is lower than the last. I wouldn't tell this to anyone other than you, but I am not sure Dad's got it in him to pull out of it again. You haven't seen him, because he refuses to see anyone but family, and the doctors. But he's a tired ghost of himself. Very little strength left. If he wasn't so damned stubborn, I think he'd be gone already."

"And watching him die means suddenly the weight of the company is all on you," Loper said.

"Yeah."

"Maybe Seinar can handle it, in concert with the board? You could step away?"

"No," Wyo said. "I know my sister. She doesn't like dealing with the board. And they don't like dealing with her. The board sees me as Dad's natural successor, and they expect me to continue in his stead. Which I've been doing. But it's the least enjoyable work I've ever had to plow through. Far tougher than any head you made me clean when I was a kid. I sometimes think I'd happily go back to scrubbing gee toilets again, just because there wouldn't be so much damned pressure."

The older man looked down at his hands folded in his lap, then turned his chair to face directly at Wyo's own.

"Would you believe me if I told you your father voiced similar sentiments to me?"

"He did?" Wyo said, sitting up straight. This was news. Dad had always seemed an implacable force where company welfare was concerned. No wavering.

"You two aren't *that* different," Captain Loper said. "As much as Wyograd is immensely proud of the business he's built—and proud of all of us who elected to share in his dream with him as foundational employees—that dream came with a fairly severe cost. Because deep down, Wyograd still wants to be that wide-eyed third-class ship's mate, newly signed on for his very first stint aboard a starliner. He wants that magic back, and he never really got it. No matter how successful the business became."

"Dad never said anything to me," Wyo admitted.

"Of course he never said anything to you," Loper said. "You are his son. For you, and your sister, he wants to be the immovable mountain. The man upon whose shoulders your reality solidly rests. But it was never easy for him. And when he got sick, and then got sick again . . . well, there are a tiny handful of us old-timers who have managed to keep in touch with him, and know the true toll that's been taken. Though, once the correspondence stopped, I knew he'd gotten so sick, recently, that this might be it for him."

Wyo studied the older man's face, and thought he saw a tear slip down Captain Loper's cheek.

"I guess I've been feeling sorry for myself," Wyo said sheepishly.

"Damned right you've been feeling sorry for yourself," Loper said sternly.

"That's not going to cut it on this trip, is it?"

"Nope," Loper said, matter-of-factly.

"So I'd probably best suck it up, and go find a way to make nice with the Lady Oswight?"

"You might consider it."

"Any advice on that?"

Loper paused, his profile looking particularly aged in the light from Planet Oswight's far home star, then he said, "Appeal to her scholarly expertise. Get her talking about the Waymakers, versus First Family business. And find enough humility to slip a genuine apology in there somewhere, okay?"

"Okay," Wyo said, then stood up, and patted the older man on the shoulder, before walking through the hatchway, back into the innards of the ship.

# CHAPTER 12

THE PICTURE:

Two orange-yellow dwarf stars, enormously far apart.

Also, two small squadrons of starships, each squadron moving rapidly away from its respective star, toward an invisible point in space on the fringe of that star's gravitational domain.

And two conventional fleets of war vessels, perpetually stationed around those points. Each fleet forever on alert against invasion. Which can happen at any moment. Or not.

Connecting the points is an alien Overspace architecture, which is newly aimed at a third point which previously did not exist—on the edge of a yellow dwarf star's territory, into which one starship has already disappeared. With no word on that ship's fate.

Commodore Iakar wasn't a betting man. In his career with the Constellar military, he'd gotten where he was through determined vigilance against unpredictable outcomes. Which was precisely how he ran his crew aboard the *Comet,* which in turn reflected how he ran his security flotilla, over which Iakar had presided for the better part of an Oswight solar year. He was boringly methodical, and he knew it. Just as he knew that his style drove many of the junior officers nuts. Which was just fine. Iakar had been one of them, once. He'd paid his dues. If somebody in his direct chain of command didn't like his style, he didn't have to care. Because while he was in charge, the security flotilla *would* be ready to repel any and all invaders. To the last DSOD ship, if necessary. No slacking off. No exceptions.

So they maintained their ships, and drilled for battle, then drilled some more, did still further maintenance, drilled for battle once again, then drilled for battle a final time, after which, there were always... more battle drills.

Thus, life this far from civilization wasn't glamorous. But there was a comfort to the routine which suited Iakar's personality. He could wake up every day knowing exactly what his job was, which meant knowing exactly what everyone else's job was too, and so long as they all did their jobs the way they were supposed to, Planet Oswight and its system were kept safe from the Nautilan threat. A threat Commodore Iakar took very, very seriously.

Until... now, Iakar's flotilla was to be broken up. Which made Iakar ferociously surly toward even those officers he normally liked. Enough so that everyone around him had begun giving Iakar a wide berth, lest the man erupt with a fresh series of expostulations about how Admiral Mikton's pending Slipway voyage to the mystery star—which would eventually entail pulling across some or perhaps even all of Iakar's carefully managed force—was going to cripple his ability to carry out his first assignment: to protect Oswight space.

The commodore imagined that his counterpart on the Nautilan side was in a mirrored state of agitation. No Waypoint security commander wanted to get caught undermanned or outgunned. The flotilla was what it was, precisely for the purpose of ensuring that any adversary trespassing into friendly territory would be met with as much firepower as possible. It didn't take a starship to mount lots of missile silos and railguns. There was no great secret to the calculus of winning, either. The battle group with the most ships, able to shoot first, usually took the day. Time after time, this was how almost all invasions—in any Starstate— had played out.

So, faced with seeing his resources halved—or worse— Commodore Iakar had to work extraordinarily hard to keep his temper in check while he communicated with Admiral Mikton and her expeditionary team.

"Still no word from the *Daffodil*?" the admiral asked, her message taking mere seconds to travel the distance from the *Catapult* to the *Comet*.

"No, ma'am," Commodore Iakar said. "Either she's waiting

patiently for you and your people to make the crossing, or she's run into trouble the likes of which we can only guess at. Which is why I am still *very* unsure about your plan, to be honest. You're going over the Slipway knowing exactly nothing about what you may face. And my understanding is you have an heir of Family Oswight with you? It's madness to take a First Family member on what may amount to a suicide mission, ma'am."

"Your opinion is noted," Admiral Mikton's visage spoke, after a few seconds' delay. "And like I've told your old friend Commodore Urrl, all things being equal, I'd like to wait until DSOD sends us a true task squadron. But since the *Daffodil* decided to risk everything for the sake of being first on the scene, I feel like we have to hedge our bets, and jump over too. Once I'm on the other side, I can ascertain what's needed to hold our new position, then send back at least the Oswight yacht to begin the process of transferring your command to the star's Waypoint."

"And leave Oswight space with only partial or no protection," Iakar said dubiously, his arms crossed over his chest while he talked to his boss—across almost a million kilometers.

For this conversation, Iakar had ordered everyone out of the *Comet*'s tiny briefing room, which was adjacent to the command module. If things got heated, he didn't want the noise spilling over to the rest of the *Comet*'s crew. People were already on edge. Listening to the Commodore quarrel with his superior wouldn't do any of them any good.

"I am willing to wager that Starstate Nautilan only has eyes for the freshly minted Waypoint," Admiral Mikton replied. "Just like we do."

"That's a hell of a wager, ma'am," he said, still not convinced.

"Yes, it is," Admiral Mikton said. "And I realize I am putting you in an unfortunate position, by making you take this wager with me. Splitting the security flotilla is not an ideal move. It's definitely not a 'by the book' defensive strategy. But the book never took into account the manifestation of new Waypoints. So, this is where I have to improvise, and hope I am not wrong."

Commodore Iakar's face twisted up in an expression of skepticism, then he nodded his head curtly, and said, "Copy your latest orders, ma'am. My ships and I await your arrival."

And with that, the connection dropped.

When Iakar resumed his seat in the captain's gee chair, all of the command module was hushed. He'd taught them to expect harshness these past few days. It was a point of extreme soreness for him, not having *Daffodil* at his disposal. She had been his only early warning system, capable of detecting Waypoint activation and use moments before any inbound starships could arrive. Now, he was limited to conventional sensors only. Which meant an enemy flotilla could cross the Slipway and emerge—missiles firing. Absolutely no time to prepare. Iakar's own flotilla would simply have to dump the entirety of their own stores in one panicked salvo, and hope it was sufficient.

Because there probably wouldn't be enough of Iakar's watch flotilla left for a follow-through strike. They'd be nuked to rubble, and the Nauties along with them—hopefully.

Strange, Iakar thought. That interstellar warfare was reduced to such a brute-force strategy. But then, he suspected it had ever been thus, dating all the way back to the ancient times. *Arrive first with the most guns,* had surely been written on some primitive war college's doorstep. Back in an age before humanity went to the stars—desperately escaping what had surely seemed like the war to end all wars.

*The last, big fight,* Iakar mused to himself, as he checked his flotilla status display, and tapped out commands on his gee chair's swing-arm keyboard. *Sooner or later, we're going to see the same thing happen too. One by one, Starstate Nautilan's rivals are going to be consumed.*

It was practically heresy to speak such fears openly among other Constellar commanders. But the mathematics seemed clear to a man who'd spent his entire life learning how to read the numbers, and extrapolate them to their most logical conclusion. The simple reality of it was that every time Nautilan took another system, it got bigger and stronger, while some other Starstate got smaller and weaker. And while all of the remaining Starstates combined—Constellar, Sultari, Yamato, and Amethyne—might have had a chance at repelling an all-out, determined push for total Waywork domination, there was almost no way any of the leaders in any of those Starstates could manage the diplomatic gymnastics required to forge a lasting alliance.

So, Commodore Iakar's only real hope—and it was an outside possibility, at best—had been for Nautilan to succumb to factors of which he was not aware. An internal rebellion within

Nautilan's own borders, perhaps? Some of the DSOD intelligence literature speculated that Starstate Nautilan spent even more on troops, ships, and equipment for internal security than it did on war fleets designed to seize new territory.

Never had Iakar thought it possible that the Waywork itself would surprise him.

A whole ship's day passed as Iakar waited for the expeditionary Task Group to arrive.

When Admiral Mikton's ships finally showed, Commodore Iakar thought them an even more fragile-looking bunch than he'd first surmised. The civilian starliners, while seemingly state-of-the-art, were nevertheless toothless in battle. The two scouts and the single, bulky frigate, would be hard pressed to run defense. To say nothing of the small, delicate Oswight yacht. Which would be swatted away by the merest gust of Nautilan wind.

"I want to wish you good luck," Iakar said to his superior as Mikton made final communication before the Slipway crossing.

"I want to wish us good luck too," she said, her image hovering in front of Iakar's face.

He did not know the admiral very well. What little he did know of her history spoke of a capable officer who'd nevertheless been overwhelmed by events. Just as it now seemed she might be overwhelmed again.

"I'll wait for the return of the Oswight yacht," Iakar said. "But in the event that the yacht does *not* come back—nor any other ship from your group—Admiral... what are your orders?"

Now Iakar could see Commodore Urrl's face moving into the picture, where he whispered quietly into Mikton's ear.

Mikton nodded once, then squared her shoulders, and addressed Commodore Iakar formally.

"In the event that no ship from this Task Group returns, you are to notify the ICC of this fact, and maintain readiness at the Waypoint proper. Do not assume anything, Commodore. Failure to return could mean any one of a dozen different things. The ICC has one courier starship in reserve, which can be dispatched to relay messages to the rest of the Starstate. It's vital that you keep the Waypoint defended, and open to friendly traffic. I say again, if we do not return, it's vital that you maintain the security of the Waypoint. The fate of systems beyond Planet Oswight's may depend on this."

"I copy your orders, ma'am," Iakar said. "I hope I won't have to follow them."

"Me too," Admiral Mikton's visage said. Then she disappeared, and Iakar was left to brood in his gee chair, wondering how the future might unfold.

# CHAPTER 13

THE LADY OSWIGHT WAS UPSET WITH HERSELF. IT WAS VERY uncouth to lose one's temper in the fashion she had lost her temper with Lieutenant Commander Antagean. Even if everything she'd said was true, she knew her father would be ashamed of her for letting the veneer of Family manners slip far enough to show a mere corporate man that, yes, First Families really *are* people after all. Special people, true, according to both law and custom. But still people just the same. And it didn't do to bring oneself down to a common level. Especially in the midst of an argument with somebody who, in seriousness, had no right to talk to Garsina the way he had. Going so far as to question the legitimacy of First Family preeminence in the Starstate, for Exodus' sake! Who by the Waymakers did that Antagean man think he was?

So, Garsina spent several days stewing her way through the ship, and ignoring the several messages which came across to her personal mailbox through the ship's intranet. Messages delivered from Wyodreth Antagean's personal account, and appearing for all intents and purposes to be olive branches extended in good faith.

*No,* Garsina thought. *I know enough about this game—from what my mother taught me—to realize that you don't take the first offer. Nor the second. Nor the third. Let him sweat over his mistake! Become unsure of himself, enough so that when next we're face to face, he will be so abashed—*

The Lady Oswight was unable to finish her thought. Elvin Axabrast appeared, and seemed anxious to get her attention.

"What?" she asked, busily reorganizing a spacer's steamer trunk—which had already been organized three times before. The various items in the trunk would have gone floating throughout the room, save for the fact that the trunk's lid was lined with grip surface. So, anything which had to be removed from the netted subcompartments inside could be temporarily held in place, while she went digging still deeper into the trunk's contents.

"Ma'am," the majordomo said, "I think you might enjoy it a great deal if you're in the command module when they activate the Key. I don't think you've ever seen such a thing up close, have you?"

"No," Garsina admitted, and slapped the steamer trunk lid closed with a *thunk,* then allowed herself to be led away. Would Wyodreth be in the command module? Even though she was certain in her soul that it was he who had been in the wrong, she wasn't sure yet how she wanted to use that fact to her advantage. She might have been the youngest Oswight heir, but she was not an idiot. Having the upper hand in her dealings with Antagean was going to be very important during the days ahead. She needed to be sure that the man grasped exactly where he stood, and that it was not on equal footing with Garsina Oswight.

After hustling through several corridors, and a lengthy lift ride down the backbone of the vessel, Garsina found herself being propelled into the civilian starliner's command module. She'd toured many military vessels and seen their command modules before, so the command module of the Antagean liner was something of a surprise. There were far fewer workstations present, and while the station for the Key seemed to be where one might expect it, the arrangement for the ship's captain was quite different. He didn't occupy a position of prominence. Merely sat in an ordinary seat among several, with flatscreen displays and a small holograph machine no different from any other.

Captain Loper rose to attention, his spacer's boots gripping him properly in place. Everyone else in the command module rose too, until Garsina forced a smile to her face, and bade them all relax.

"Would it be a problem if I observed during the crossing?" Garsina asked.

"No, ma'am," Captain Loper replied. "We'd be honored to

have a distinguished spectator for this, surely the most historic Slipway crossing since the very first performed in the Waywork. Ma'am, if I can direct your attention to our trusty Slipway pilot, who's got his hands on the Key at this very moment, we can watch him do his thing. I only ask that you save your questions until after he's through. This takes a bit of concentration."

Garsina knew the technical details. The Waypoint pilot did not control the Key like an ordinary pilot. It was mental work all the way, accessing the Key's functions through a seemingly telepathic interface which human scientists still didn't understand. They only knew that it worked. And that not everyone was suited—innately—for the vocation. Garsina herself had always been curious to find out if she had the aptitude, but like so many things in life, her father had considered it beneath her station. So she had been content to study the Keys as an academic. A discipline for which there was abundant speculation and theory, but precious little hard data. The Waymakers had left so little of themselves behind for humanity to study. And what they *had* left, didn't tell Garsina—or anyone else—much.

The civilian pilot's forehead was damp with perspiration, and his eyes were closed. His hands moved across the Key in an almost intimate fashion. And his lips moved ever so slightly, as if to make words without sound. Garsina held herself steady near the Waypoint pilot's gee chair, with Elvin peering over one shoulder, and Captain Loper peering over the other. Neither man said a word. They all just waited silently for the Waypoint pilot to make the next move.

"Sir," the Waypoint pilot finally said, "we're now in an optimal position within the Waypoint envelope."

"How about the other ships?" Loper asked, this time directing his question to one of the Antagean Starlines personnel who stared into a traffic-control hologram.

"Everyone's lined up and awaiting the order to execute," the young woman said.

"Signal our readiness to the other two Antagean liners. Then give our status to the *Catapult*. We'll wait for their order."

The crossing would be almost simultaneous. As soon as the Waypoint pilot received clearance to proceed, he would activate the Key. What that looked like, precisely, in the pilot's mind, was unclear. Most Waypoint pilots described it like a waking dream, wherein the dream's contents were directly touchable through force of will. The web of the Waywork would be stretched before them, all of the many Waypoints connected to their closest neighbors by a skein of pathways. Traveling great distances required using several Waypoints in succession. But there was never any danger of congestion on the Slipway proper, because the moment the Key was activated, the starship in question instantly ceased to exist at one Waypoint, and came into existence again at the far Waypoint.

Garsina knew the theoretical physics behind the maneuver. Every particle of ordinary matter on the ship, in the ship, and attached to the ship, would be translated across an Overspace which could not be accessed with ordinary human technology. In the Overspace, ordinary time did not exist, nor did ordinary distance. The ship—and everyone aboard—would experience an immeasurably small moment of what could only be called singularity within the Overspace, and then would promptly pop back out into normal space at the target Waypoint. With no conventional time having elapsed.

If the pilot removed his hands from the Key at the instant of activation, or there was a power failure of some sort, the ship merely remained in place. No movement would occur. Experiments had been performed countless times, testing to see whether or not having multiple people touching the Key at once, or providing the key with an excess of power from ships' reactors, made any difference in a Key's performance. It apparently didn't matter how much power you dumped into the operation. Any given Key could only jump one Slipway per execution, and whoever touched the Key first had command of the device. No other mind could access a Key at any one time. Therefore there was no daisy-chaining possible. You activated the Key, found yourself on the other side, and had to begin the attune to the Waywork all over again—at the Waypoint pilot's mental level—for the next crossing. Which would take minutes, at best.

Meanwhile, the ship's human-built computer would be loudly broadcasting encrypted FRIENDLY codes on known Starstate Constellar identification frequencies, to avoid being mistaken for a hostile vessel. Ships failing to properly identify, or identifying with outdated codes, risked being fired upon with extreme prejudice. Because every Waypoint in the Waywork was defended by a security flotilla similar to that of Commodore Iakar's.

So, ensuring that all starships were constantly updated with the correct code scheme was vital to ensuring ordinary civilian and military traffic proceeded without incident.

Which did not concern Garsina nearly as much as the fact that nobody really understood how or why the Keys could access Overspace in the first place. There were no conventional instruments capable of plumbing Overspace's dimensions. And no one outside of the Key-adept had direct access to a Key's functionality—with a price. The Keys had not been built to interface with human minds. Sooner or later, all of the Key-adept were forced to retire. Often while still quite young, lest constant mental contact with the Keys drive the Key-adept insane.

Or was it the Overspace itself which drove men and women mad?

Garsina once visited a DSOD veterans hospital where several Waypoint pilots had been committed. They had each been sad souls, drifting in and out of coherency. Most of them claimed to still be able to reach the Waywork, even without the Keys. And that it was the Waywork gradually pulling them across—their minds, one bit at a time—without conscious effort which made them crazy.

Eventually, they all dropped into comas, and died within weeks.

Every starship in the Waywork therefore carried medical personnel specifically tasked with caring for the Waypoint pilots. Ensuring that they all got plenty of rest. Painstakingly logging each and every hour of work. There wasn't a hard limit on how much exposure the human mind could stand—to Key work—before going unstable. But a general range had been identified. And anyone hitting the lower end of that range was promptly taken off the job, and never returned to Key work again. Which did not eliminate unstability, especially among prior service military personnel. But it did cut down on the total number of Key-adept being forcibly institutionalized.

Some former Waypoint pilots—the ones who quit in time— retired from space duty altogether. Others went on to other space work, just not involving Keys. A few matriculated to academics, which is where Garsina had spent her time immersed in Waymaker lore. The other students, and a tiny handful of instructors, who had been Key-adept had seemed normal enough to her. Though a few of them had confided that doing work with the Keys had permanently changed their sleep patterns. It was not uncommon for veteran Waypoint pilots to suffer from insomnia, which itself had to be remedied through a variety of different medicines and techniques.

Virtually all of the former Key users whom Garsina knew through the academic world were proficient meditators. Men and women who'd forced themselves to achieve monk-like levels of mental discipline. Simply out of self-preservation.

Garsina almost felt sorry for the Antagean Starlines employee seated before the Key, whose face was even younger than her own, but who seemed to carry an invisible burden while his hands kept sliding over the Key's smooth surface.

"Clearance to cross, affirmative," said the command module crewperson watching the traffic hologram.

"Go," Captain Loper said.

Garsina watched, breath held, as the Waypoint pilot's lips thinned into a tight line. His hands froze for a moment, and then the Key's surface illuminated . . . and it was an experience difficult to describe. Like the whole world becoming a negative image of itself, just for the smallest fraction of a second. Before suddenly everything was back to normal again. Not a hair out of place.

Except the Waypoint pilot's whole face had gone damp, and he practically panted for air.

"Something wrong?" Captain Loper said, gently pushing past Garsina's shoulder to rest a hand on the young Waypoint pilot's arm.

"Nossir," the Waypoint pilot said, his breathing gradually coming back to normal. "That was *weird*. It was like having to run wind sprints, except sitting perfectly still. The crossing doesn't normally take that much effort. I don't know why it did this time."

"Log it with the surgeon," Loper ordered. "Meanwhile, navigator, get busy making sure we ended up where we thought we should end up."

Garsina turned to look at Elvin Axabrast, who'd observed the whole affair, and the old man merely gave her a shrug. He was a prior soldier, not Key-adept, and while spaceships were a pet fascination for him, the Keys were a mystery forever beyond his reach, so he didn't have the same kind of interest in them that Garsina did.

A pair of new faces appeared behind Elvin's.

Wyodreth Antagean. And Zoam Kalbi.

"Everything go okay? Sorry I missed it," Antagean said to Loper.

"Seems fine so far. How about it, Darl? We wind up where we're supposed to be?"

The traffic control crewperson was rapidly typing keys on her keyboard.

"The starfinder is still sorting itself out . . . wait, got it. Yes, we appear to be where we ought to be. We're drifting just inside the new Waypoint's operational envelope."

The lighting in the command module suddenly went orange, and a computerized *bong-bong-bong-bong* began to sound.

Zoam Kalbi—equipped with a video and audio recorder— swiveled his head around and asked, "What's that? Was the ship somehow damaged?"

"Nossir," the young Antagean employee working traffic control replied. "The computers are simply telling us that no encrypted traffic pattern channels are live in this system. It thinks we're at risk of being mistaken for hostile by this system's security fleet."

"Do you see any such thing?" Wyodreth ordered, before Loper could even open his mouth. "Now that we're across, we have to know if there is anyone waiting for us."

The hologram over the young woman's workstation, quickly populated with small visual signatures—all of them glowing happily blue.

"Nothing but the rest of the Task Group," she said, and exhaled with relief.

"Signal the *Catapult* that our status is nominal," Captain Loper ordered. "And check with our other two ships, to see if their Waypoint pilots had the same experience as our own."

"Fascinating," Zoam Kalbi said, moving with care as the pair of glasses he wore merely served as the eyes for his recording equipment, tucked discreetly into his beltline.

Garsina took a moment to look at Wyodreth Antagean, who'd quickly pulled himself over to one of the empty command module workstations, and plugged in a slim headset. His fingers were a blur, moving across his station's keyboard, and he didn't look up as she continued to watch him.

The orange light returned to normal white, and the aural alert ceased.

"There," Wyodreth said. "My override appears to have worked. Though the computer is very confused by the fact that there's no traffic control to talk to on this side of the Slipway. I've ordered computers on all three of our ships to slave to the *Catapult* for the duration. That's our authority until we cross back to Oswight territory."

Now Wyodreth's eyes did come up, and he looked Garsina square in the face for the first time. Their unflinching gaze was mutual—for a moment which seemed just a bit longer than necessary—then Wyodreth dropped his eyes back to his displays, and returned to typing.

# CHAPTER 14

KOSMARCH GOLSUBRIL VEX SWEPT INTO THE COMMAND MODULE of the *Alliance* as if she, and not General Ekk, were in charge. Having dispensed with her subdued travel uniform many days prior, she now wore the more elaborate and formal kosmarch's state dress—with the sigils of her authority circling her forearms at the cuffs, and a bright red band of silk running around her collar to match that of Starstate Nautilan's proud national banner. When the eyes of the command module crew looked up, they met Vex's just long enough to realize who she was, then they immediately looked down to their various keyboards and screens. Afraid—she knew—to hold her gaze too long, lest she become overly interested in them specifically. A predicament which few officers enjoyed, even at the higher ranks.

All except that sickly colonel, who seemed to delight in meeting Vex's gaze, almost daring her to say something to him. Had he been any ordinary soldier, or even a common citizen, such impertinence would have been lethal on his part. But Colonel Jun came with General Ekk's seal of approval, as their best—indeed, only—expert on Waymaker knowledge and lore.

So, the kosmarch tolerated the colonel. But only barely.

Having arrived at the Waypoint for Jaalit's home star, Vex was eager to get on with the project at hand. And because she so seldom had the opportunity, she wanted to observe the crossing from the standpoint of a Waypoint pilot. A discipline for which Vex herself had initially tested, upon first entering government service. But she had not possessed the natural aptitude, so her abilities had been directed into other areas. Which had ended up suiting her just fine, in the long run. Waypoint pilots were expendable assets. A skilled kosmarch was a vital tool of the Starstate. Irreplaceable. Especially one about to embark upon the journey of a hundred lifetimes.

"Are all ships prepared to enter the Slipway?" Vex asked General Ekk, as the older man greeted her formally.

"They are, Madam Kosmarch. We only wait for your command to begin Waypoint passage. I admit, I was not prepared to entertain your presence here in the command module. You could have given the order from your quarters, if that would have been to your preference?"

"It would not have," Golsubril sniffed. "I wanted to see the crossing from the standpoint of those who do the work. Specifically, I wanted to see the Key during Waypoint activation."

"Interested in the Waymakers' great gift to us?" Colonel Jun asked, inviting himself into the conversation, despite the fact that Golsubril had not included him.

She slowly pivoted in the air, using handholds to guide her way, and allowed the shorter man to enter the small circle with herself and Ekk.

"Yes," Vex replied coolly. "Knowing that a thing functions, and observing its functioning firsthand, are different, don't you agree?"

"Most definitely," the colonel said, not adding the customary *madam kosmarch* which all subordinates reflexively attached to their speech when addressing Vex.

Golsubril looked at the colonel. Jun's file said he came from very old, very loyal Nautilan stock, which stretched back to the very beginning of the Starstate. Unlike so many of the conquered peoples, who very often made poor soldiers, and were fit only for regional subjugation on their individual worlds of origin, Jun's folk had been Nautilan from the start. His father had served ably in the echelons of the previous kosmarch's administration. Nothing about the man's breeding spoke of intemperate nor seditious tendencies. And yet he insisted on a level of informality—around Vex—which bordered on scandalous.

How much longer should she allow it to continue, lest it degrade the level of discipline among the other officers and staff?

Allowing oneself to tolerate an ignored standard, she knew, was essentially setting a new one.

But—and this was Ekk's pleading—Jun did know a lot about the Waymakers. As much as could be reasonably known about them, based on what little technology had been left behind *other* than the Keys which gave humanity access to the Waywork.

The trio used handholds to pull themselves over to where *Alliance*'s current Waypoint pilot was seated at her control board—the spherical Key resting in a pedestal-like installation which rose from the deck. The pilot's gee chair was like any other in the command module, but unlike the other officers, this pilot's uniform was stained with perspiration. Her hair was pulled back into a tight bun, and beads of sweat were scattered across her face. In microgravity, the fluid merely collected on the surface, versus running down.

"Are you too fatigued to perform the crossing?" Golsubril Vex asked seriously.

"No, ma'am," the young woman said. "I am fully prepared and capable of doing my duty until it is time for me to be relieved."

"Very good," Vex said. "I like a woman who can persevere under adverse conditions. Does my presence in the command module add to your burden?"

The young woman's eyes darted from Vex's face, to General Ekk's, then to Colonel Jun's, and back to Vex's.

"It does not, Madam Kosmarch."

Vex allowed herself a small smile. The Waypoint pilot was lying, just as they all lied. But it had been a brave lie. Being able to control and suborn one's discomfort—enduring a superior's scrutiny during the carrying out of one's operational duty—was the mark of a quality Nautilan individual. Such underlings were always valuable, in any capacity they could be had.

"Continue, please," Vex said. "I would merely like to watch as you explain."

The Waypoint pilot swallowed twice, without lifting her hands from the Key's spherical, smooth surface, and turned her eyes back to her status display.

"You won't be able to see what I see," the woman said, working to keep her voice calm, "but right now I am accessing the Waywork, and readying the Key to execute the crossing over the Slipway to the target star's Waypoint. Everything at this stage in the process looks and feels nominal."

"Feels?" Vex said, the tone of her voice implying her intrigue.

"Yes, Madam Kosmarch," the Waypoint pilot said, before swallowing again and continuing. "Much of what I do—what every Waypoint pilot does—is an act of intuition. You know that we are tested before entering the school to become Waypoint pilots. Very few people have the gift."

"You consider it to be a talent, then?" Vex asked.

"Madam Kosmarch, I do. A talent which has made me valuable to the Starstate, thus my family can be proud of me, and we can be proud together."

"Very good," Vex said. "That is correct. You may continue."

"As the *Alliance* moves to within operational distance of the Waypoint coordinates, I can *feel* the Waypoint's proximity, as well as the Slipways which stretch across the light-years to the nearest connecting Waypoints around other stars. Once these connections are solid in my mind, I will use this control interface in front of me to divert a great amount of the ship's power into the Key itself. No conventional thrust will assist me in what I have to do next. Once the Key is primed for activation, I must devote my attention utterly to bridging the two Waypoints—*feeling* the ship across the Slipway—so that the energized Key can do its work. After that, everything happens too quickly to describe. We simply cease to be one place, and arrive at another."

"Does it hurt you?" Vex asked.

"Not physical pain per se, Madam Kosmarch. Rather . . . there is an intense sensation of expenditure. Although the headaches are something every Waypoint pilot experiences so frequently, we just learn to live with them while on duty. That too is part of the screening process, before you can be schooled in Waypoint use."

"Madam Kosmarch," General Ekk said, "we're moments now from executing the maneuver."

Vex watched as the Waypoint pilot's eyes lost focus, and suddenly the young woman seemed to be very far away. In her mind. A slightly knit expression formed on the Waypoint pilot's brow, while a tiny groan passed from her lips. Followed by the ordinarily smooth, opaque surface of the Key doing something Vex had never witnessed in person before. The sphere seemed to illuminate from within itself, but only enough for the surface to take on a translucent quality. Just beneath the semitransparent surface, a geometry of regular lines became visible. Not machinery, per se.

But rather, a network of fissures in the substrate, each of them giving off a faint, sea-blue light. Which glowed up through the actual surface of the Key—over which the Waypoint pilot's hands appeared to float, as if she were not even touching the device.

There was a flashbulb moment, which crossed the kosmarch's consciousness so quickly she couldn't be sure that it registered.

Then the surface of the Key snapped back to its familiar, metallic, pristine self.

The Waypoint pilot practically rolled up in her gee chair, chest rising and falling with deep, sucking breaths of air.

Vex looked to Ekk, who looked to the conventional pilots in the command module. They were busy using the *Alliance*'s sensor modules to recalibrate position—based on relative starfield shift. After a few moments, one of them turned his head and announced, "We appear to have successfully made the crossing to the unexplored system, sir."

Before anyone could reply, the Waypoint pilot's hands reached out, clutching wildly for anyone or anything to grab onto, until she ultimately latched onto Vex's outstretched arm. The young woman's skin was cold and clammy, almost to the point of being disgusting, but Vex kept her revulsion in check long enough to ask questions.

"It's not always this hard," Vex intuited. "You were surprised by that?"

"Yes," the Waypoint pilot whispered. "It's not . . . you don't have to . . . I had to *pinch so much* for that one. It was almost too difficult to stand. I don't know why."

"Was there something or, perhaps, someone in the way?"

"Yes and no," the Waypoint pilot said, her eyes closed, and a look of extreme fatigue settling over her face—which almost seemed to be aging before Vex's very eyes.

Ekk raised a hand, and two of the security personal flanking either side of the command module door used handrails to float over to the Waypoint pilot's position.

"Take her away for double the ordinary recovery period," Ekk ordered. "And have the next Waypoint pilot on the rotation report to the command module *now*."

The young woman allowed herself to be floated out of the command module without protest, leaving Ekk to stare at the Key nervously, while Vex evaluated what had just happened.

"Extraordinary," whispered Colonel Jun.

"How so?" Vex demanded.

"An experienced Waypoint pilot should have had no more trouble crossing this Slipway than any other in the Waywork. Yet, if her reaction is any gauge, there was something about this particular Slipway which resisted her effort. That's either a function of the Slipway itself—perhaps being so newly formed, it requires some form of roughening out, before it smoothly accepts our use of it—or we may be dealing with an opposing force *other* than conventional."

"And what does *that* mean?" Ekk asked the sickly Waymaker expert.

Jun coughed many times into a handkerchief before neatly folding it and placing the cloth back into a pocket on his uniform.

"We've always assumed that the Keys and the Waywork are neutral," Jun replied matter-of-factly. "We've never seen anything to make us believe that the Waymakers themselves might not want us using their technology. But if something has changed in this regard . . . perhaps some kind of failsafe has been triggered? I am guessing, really. But that Waypoint pilot put herself through extreme strain taking us across. I've never seen any of our Waypoint pilots have to fight so much to execute Slipway navigation. Especially one as youthful as she was. I suggest we proceed with caution. Now that we're on *their* side, we can't be too careful."

"You speak as if the Waymakers are no longer a past-tense part of the equation?" Golsubril Vex remarked.

"Maybe they're not?" Colonel Jun replied.

# PART TWO

# CHAPTER 15

THERE WERE NO EXTERIOR PORTHOLES NOR OBSERVATION BUBBLES in the *Catapult*'s command module. The entire thing was up-armored, with triple-integrity hull reinforcement, to safeguard against decompression during battle. Which did not make the command module invulnerable. But did make it so that Admiral Mikton couldn't get an immediate naked-eye view of the new star system into which she and her small Task Group had ventured.

She hastily made her way—with Commodore Urrl in tow—to one of the *Catapult*'s lifts, which ran up the center of the ship, and departed for the nearest module which did have windows on the universe.

When they arrived, she discovered they were not the only ones with the same idea. Though space itself technically looked no different from the way it had just a few minutes before, everyone was eager to get a look at uncharted territory. They were, so far as they knew, the first human beings to ever cross to this specific Waypoint. No people had ever before observed the galaxy, unadulterated, from this place in the universe.

A crowd had gathered to look out the bay observation dome, and was speaking in hushed voices as they stared at the sand-scatter of bright, seemingly fixed points against a field of pure midnight black.

One star in particular was just a bit brighter than all the rest. And though Mikton could not be completely sure, she thought she saw just a hint of occlusion—the superjovian, which had been seen by the planet-finders, orbiting close to its home sun. Only this time you could actually witness it without instruments. An off-color mote drifting over the face of a yellow-white disc, many, many astronomical units away.

"Can't linger too long," Urrl said quietly into his boss's ear.

"I know," Zuri whispered. "But this is part of the reason we all came out here in the first place, isn't it? With DSOD? Nobody comes strictly for the chance to fight. Or at least, I've never believed that's the only reason."

"Probably true," Urrl replied. "I think for me, it was about wanting to go to space, and then once I'd experienced my first combat engagement, it was about wanting to make sure space stayed free."

"No space in the Waywork has ever been *this* free," Admiral Mikton said. "Think of it. This system belongs to no one. No government in human history has ever ruled it. That's a remarkable idea, when you get down to it. Now that we're here, I am almost ashamed to claim it—assuming there's anything worth claiming."

"Once we get in touch with the *Daffodil,* we ought to have a fuller picture."

"Right. Let's go check on that."

Reluctantly, Zuri returned to the command module, where the Task Group control officer reported that all ships—military and civilian—had reported in. The crossing went well. Except for the fact that all of the Waypoint pilots each reported some degree of difficulty during the crossing proper. When Zuri ordered the on-shift Waypoint pilot to report, he merely spoke of a *resistance* which could not be described very well, except for the fact that he came out of the experience even more sweat soaked than before. His replacement had been called up ahead of schedule, and the exhausted young officer—who'd just taken *Catapult* over the Slipway—was bidden to report for off-shift recovery, with Admiral Mikton's personal thanks for his work.

The fresh Waypoint pilot reported that the Waypoint—on this side—remained stable. No discernible perturbations—as detectable through the Key—could be sensed.

"Order the Task Group to keep formation," Zuri commanded, "with all ships broadcasting for *Daffodil*'s awareness. Since she's not in the immediate vicinity, we need to locate her, and get a report. Meanwhile, order all Waypoint pilots to stay sharp, and alert their respective captains to *any* Waypoint activity of any sort. We don't know who might come through behind us. If anybody. Friend or foe. Though, I think we can safely assume that, because the Nauties aren't already here, and already shooting at us, we've been lucky enough to arrive ahead of them."

"Probably," Urrl replied in agreement.

"Which means when they *do* arrive," Zuri speculated, "we're going to have an immediate problem on our hands. When's the earliest we can get the Oswight yacht back across the Slipway? The sooner we begin moving the security flotilla to our side, the better."

Some discussion went on between several junior officers.

"Ma'am," said the *Catapult*'s captain, "the *Hallibrand* reports she will be turned around and ready to recross within fifteen minutes. Though her captain says he's not eager to go home just yet. Wishes he could loiter and have a look at the new system along with the rest of us."

"Tell him I fully sympathize," Zuri said, with a small smile on her lips. "Hopefully if our luck holds, there will be time for everybody to do some sight-seeing. But first things first. The security flotilla is our only chance to hold this system against Starstate Nautilan. Or any other Starstate, for that matter. I have to think all of them are going to try to find a way to cross at some point, though they won't be doing it through Constellar space without some gymnastic diplomacy."

"Maybe the Nauties *won't* be interested in a gun fight?" Urrl speculated.

Zuri sighed. "Would be nice. For a change. But you and I are both too old to rely on hope alone to guide our judgment. So, let's get busy bringing our security ships over, and hope *Daffodil* doesn't take too long to report back."

"Assuming she *can* report back," Urrl said, eyebrow raised.

Zuri opened her mouth to reply, then shut it promptly. Her exec had made a cogent point, which she didn't really have a rebuttal for. They would simply have to loiter and wait. Until or unless the Key-equipped monitor reported in, the first priority would be acting as an armed toehold on the new Waypoint's periphery. Betting that the Task Group could bring in enough security firepower to give Starstate Nautilan second thoughts about a battle, once Nautilan arrived.

The Task Group command network came up, with Wyodreth Antagean and Lady Oswight both occupying separate squares on *Catapult*'s tactical command wallscreen.

"Ma'am," Lieutenant Commander Antagean said, "we're ready to begin burning for the inner system."

"Not just yet," Zuri said. "I want to wait until we've got word from *Daffodil*. Or, failing that, I want to move a few armed assets over, to augment our force, prior to departing the vicinity of the Waypoint."

"Ummm," he said, his mouth puckering slightly, "Lady Oswight made it quite clear that she expected to be able to begin reconnaissance of the new system as soon as we were safely over the Slipway."

Zuri sat back in her gee chair, both eyebrows raised. This was the part she had been least looking forward to. Technically, she owned the Task Group, and Lady Oswight was merely a knowledge asset. But if Lady Oswight began throwing the Family name around, demanding concessions, to what extent could Zuri refuse? If things began to get heated, there was significant risk of causing a row between Family Oswight and DSOD proper. Admiral Mikton was already making a lot of from-the-hip calls, as things stood. Pushing back too hard on Lady Oswight's wishes might cause the admiral a lot of unwanted trouble.

Zuri cleared her throat, and addressed the square containing Garsina Oswight's face.

"I know you're eager to begin a survey, madam, but your safety demands that I not allow any of the Task Group to depart the periphery of the Waypoint before we've received some kind of communication from the monitor *Daffodil*."

"If that ship is far into the inner system," Lady Oswight replied, "it could take hours, or even days, to get a response. There is no system-wide network supporting comms here. Since *Daffodil* is clearly not waiting at the Waypoint for our arrival, we have to assume she's engaged elsewhere. I would like to take the Antagean ships, and join in *Daffodil*'s effort."

"But securing the Waypoint—"

"Is a task best suited for ships with the weapons to do the job," Lady Oswight said, cutting Zuri off. "None of the Antagean ships will be any good to you in a fight, Admiral. The longer we linger here, the more time we waste. Better to let us leave, and spread out our ships. Besides, if we *are* to be attacked at the mouth of the Waypoint, and all of us are obliterated, who will warn the *Daffodil* of what's happened? It makes sense, Admiral. And Mister Antagean—excuse me, the lieutenant *commander*—has assured me that his crews are ready to go. With DSOD personnel backing us up."

Zuri's face had become a creased button of indecision. She had to admit, Lady Oswight did make sense. Antagean's ships would not be able to shoot back, if Starstate Nautilan—or anyone else—came through the Waypoint. The *Gouger* and *Tarinock* would be hard-pressed to intercede on Antagean's behalf. Maybe it did make more sense, from a purely tactical standpoint, to send the unarmed starliners on their way?

But...

"Madam," Zuri said, "all of this assumes hostile forces have not already crossed ahead of us, destroyed *Daffodil*, and now lie in wait."

"Is there any evidence of this?" Lady Oswight asked. "I know a starship, recently arrived at a Waypoint, leaves a lot of hydrogen plasma in its wake when it begins thrusting. If a hostile force did come ahead of us, is there any discernible evidence that they were recently here? Have your military sensors detected any other ships in close proximity? Antagean's civilian sensors—on all three of his ships—can only find the scattered, cooled wake of a vessel which crossed many days ago. I deduce this is the *Daffodil*, and that nobody else has crossed since. Can you verify, please?"

"One moment," Zuri said, and used a switch on her gee chair's keyboard to mute the tactical feed. She quickly ordered *Catapult* to perform a full sensor checkout, to determine if what had been reported by the Antagean ships was accurate. After several minutes, during which Zuri gnawed at the thumb on her left fist, *Catapult*'s command module crew unanimously confirmed Lady Oswight's report. Evidence for a single ship's passing was detectable, but only a single ship. Not the fresher, newer tracks which would have been made by another group of vessels.

Zuri switched open the tactical feed again.

"All right," she said reluctantly. "Proceed, madam. But understand that Lieutenant Commander Antagean is in full control of the detachment. Those are his company's ships, but he's carrying several hundred of *my* men and women with him. In addition to yourself. He's responsible for all of it. Antagean, is that understood? You've got detachment command until further notice. I expect you to stay in touch with the Task Group throughout. And the moment you see or hear anything of *Daffodil,* we want to know immediately. Is that clear?"

"Perfectly clear, ma'am," Antagean said, reflexively dipping his chin to his chest in acknowledgement of the order. "Both Lady Oswight and the detachment personnel aboard my ships, are in good hands. We won't do anything foolhardy. Captain Loper and I have already been plotting a conservative reconnoiter approach which should give us a look at two of the outer jovian planets before we close on two of the inner terrestrials—with an eye to finally winding up in orbit around that big superjovian close to the main star."

"An astronomer's dream," Zuri remarked. "Too bad we didn't bring any of *them* along."

"I'm the eyes of the university faculty," Lady Oswight said, breaking into a grin. "Lieutenant Commander Antagean assures me that the telescopes and other sensor module equipment, on each of his ships, is up to the task of giving this system a proper first look. I am eager to collect as much data as possible. And, hopefully, we find out something new about the Waymakers themselves."

Zuri nodded her head in understanding. Underlying the Lady Oswight's excitement for the survey was the hope all of them felt—that something new here, some dramatic clue, might give them a better understanding of who the Waymakers were. Or, at least, how their technology worked.

"Proceed," Mikton finally ordered. "May God favor the bold and the free."

"Victory with honor, hurrah, hurrah," Wyodreth Antagean responded loudly, though Mikton was sure she heard the Oswight majordomo again shouting the response to the motto, just off-screen from Lady Oswight herself.

The squares for both Oswight and Antagean went black.

"Are you sure that's a good idea?" Urrl asked, from his gee chair next to Mikton's.

"No," Zuri said. "But she did make some good points. And I'd rather cut her loose to go exploring than have to sit here for the next few days taking increasingly angry and impatient calls from some girl who can potentially have all our careers on a platter, assuming we get back and she goes running to her father about how Mean Old Mikton wouldn't let the Lady Oswight go and play."

"It's not even her I am concerned with," Urrl grumped, coughing into his fist.

"Ah," Zuri said, now tracking what Urrl was actually saying. "You think Antagean's not up for running the detachment? They are *his* ships after all. And he's not some young ensign who's never even done a watch before."

"Maybe send *Tarinock* to chaperone?" Urrl suggested.

"If we had more of Iakar's force here with us now, I'd send *Tarinock* and *Gouger* both. But until the Oswight yacht brings us some additional firepower to form the nucleus of a security force for *our* Waypoint, we need to keep all three DSOD ships here. Where we can concentrate our attack pattern—such as it is."

Urrl nodded his head in understanding, then sighed, and went back to typing on his own gee chair keyboard.

"Damned shaky thing, being out here on a limb like this," he said.

"Don't have to remind me," Zuri replied. Then she raised her voice, and addressed *Catapult*'s captain. "Is the *Hallibrand* ready yet?"

"Almost," the captain replied. "Couple more minutes."

"Iakar knows the priority of fill," Zuri said. "So there ought to be no confusion, nor dithering, back in Oswight territory."

"I'll make sure the DSOD liaison aboard the *Hallibrand* understands your intent," the captain replied, and started speaking into his headset.

# CHAPTER 16

LIEUTENANT COMMANDER ANTAGEAN WAS FURIOUS, AND COULD not show it. Having excused himself from the command module of his starliner, he silently hurled obscenities at the bulkheads. Taking his ships to the inner system, without armed escort, was an extreme gamble. Lacking a recon report from the *Daffodil*, he had no idea what any of them would be getting into. And while he didn't doubt the heartiness of the civilian crews, or their DSOD counterparts for that matter, it wouldn't do any of them a lick of good if they met foreign warships along their route.

And all because Garsina Oswight didn't want to wait.

She didn't seem to appreciate the risk, whereas Wyo was now painfully aware of the numbers in his head. If even one starliner became disabled or, God forbid, destroyed, he'd be looking at over sixty Antagean personnel dead, along with almost two hundred DSOD troops. And *he* would be the one responsible. Not the Lady Oswight. Ohhhhh, no. She could flex her Family name all she wanted, but when things went sour, Wyo knew he was going to be the man who had to live with those deaths on his conscience.

He stopped at one of the berthing modules, and stepped out into a small sea of Antagean and DSOD people sprawled on their gee bunks. Now that the ship was back under thrust again, using handholds and grip boots was unnecessary. Everybody was thankful to have a modicum of gravity.

One of the senior sergeants noticed Wyo walking into the bay, and he snapped up out of his bank and hollered the entire bay to attention. Dozens of feet quickly slammed to the deck, while the civilian ship's compliment hopped up as well.

"Sir," said the veteran noncommissioned officer who'd so expertly brought the entire bay to its feet. "Ready to deploy when you need us."

"Thank you," Wyo said, still unused to the formal regard given him when he was wearing a DSOD uniform. Wyo *liked* the casual approach of the civilian world. He thought it calmer, friendlier, and in the end, more efficient. Military discipline was for people who *needed* the reinforcement, which few Antagean employees did. Or they soon discovered they weren't employees anymore. Wyo—like his father—preferred to run the company according to the grownup standard. There were bigger operations in Starstate Constellar, but Antagean paid the best of any of them. So Antagean could afford to be picky.

Deep Space Operations and Defense—like all militaries throughout history—was more of a mixed bag. Some really good people, mixed with the usual lifers who did just enough to keep advancing in rank, and then there were the duds. Men and women who really didn't have anywhere else to go, nor much else they could do. Especially among the ranks of the Tactical Ground Operations division. Like Oswight's majordomo, who'd clearly never *left* the TGO—in his heart—and wore this sentiment on his sleeve.

Wyo studied the faces in front of him while his arms hung uselessly at his sides.

"We've been ordered to proceed *without* protection," Wyo said matter-of-factly.

"Figured it might be that way," the NCO said crisply. Unlike Wyo, who wore the one-piece spacer's flight suit common in the ship's command module, the NCO was dressed in a battle zipsuit not too different from the one Lady Oswight herself had been wearing the entire time she'd been aboard. His rank chevrons were prominent on both shoulders, and the zipsuit appeared to have been well maintained, with bulkier shielding than was customary with civilian editions. Including lock-and-interface points for a full set of combat armor, in the event that such armor became needed. Wyo himself had such a zipsuit, with matched armor plate, stowed in the military trunk which had been put together for him and brought aboard before departing Planet Oswight's orbit.

"I hope we find something in this system worth our time and trouble," Wyo continued. "Until we do, I don't have much to tell your company commander. So, I am afraid everyone has to play the hurry-up-and-wait game."

"Copy that, sir," said the NCO. "This wouldn't be the first time, for many of us. It's all right. We're enjoying the civilian accommodations while we have them, including your galley. It's a step up from what we'd find on an ordinary DSOD battle transport."

"Yes it is," Wyo said, smiling. "Courtesy of Antagean Starlines, I would add. Consider it a modest perk, working with the company."

"So if you don't mind my asking, sir, in what capacity are you paying us a visit today?"

"Both," Wyo said. "Most of the Antagean crew already know me, or at least know my reputation. But TGO personnel probably don't know me from a hole in the bulkhead. And since we're going to be potentially seeing a lot of each other over the coming days, or perhaps weeks, I am hoping to at least make my presence known. Admiral Mikton's placed me in charge of the detachment while we're separated from her Task Group, and this means I'll be a lot more involved in your company commander's battle rhythm. And also that of the NCOs. Especially on this ship. So, maintain readiness, enjoy the civilian-upgraded lifestyle while it lasts, and I will do my best to make sure that all of us—all three ships—not only complete this mission in one piece, but return to Oswight space able to tell the tale."

"Victory with honor, hurrah, hurrah!" sounded the lot of them.

Wyo was almost embarrassed, but repeated the second half of the motto with as much gusto as he could muster. The NCO saluted, Wyo saluted back, and then stepped out of the bay, to go repeat his performance elsewhere on the ship. Each time, he told the men and women what he could, and when he finally returned to the command module, his nerves had settled down enough that he wasn't ready to chew through a bar of hull steel.

"How are people handling themselves?" Captain Loper asked as Wyo settled gratefully into his gee chair.

"Okay so far, but nothing bad has happened yet. When something bad happens, *then* we'll see what we've got."

"Talking to Admiral Mikton's exec," Loper said, "I get the impression he thinks the same of you."

"Oh?" Wyo said, sitting up a bit.

"He didn't come right out with it, in so many words," Loper admitted. "I can just tell, one old starship jock to another old starship jock, that Commodore Urrl isn't exactly thrilled with the idea that you—and you alone—are carrying the flag for this so-called detachment we've created."

Wyo's mood instantly grew uncivil again. He quickly looked around the command module, to be sure there were no First Family ears to hear him speak seditiously, and then he cut loose.

"Next time you have to talk to Urrl, or anyone else from Admiral Mikton's staff, you make it known precisely how much I disapprove of this adventure—and that it's all the Lady Oswight's damn idea. I'd have preferred it if we stayed put with the rest of the Task Group, and awaited some actual armed backup, before taking off to explore this system. I mean, the job is the job, and we're obviously equipped to put boots on the ground, wherever it's required. But I told Mikton's staff from the very beginning that our starliners will present big, juicy targets for any Nautilan force sent to interdict us. If Mikton and her people are wrong—if Nautilan or one of the other Starstates has managed to put ships into this system ahead of us—our starliners may pay the price. Not something I happily risk by choice, that's for goddamned sure. And it's because we can't tell that First Family idiot to go airlock herself when she has no idea what she's dragging us into!"

Wyo had practically shouted his last sentence. He looked at the half dozen Antagean employees surrounding him, and added, "If even one of you leaks back to that woman what I said just now, you're fired."

A ripple of laughter went around the command module, then Captain Loper said, "What gets said between Antagean folk, stays among Antagean folk, right?"

Murmurs of agreement.

Wyo sank lower into his gee chair, and rubbed the heels of his palms into his eyes. "By the Exodus," he said, "this mission is going to put a decade on me before it's over."

"So . . . it's safe to say you never got around to that apology I suggested," Loper remarked, as he idly scanned one of the ship's manifests on his flatscreen.

"Nope," Wyo said.

"And based on the way you two argued, prior to our detachment from the Task Group, I imagine there isn't going to *be* an apology."

"Nope. Lady Oswight is getting what she wants. An unguarded expedition to the center of the system. She has her way."

"Well," Loper said, coughing uncomfortably, "she *is* a beautiful young woman. In my experience, beautiful young women almost always have their way. Even with young men who don't want to give it to them. Or should I say, *especially* with young men who don't want to give it to them?"

"I'm at least a dozen years her senior," Wyo scoffed, "and you think I haven't learned how to handle beautiful women? If I had a starliner for every climbing socialite who's tried to get at me since I turned twenty, Dad could double the size of his fleet! They look at me, and they see money. A quick path to financial independence. I've had to fend off much prettier, and much more aggressive, females than Oswight."

"Yeah," Loper said, "but none of them had the authority to boss you around if they wanted. The Lady Oswight *does*. Or at least, she does through her Family connections. Which takes us back to that apology which never happened. It seems to me that you could afford to reconsider mending the fence. If for no other reason than the fact that all of us are going to have to be working with and for this person until we take her home."

"And that pet brute she brought with her—" Wyo began, but was cut off.

"Is just a doting old trooper who guards her the way he'd guard his own child," Loper said sternly. "It wasn't *that* long ago when your father gave me a similar responsibility. And let me tell you, you were both arrogant and insufferable."

Wyo sat back up again, feeling heat in his cheeks.

"You never told me that," he admitted.

"Well, now you're gonna hear it, kid. When you first came aboard, almost two decades ago, you thought you knew everything. Your father was the boss, and you were the boss's kid, and you thought you had the run of the place. When I slapped you down hard—and had to *keep* slapping you down hard—you just got more and more pissed off about it. To the point I contacted Wyograd and told him it was probably a bad idea to keep you out on the ship with me. You seemed to hate it, and to be honest, I kinda hated you."

Wyo listened intently, staring at the face of his mentor. In all the years he'd known Loper, the man had never said anything remotely like this before. Oh, sure, life had been tough the first couple of years Wyo had been under Loper's supervision, but Wyo was proud of the fact that he had toughened up quick. Grown into himself. Learned to do hard work, on hard days. The kind of work somebody like Garsina Oswight had never, ever had to perform in her life.

But now Wyo was being told things about himself which gave him pause.

"Obviously Dad told you no," Wyo said.

"Not only that," Loper said, "he told me to beat on you *harder*. He said to me, 'That damned boy is soft, and he's not going to stop being soft until he learns he's not the center of the goddamned universe,' end quote. So, if you're feeling particularly irked by our First Family girl, remember that you weren't terribly different from her once. And it took running you through the ship's proverbial recycler a few times to clue you to the fact that your bowel movements stank to the same degree as everybody else's. I have to assume Lady Oswight has never stepped far from her sire's shadow. I sense a lot of proper finishing with her. But also a great deal of resentment. Mixed with inexperience beyond the regimented protocols of Family life."

"So?" Wyo asked, becoming somewhat exasperated.

"So...maybe instead of hating her guts for who she is, Wyo, you can have a little sympathy? I know neither you nor your father think as well of the Families as the Families would like you to. But that Oswight girl, she's trying to establish a footprint. Apart from her name. I know. I've chatted with her enough—away from the watchful eyes of Mister Axabrast—to know that she's eager to make her mark well *beyond* the Family title."

Wyo considered. He'd never looked at the problem in that light before. It did explain why Lady Oswight was willing to risk going to the inner system without protection. In a sense, she was eschewing Admiral Mikton's umbrella the way she sometimes eschewed Axabrast's umbrella. Wyo searched his memories of adolescence, and could recall how freeing it had been to be out among the stars. Even if Loper had been a taskmaster. At least Wyo had been granted time to find himself. And ultimately go back home—being his own man.

"It's still a bad idea to be doing this," Wyo said.

"Yes it is," Loper said. "Just like it's a bad idea for any of us to do half of *any* of the things we do in life, for the sake of potential reward. But then again, how boring would it be to never take chances? Your father took many during the early years of the company. Once or twice, I thought he had literally broken us. But it all worked itself out in the end, and the company pushed forward. Largely on Wyograd's will to not fail. And the fact that he always made sure to do right by the employees who had done right by him. People can stick together through almost anything, provided they trust each other."

Wyo looked hard at his former mentor, and realized that even after all these years, the older man still had things to teach, and Wyo still had lessons to learn.

"Thanks," Wyo said, and promptly got up out of his gee chair.

"Where are you off to now?" Loper asked.

"I've got to go change into something a bit more appropriate," Wyo said. "Then I am going to go see if I can build a bridge."

# CHAPTER 17

GARSINA OSWIGHT COULD BE A HARD WOMAN TO FIND WHEN she wanted to be left alone. Having reassured Elvin Axabrast that she was just going out for a bit of exercise, she took a lift car straight up to the cargo spaces located directly under the starliner's mushroom-shaped shield dome. The dome was a huge, thickly-concave battering ram, intended to absorb whatever dust or debris crossed the ship's path. Even very small particles, traveling at interplanetary or interstellar velocities, could seriously hurt the ship. So, while under thrust, the dome took the brunt of the damage. Making the area directly under the dome perhaps the safest place one could find aboard. Half of the starliner's fuel was nestled there, including storage for sensitive or volatile cargo.

Presently, Garsina wandered among rows of gee-stacked military crates—each crate magnetically locked to the others, which in turn were magnetically locked to the deck—all of which were labeled with various DSOD hazard warnings. Either because of explosive potential, or radiation danger. An armed guard had let Garsina in, largely because the guard didn't know what to do with a First Families heir. Garsina had promised to behave herself, then began walking among the containers. Not looking for anything in particular. Mostly enjoying the sensation of vigorous movement after days spent in slightly uncomfortable micrograv-ity. Getting her blood moving, with her arms and legs swinging rhythmically, was good for body and mind alike.

Convincing both Wyodreth Antagean and Admiral Mikton

to allow Garsina to depart the Task Group unescorted had been something of a coup. But diplomatic maneuvering, and the subtle—or not so subtle—application of Family force, was something she didn't do easily. Her interest on this expedition was purely scientific. The fact that Constellar was still on a war footing against Nautilan merely complicated what should have been a straight-forward project. She understood the risk. But she also believed that nothing ought to stand in the way of increasing humanity's knowledge where the Waymakers were concerned.

The opportunity to examine a fresh set of worlds, orbiting a new star, was too important. All her years of painstaking study had built up to this moment in her life. Though she had not known it as an undergraduate. Would she be disappointed? Or were there treasures here, the likes of which she could not even dream of?

Even a few fossils would suffice. Humanity had never known what the Waymakers even looked like. The aliens left no dead behind. No bones, nor any statues. Some of the inert tools suggested possible shapes for hands—or at least the Waymaker equivalent. But there wasn't any way to be sure. Almost as if the aliens had deliberately removed any trace of their corporeal selves before abandoning the Waywork—for humanity to eventually stumble upon.

Had the Waymakers known humans would be coming? Had they known about Earth? Was the Waywork constructed purely for human benefit? Or was it actually—as some pessimists had opined—just a trap? Into which humans, fleeing Earth, had fallen.

There were some who speculated that the Waymakers were behind the war which had sparked the Exodus in the first place. Their reasoning went like this: humans are confusing, or fascinating, or dangerous—to a truly alien mind—so get people off Earth, then *destroy* Earth, and herd the survivors across the stars. Until they can be safely contained in a closed environment. Unaware that they are being studied. A cosmic petri dish.

Was that why the Waymakers had left so few traces? So as not to overly contaminate their experiment? If so, why leave the Keys at all? Unless the Keys themselves—and what little Waymaker technology had come with them—were just part of the project. Intended for humanity to discover and use. With an explicit lack of faster-than-light escape routes.

Not that there was anything to prevent a conventional expedition to systems beyond the Waywork. But those voyages took a hundred years or more, just to go one way. Who in their right mind wanted to embark upon a journey of such tremendous length, even for the chance to see foreign worlds in foreign space? When you returned—assuming you *could* somehow live long enough for a round trip—almost nobody you knew or loved at the beginning would be around to greet you.

Still, a handful of such attempts had been made, replicating some of what was known about the arks which came from old Earth. But those missions had failed. Or, at least, were never heard from again. Was it deliberate? The people on the arriving side, wanting nothing to do with the Starstates anymore? Had the children of the original voyagers felt no kinship to those within the Waywork, and set about creating separate societies for themselves?

Or was it simply impossible to survive the trip? Nobody could consider *every* contingency when planning such a lengthy and complex journey. No machine worked perfectly. Not even for a span of months. Much less the century, or more, it took to reach some of the nearest systems. And while automation and self-replication could solve part of the mechanical problem, what about the people themselves? A slower-than-light voyage was a recipe for mental illness. Nowhere to go but inside the ship itself. Everyone and everything you knew, left behind. Homesickness would be rampant. And even a very big ship—maybe, perhaps, a converted comet or asteroid?—could eventually seem insufferably small. Given enough time and restlessness among the crew.

People might have gone mad. Or gotten sick. Long-term exposure to cosmic radiation was still a problem many worlds across the Waywork struggled with. Cancer of one form or another was perpetually taking lives, despite the best modern medicine could do. Unless you lived most of your days underground, deep within the crust of a planet. Which is perhaps where the survivors of those lost expeditions had ultimately fled? Burrowing. Hoping to outlast the danger. Watching critical systems gradually fail. Along with hydroponics crops. The mass death of livestock brought along for the trip. Friends and loved ones succumbing to the end. No hope. A slow suicide.

Practically speaking, every problem faced by any inclement world in the Waywork was magnified tremendously when you extrapolated such problems for potential interstellar travel. Which meant the cost for even a single trip, using a single ship, had almost broken several of the Starstates' economies in the distant past. So, when the first few attempts yielded no results, future attempts were abandoned. There had been no payoff for so great a gamble. And there was plenty of virgin territory—back then, within the Waywork—worth claiming.

At least until one Starstate had grown so large and so hungry, that all the other Starstates were unable to escape their oversized neighbor's appetite for perpetual expansion.

Garsina knew—along with her brothers—that the Constellar Council had been discreetly reconsidering the slower-than-light dilemma. If it came right down to it, what choice would the First Families have? When every last Constellar planet had been seized, where could any of them hope to go? Nautilan policy regarding previously captured Constellar worlds was supposed to be brutal. Political executions, or so the stories said. Precious little actual data got back to Constellar from within Nautilan proper. And what did come back—from worlds taken, and transformed in the Nautilan model—gave an impression of unutterable tyranny. First Family holdings and estates ransacked. Family members killed, or driven into hiding. Whole populations threatened with death by airlock, or manual labor in the factories, if they did not reform according to Nautilan directive.

It hurt Garsina, knowing that there were children now being born on former Constellar worlds who knew nothing of their past. Of Constellar's rich and noble history as a country. Of the valiant effort to preserve Constellar culture.

Those lost children would, in fact, be raised to hate their own people. On the other side of the Waywork. Men and women who were estranged cousins, but Nautilan regarded them as enemies.

The worst stories said that former Constellar worlds which openly rebelled were eventually wiped clean of human life. Every last person, regardless of age, made to eat vacuum. Their corpses left to freeze-dry. Until Nautilan recolonization could begin anew. As if that world had never had a history, nor a civilization, all its own. The culture having been effectively erased. Not just exterminated. But removed from the Waywork in total.

Except in the archives of the Constellar Council's Hall of Remembrance. Where each and every former world, and former system, was reverently commemorated. Names and images of families stored. Lineages too. Their fates, and the fates of their descendants, largely unknown.

Dwelling on these morose thoughts, Garsina almost collided with Zoam Kalbi as the short man rounded a stack of crates—his head craning to get a better look with his video spectacles.

"I'm so sorry," he said, taking three steps backward. "The guard told me you were in here, but after a few minutes of looking around, I became fascinated by the contents of these shipping containers. It's a bit unnerving to think we're surrounded by so much potential destruction. Some of these metal crates contain tactical nuclear warheads. If just one of them exploded, it could take half the ship with it."

Kalbi rested a hand on the box nearest him, but gently—as if the metal were hot.

"I should probably get back to the executive suite," Garsina said. "Mister Axabrast will be calling for me soon, if I don't call him first."

"Do please extend my courtesies to the man," Zoam said, his thin lips approximating a smile—while his eyes did not.

Garsina instantly snapped back into diplomatic mode.

"Of course I will," she said.

"It was not my intention to upset your servant."

"He knows that," Garsina said. "But you have to understand, Elvin thinks it's his job to be a little bit grumpy about *everything*. Behind the roughness, he has good intent."

"Thank you for the reassurance," Zoam said.

"Have you been able to interview Antagean's personnel like you wanted?" she asked.

"Mister Antagean's employees have been willing to speak to me every time I've asked, but the answers I am getting to my questions seem to be...a bit too self-aware. No doubt Antagean Starlines has a company policy regarding its workers talking to informationalists. I was hoping to better capture their fear, as well as their anticipation, on this journey. But they've been much too professional for that, thus far. We'll see if they maintain that professionalism, in the event that there is real trouble."

"You say that so calmly," Garsina objected, "as if 'trouble' for them doesn't mean trouble for all of us? Especially you. You're here by yourself. Nobody really knows you. Except by reputation."

"Occupational hazard," Zoam remarked. "Infotainers are known to work alone. It's really a matter of rights. One informationalist with good recording equipment can gather all the audio and video feed necessary for a fine infotainment production, and have to share none of the compensation. Having multiple people covering a single event tends to dilute the value of the stories which follow. Because when everyone is reporting on something, nobody is reporting on something. Does that make sense to you, Lady Oswight?"

"I think so," Garsina said. "Still, if I had to come on an expedition like this, and do it without any prior connections to *anybody*, I think I might be a nervous wreck. At least until I made some friends. Hopefully."

The corners of Kalbi's mouth crept upward slightly. "Perhaps you and I could become friends," he said.

"Yes, perhaps we could. Though, I understand infotainment requires you to also maintain some professional distance too."

"Yes, it does. You seem to understand my profession better than the average Constellar citizen."

"I have to," Garsina said. "I am part of a First Family."

"Of course," Zoam said.

Both of them waited for the other to continue speaking. Then, in somewhat awkward silence, Kalbi went back to his recording.

Garsina turned to begin walking for the exit when Lieutenant Commander Antagean approached. He'd dispensed with the one-piece spacer's flight suit, and put on the more formal, two-color uniform she'd first seen him in back on Planet Oswight's surface. Knowing what had transpired during their previous interactions, and that she still had to carefully maneuver against the man's inherent, anti-Family prejudice, she elevated her diplomatic personal shields even more, and assumed a stance of dignified disinterest.

"Lady Oswight," Wyodreth said as he approached. The look on his face told her he was slightly nervous. And, having heard Antagean's approaching boot steps, Kalbi had switched from examining the gee crates to focusing on the conversation.

"Lieutenant Commander," she said coolly.

Wyodreth looked at Zoam, and raised an eyebrow.

"This is a secure area," he said. "I don't think civilians are authorized here."

"What about her?" Zoam objected, pointing to Garsina.

"First Family exception," Wyo said. "Which doesn't cover infotainers."

"Article Thirty-six covers a *lot* of things," Zoam said, baring his teeth in a grin Garsina could have sworn was meat-eating.

"Even so, with these kinds of weapons, I don't think it's a good idea for you to go probing."

"Mister Antagean," Zoam said, ignoring the Reserve officer's title, "do you somehow think I am going to set one of these bombs *off*? I wouldn't know where to start. And I can't exactly steal them, now, can I? They each weigh more than I do. And these crates are security sealed, not to mention magnetically held to the deck. Nothing short of a conventional explosion could dislodge them. And I am not hurting anything coming here to see just what kind of munitions your Tactical Ground Operations soldiers might employ. Curious, that they thought it necessary to bring weaponry like this. What could possibly be so threatening in this system that a surface army need employ fusion bombs?"

"You'll have to ask the resident TGO company commander that question," Wyo admitted. "My orders are to safeguard everyone aboard, since our departure from the Task Group. What the TGO company commander, or the battalion commander who is on one of the other Antagean Starlines ships, has in mind...is your guess as well as mine. I suspect they're thinking it pays to be prepared for even the most unlikely combat scenarios. Better to have and not want, than to want and not have. Or at least my father liked to say that, when he taught me about running maintenance depots."

"But, are you *ordering* me to depart?" Kalbi asked pointedly.

Wyodreth's eyes scanned the crates, then looked at Garsina, before returning to Zoam's face.

"No. Just please be careful."

"I had no intention of being anything else," Zoam said, and then pivoted cleanly on a heel before walking quickly away.

Garsina watched the expression on Antagean's face gradually relax.

"Informationalists serve the public trust," Garsina said. "Even the First Families acknowledged this when the Starstate was founded. If our society is to be one built on principles of liberty, a certain amount of transparency must be maintained."

"If that's *all* it was," Wyodreth said coldly, "I don't think myself or my company would have any issue with Zoam Kalbi.

But he's here *looking* for problems. And I suspect if he can't find any problems, he'll *invent* them. That's the nature of the infotainer. Merely reporting the facts is not enough. It's about the audience too. You don't maintain a fan base by giving them boring material. Kalbi wants *dirt*, Lady Oswight. Dirt on me. Dirt on you. Dirt of any kind that can be used to spice up his rendition of events upon our return. And if this causes marketing problems or public embarrassment for either you, or myself, or the DSOD, Zoam Kalbi doesn't have to care."

"That's a remarkably cynical viewpoint," Garsina said. "For a man who's been charged with safeguarding all of us, you seem to take a particularly dim view of at least two VIPs in particular."

Lieutenant Commander Antagean opened his mouth to object, then seemed to think better of it, and closed his mouth. He stepped from foot to foot for a couple of seconds, then forced a small laugh out of his throat.

"You're right. And I am sorry. In fact, that's the whole reason I came looking for you in the first place. Axabrast wanted to throw a fist at me when I inquired about your whereabouts. So I used the ship's secure network to put out a quiet all-points bulletin, asking if anyone had seen you. Coming up here, I knew it was risky. Because you've got no reason to want to get along with me. But I *am* hoping that I can convince you to trust me. Not just as an Antagean. But as a man who takes his duty with the DSOD seriously. Admiral Mikton put this rank on my collar, and I intend to do right by her. To the utmost of my ability."

"We all intend to perform our duties to the utmost of our ability," Garsina said, still maintaining a pose of dignified detachment. Her eyes looked past Antagean, then scanned the crates nearest him.

"Anyway," Wyo said, seeming to realize that she wasn't in a mood to be placated, "I came to offer you a sincere apology for how I've handled myself so far. My father taught me better, and so did the DSOD. I suppose this entire expedition simply caught me completely off guard. My father's been sick, and most of his responsibilities have fallen to me—until now. I don't like having to drop everything and run off, leaving my sister to carry the company load all by herself. It's made me brittle, and I am afraid you've caught some of the worst of that brittleness. I hope to do better in the future. By your leave, Lady Oswight."

Antagean snapped his heels together formally, and dipped his chin to his chest.

"Wait," Garsina said, despite herself. "Don't leave yet. I didn't realize your being called up for this expedition was a source of personal crisis."

"It is," Wyodreth said, coming to parade rest.

"That I *can* understand, Lieutenant Commander. I suppose I've been so completely focused on this opportunity to do additional research on the Waymakers, I didn't bother to consider how the lives of others were being disrupted. You don't want to be here, do you?"

"Not really, to be honest. No."

"Not even for the chance to make history?"

"Lady, I am a practical man. I'd have been content to observe the results of this mission from the desk in my father's office. Antagean is proud to serve Starstate Constellar, no question. But as you may have noticed, Captain Loper is more than capable of running this detachment. I, on the other hand, should be back home, running the company in my father's absence. The longer we're here, the more difficulty my sister will encounter. And if something happens to us, and I don't return, the future of Antagean Starlines will be in doubt. My father built the company from the ground up, and unless I am there to see his directives carried out, the company could crumble. That's not fair to my sister. And it's especially not fair to our employees. Some of whom, like Captain Loper, have devoted their lives to the business."

Garsina considered. In an unexpected way, the situation—as described by Lieutenant Commander Antagean—mirrored that of Family Oswight. Just on a different scale. In both their cases, their parents were depending on them to carry on the family name. An obligation neither she nor Wyodreth had asked for, but which had been placed on them regardless. Purely through an accident of birth.

She noticed again that Antagean seemed to have premature wrinkles around his eyes.

"You don't enjoy giving orders," she said matter-of-factly.

"Enjoy it, Lady Oswight? Why would any sane person enjoy the burden? I always tell this to my new employees, who constantly gripe about how things could be run better: everyone thinks they can do the boss's job better than the boss is already doing it, until *they themselves* are suddenly on the hot seat—then it becomes a whole other question entirely. Management is not something I aspired to, yet it's come down to me in time. Just as a military career was not something I aspired to. But my father felt it would be good for me—for the family name—if I put in my time.

"In spite of what I've said to you about what I think of the First Families, the Antageans *are* patriots. We believe in the Starstate. We also believe in the Council. We want to do everything we can to keep Constellar free. But that doesn't mean I, personally, get a kick out of giving orders. Just the opposite, in fact. Giving orders means taking responsibility—both for good, and for bad. My mistakes affect other people's lives. Now, more than ever. That's about the furthest thing from 'enjoyment' I can think of."

In that moment, Garsina felt something stir. Deep down within herself. Being surrounded by First Family apparatchiks who endlessly aspired to greater degrees of authority and influence, she'd come to assume that *all* men craved the same. But here the lieutenant commander was, plainly stating he did *not* want the authority, and for reasons which made perfect sense to boot. Remarkable.

Now it was her turn to laugh. Just a little.

"What's so funny?" he asked.

"You and me," she said. "My father begged me not to come. And you? You're here against your will. How ironic is that?"

"I suppose it is," Wyodreth admitted, smiling slightly. "Do you ever catch yourself daydreaming about a time when owing things to your parents won't have to be a primary consideration?"

"Parent," Garsina replied. "My mother is dead."

"I'm sorry about that. Mine too," Wyodreth said.

She looked at Wyodreth carefully—at that unbidden smile, and the premature eye wrinkles—and thought him handsome. Not in the polished manner of the many and sundry suitors who'd lately come calling on Family Oswight seeking a power marriage. But in an essentially masculine way. And not just because of the quality of his voice. He was, apparently, a man who did what he had to do, because he *had* to do it. This resonated with her. And she found herself glad for the revelation.

"Apology fully accepted, Lieutenant Commander Antagean," she said formally, matching his unbidden smile with one of her own. "I think *both* of us could afford to be more charitable with the other. Let's make that part of the mission, yes?"

Now it was her turn to click her heels together, and dip her chin to her chest.

"Yes, Lady," he said, somewhat startled. "Very magnanimous. I appreciate your willingness."

With that, he spun on a heel, and strode off purposefully toward the exit.

In the back of Garsina's mind, she could almost hear her mother *tsk-tsking* at the fact that Garsina had allowed his candor to disarm her. But then she quickly dismissed the matter, and breathed a great sigh of relief. She took no pleasure in maintaining an adversarial relationship where none need exist. Because the honest truth of it was, Antagean was right. She *did* have to trust him. And he had to trust *her.* If both of them were going to escape from this adventure in one piece.

# CHAPTER 18

JUST AS THRUSTING OUT TO THE OSWIGHT SYSTEM'S WAYPOINT had taken the better part of two weeks, descending to the center of the uncharted, new system was also going to take the better part of two weeks. Some of that journey would be spent with the reactor nozzles aimed at the stars, and some of that journey with be spent with the reactor nozzles aimed at the sun. All along the way, each of the Task Group captains would have to carefully monitor fuel and fluid levels—the two being synonymous in the age of high-efficiency hydrogen-fusion motors. One of the first things Admiral Mikton set about doing, while the search for the *Daffodil* continued, was conduct a survey for nearby comets which might be harvested for distillation of hydrogen—or one of its several isotopes. All of the Task Group ships, even the Antagean starliners, had the necessary distillation equipment. Assuming one or more suitable comets could be located, and nudged into a trajectory which more or less matched the Task Group's own. All of the ships could slowly replace their fuel and fluid losses. But finding a comet to do the job required additional expenditure of resources. And while both the *Gouger* and the *Tarinock* were specifically built for long-range scouting, they were also the only two ships—other than the *Catapult*—capable of mounting a defense if the need arose.

So, Mikton dispatched them singly, confident that positive results would come back, if only the scouts kept looking. Meanwhile, the first of several ships from Commodore Iakar's security flotilla arrived on the scene. And Mikton could devote her mental energy to devising what seemed like a coherent defense strategy. Because the grace period of merciful silence—no foreign vessels yet arriving—would end eventually.

At approximately twenty-eight hours post-arrival in the new system, with three more ships moved over from the security flotilla, word finally came back from the Antagean ships that the *Daffodil* had been located. She was responding with message laser only, in reply to the wider radio hails that all the Task Group ships had been sending. When Admiral Mikton finally had the captain of the *Daffodil* on-line, she reassured the man that no hostile forces had arrived on the scene, and that they could afford to have a detailed conversation.

As it so happened, the *Daffodil* was less than a light-minute distant, orbiting the outermost jovian planet—by which the Antagean detachment was soon to pass. *Daffodil* had been running dark to avoid potential detection, but now happily greeted friendly forces and began relaying information.

The planet-finders in Oswight space had been correct. All of the new system's basic data—on star type, and the total number of planets—had been correct. But the exciting part was the discovery of a potentially clement terrestrial. *Daffodil*'s crew had performed a flyby. The images they were uploading to Mikton's Task Group were stunning: huge water seas, majestic whorls of white clouds covering what appeared to be several significant land masses, and thousands of smaller islands. Spectroscopic analysis indicated an abundance of both nitrogen and oxygen in the atmosphere. If such a planet had been discovered within the Waywork itself, it would have been a jewel of almost limitless value. People had taught themselves the trick of living on harsher worlds, yes. But to make a nation thrive—with booming populations, and an outlook to match—you needed planets which would foster growth. Naturally fertile land for farming. A sky not domed over with plastics and metals. The kind of free acreage where a hearty soul could sink a shovel into the soil and begin creating anything from nothing.

"Ours," Zuri Mikton murmured to herself, savoring the idea of claiming this world for her country.

"Perhaps, but not quite," remarked Lieutenant Commander Antagean over the Task Group's tactical net.

"What do you mean?" Zuri snapped, taking her eyes off the imagery of the clement planet, and aiming them at the broadcast picture of the former civilian.

"Check your data from the *Daffodil*," he simply said.

"He's right," the captain of the *Daffodil*—face filling a different square—said reluctantly. "We picked up ordinary radio broadcasts coming from the coast of the second-largest continent."

"What do you make of them?" the Admiral asked sharply.

"Not sure, ma'am."

"Could it be alien in origin? Possibly even Waymaker?"

"They're repetitive. Looping over and over. Audio only. It sounds like human speech, albeit a form of human speech I've never heard before. Doesn't match with any dialect myself or my officers have ever heard."

Admiral Mikton used her controls to quickly capture audio feed being sent over by the *Daffodil*. The captain was right. The somewhat distorted sounds were definitely not familiar to her. She amplified them over the *Catapult*'s command module speakers, and each of her people shook their heads negatively. Nobody had any clue what was being said.

"So, we've found a lost colony," the Admiral opined. "With people who may or may not be friendly to our cause?"

"More than that," *Daffodil*'s captain said. "We got as close to the planet as we could, with the time and fuel afforded to us, and had some clear air over the source of the broadcasts—no clouds to obstruct our view. Our telescope footage shows us something quite remarkable."

Zuri snagged the graphics being fed into her ship's computer, and set several streams of images flowing, until she jabbed out a finger and stopped the feed on a particular picture which made her mouth hang partly open.

It been a vessel, once. Gargantuan. Its titanic metal ribs rose like stone arches high into the sky. Given the limited resolution, scale was difficult to determine. But the ship was practically beached on the shoreline of the second-largest continent. Nearby, an even larger object projected mightily into the air—at least two kilometers? Maybe more? The pyramid was smooth sided, save for a barely discernible pattern of repeating, geometrically uniform lines crisscrossing each of the four faces. Which presented a stark contrast to the crumbled, skeletal hull of the vessel.

What appeared to be highways randomly spoked away from the pyramid's base. There even seemed to be buildings of roughly square and rectangular construction nestled among the roads. Though these also seemed to share the disused and deteriorating quality of the beached ship.

Whoever lived there—*had* lived?—they weren't doing much to keep the place up.

"Look like anything out of any drydock you're familiar with?" Lieutenant Commander Antagean asked from his own ship's command module.

"No," Zuri admitted.

"She's far bigger than anything we could ever hope to build in a reasonable commercial manner," the younger officer said, his thumb absently rubbing at the edge of his lower lip. "In fact, I'd say whatever size it was at the start of its service life is probably larger than this imagery can tell us. Time took a toll. The spaceframe has partially collapsed under its own weight. Possibly sinking into the wet ground? Or maybe it washed out with the tide? There's a sizeable moon orbiting the world, and the moon itself seems to have a moon too."

"What's your back-of-the-envelope guess? Final ship's size," Zuri asked.

Antagean considered, then said, "Figure, one-third to one-half again as large. With huge fusion thrusters and reaction mass tanks to get it down to the ground."

"But why land anything of that magnitude?" Zuri asked. "You'd never get it back up into the sky again. Much less reach orbit."

"They probably never intended to take off again, ma'am."

"So...whoever landed on that world intended to stay for keeps?"

"I think that's a fair assumption."

"They landed, maybe partially dismantled their ship—for materials, tools, computers, and other things—then built the pyramid?"

"Negative," the *Daffodil*'s captain said, shaking his head.

"Explain," Zuri demanded, her eyes darting from one man's image to the next.

"Ma'am, the radio repetitions seem to be coming from the shell of the downed ship, but we get nothing off that pyramid. Nor are we entirely sure what it's made from. Spectroscopy isn't telling us anything. It's not metal. It's not stone. It's not a polymer, nor anything artificial like we could make in a Constellar lab. Until we land and try to gouge out a sample, I think we have to conclude that humans—if they're down there at all—didn't have anything to do with the pyramid."

"Alien," said a new voice. The Lady Oswight had spoken not at all to that point. Merely listened. But now the picture of her face was set in a stern expression. "Undoubtedly Waymaker in origin."

"How do you deduce that, if I may please ask?" Zuri said, being careful to temper the commanding tone in her voice when addressing the Family heir.

"Consider the Keys themselves," Garsina said. "We've never been able to figure out how they were built, or what they were built from. I'm going to bet that we'll have the same problem trying to analyze the pyramid's construction. The Waymakers used materials far in advance of anything men ever learned to make. That's probably why the ship landed where it did in the first place. They saw their chance to examine a significant Waymaker artifact, and they took it."

"And it cost them . . . how much?" Lieutenant Commander Antagean asked, his voice grave. "For all we know, the whole site is now an open-air mausoleum. We're not getting anything like what I'd call a live transmission. Just the repeating, automated radio broadcast. And while I can't make out a word of what the lone voice is telling us, I'm going to wager it's a warning."

Zuri considered, eyeing the grainy images of the pyramid—and the broken hulk of the vessel resting next to it, with spars trailing off and down into the crashing waves of the sea.

Suddenly, the *Catapult*'s automated threat board lit up. A dull *bong-bong-bong-bong* sound began to fill the command module.

"Status," Admiral Mikton said, sitting up straighter.

"Signals coming in from the Waypoint," said one of the junior officers. "Unidentified vessels emerging into space. Not broadcasting Constellar identification codes."

"Damn," Zuri said, closing her eyes. "Didn't take them long, did it?"

For a moment, Zuri Mikton flashed back to Cartarrus. The achingly futile feeling of retreat. Watching ships—and people—die, so that other ships and people might live. All the while, losing a whole system which had proudly flown the Constellar flag since its settlement. A population crushed beneath the heel of Starstate Nautilan's bottomless hunger for total domination of the Waywork. Relentless. Unyielding.

"No," Zuri whispered to no one in particular. "Not this time."

"Ma'am?" asked *Daffodil*'s captain, his tone edged with fear.

"We're going to stand our ground," Zuri ordered.

"But—" Lieutenant Commander Antagean began to say, and was cut off.

"Let the word go out to every single soul in every single ship in the Task Group. Now that we're here, we're not leaving. Not while there is a Constellar citizen who still draws breath. If Nautilan is going to take this discovery from us, they will be made to pay a price. Give them a lesson in what the final war is going to be like. The war for home. It begins now. Am I understood?"

The command module was silent.

"I said," Zuri repeated, projecting from her diaphragm, "Am I *understood*?"

The entire command module crew chorused their affirmatives. As did the captain of the *Daffodil*, and the other officers from the other ships on audio only. Leaving Antagean to say it last, and not without reluctance.

*Urrl's right*, Zuri thought, *that one has never fought. But now we'll see how he handles himself.*

"How many?" Zuri asked, as Commodore Urrl began relaying battle instructions to the three Task Group ships and four security flotilla craft, presently standing watch at the Waypoint's periphery.

"Uhhhh," the *Catapult*'s captain said, unsure of the readings on his display.

"Come on, come on," Zuri snapped. "We need to know what we're dealing with."

"They're stealthing us," the captain complained. "If it weren't for the scouts and their advanced sensors, we couldn't get any readings at this distance. But, uhhhhh, I think we're looking at half a dozen ships. No, correction. Just *over* half a dozen. Say, destroyer size. We'd be able to tell more if we were in visual range."

"If we were in visual range, we'd probably be dead by now," Zuri said, thinking furiously. If it was Nautilan—and she had no reason to believe otherwise, given the fact that the Jaalit system was the only other system in the Waywork to present a Slipway to the new system—they hadn't come with as many ships as Zuri had expected. Whoever was running the Nautilan side of things was eschewing traditional Nautilan attack-and-overwhelm doctrine by employing such a downsized force.

Still, with just seven modest warships of her own with which to fight them, Zuri didn't feel greatly reassured. Especially since the Oswight yacht was now stuck on the wrong side of the Waypoint. There would be no more of Iakar's security flotilla coming to help. Not until or unless the Waypoint was cleared of hostiles.

"I think they're dividing their fleet," Urrl said.

Zuri furiously pounded the keys on her gee chair's keyboard, switching the tactical wallscreen off and activating the larger holographic unit which could project three-dimensional imagery over the heads of the command module staff. Within that now-glowing space, numerous little signatures appeared: some of them blue, for friendly ships, and others bright red, for the newly arrived vessels. Urrl was right. The nine red ships were dividing up into two groups, with four of them vectoring away from the Waypoint.

"They're going for Antagean's detachment," Zuri said.

"What do you want Antagean to do?" Urrl asked.

"Run," Zuri said plainly. "It's the only thing they can do now. Get to the clement planet. Put our forces on the ground. Even if we can't overwhelm the Nauties in space, we can challenge them to a stand-up fight for the prize soil."

"And the *Daffodil*?" Urrl asked.

"She went dark once," Zuri replied. "Order her to go dark again. She's not toothless, but she's not built for battle like her sisters from the security flotilla, either. We might need her to get back across the Slipway, assuming we can punch a hole through the five ships facing us directly. They're bigger than any of ours. Very probably better armed, and better armored. It'll take all of us working in concert to match them."

"Shouldn't we try to intercept the ships vectoring on Antagean's trio?"

"No. Antagean has a nice head start. They can see him, but they can't close the distance very easily. Our best shot is to try to beat the five who remain, and hope there's enough of us left to use the Waypoint again. Get word back home. Maybe even bring some more of the security flotilla over. *Then* we can look at tackling the four ships detailed to chase Antagean."

Zuri hated the idea of letting Antagean's three ships go it alone. But they had so much distance between themselves and the Waypoint now that there was no practical reason to try to send help. The vastness of space would protect Antagean, his ships, and Lady Oswight. At least until they could reach the new world, where it seemed men had once walked. And might walk again?

The logical move was to keep the armed Task Group together. If they hit quickly and hard enough, they might be able to gain the upper hand. It only took one lucky nuke hit to seriously damage a destroyer—even some of the top-of-the-line stuff that Nautilan shipyards were putting out these days. Chances were high that Zuri would lose some ships too. Especially the little scouts. But so long as it was seven to five, she at least maintained a degree of numerical advantage. And that meant enemy forces shooting at more of hers, and hers shooting at less of them.

Nothing would happen instantly. The Task Group was far enough removed from the edge of the Waypoint that it would be hours before anyone saw any action. Plenty of time for all of the crews to make ready, and for Zuri especially to disseminate the order of battle to her other ships.

# CHAPTER 19

THE NAUTILAN SHIPS EMERGED FROM THE WAYPOINT IN FORMATION: nine warships forming three sets of three ships in arrowhead configuration. Almost immediately upon their arrival in the uncharted system, General Ekk—from his gee chair in the command module of the *Alliance*—ordered a prompt sensor sweep. Their default assumption prior to crossing the Slipway had been that they would encounter armed Constellar resistance. And this assumption had proven correct. The *Alliance* quickly detected a number of other ships. Some of them appeared to be military configuration, while three of them were distinctly civilian.

"Starliners?" Kosmarch Golsubril Vex remarked, from her gee chair which flanked General Ekk's own.

"It would appear so," he said. "Put us on combat alert."

Promptly, the light in the command module went from white to yellow, and a low, repetitive klaxon began to fill the air. Several command module personnel scrambled to get to their gee chairs—having been formerly floating, using grip boots or handholds—while the conventional navigator performed checks on distances to the foreign ships, and read them off to both the *Alliance*'s captain and General Ekk.

"They've split their force," Ekk said. "But I admit I don't understand why the three civilian craft departed the Waypoint without armed escort. That's foolish."

"They simply assume there's no one deeper in the system to challenge them," Vex remarked. "We don't know how long they've been here, or how much reconnaissance they've managed to do. Can we be sure they don't already have assets closer to the home star? Ships undetectable at this range?"

"No we can't," Ekk said. "But if I may offer an opinion, Madam Kosmarch, the makeup of their security group seems slapdash at best. Two scout-sized ships. What might pass for a destroyer, on the small side. And four conventional close-patrol ships, which are almost certainly from the security group guarding their Waypoint on their side of the Slipway."

"Your point, General?"

"Madam, their plan is a hasty plan. They brought over everything they *could* bring over, as soon as it could be brought. And it still won't be enough to save them. We outgun them in every instance, ship to ship. The upper hand is ours."

"Unless they move more assets across the Slipway," she said guardedly.

"If they could move more, especially en masse, they'd have done it already. Madam Kosmarch, I recommend we attack *now*. Finish them here. Claim the Waypoint. And that will give us time to perform a proper reconnaissance of this system, at our leisure."

"You're that confident we can take them?" Vex said.

"Yes, Madam Kosmarch, I am."

"And the three civilian craft? They appear to be almost two days ahead of us, even thrusting at full gee. Does that not concern you?"

"They can't shoot at us. What harm could they cause? We can pursue them later, once the Waypoint is ours."

Vex thought about it. The tactical-command hologram suspended in the air of the command module showed the relative positions of both the foreign ships and Ekk's triple-wedge battle squadron. The civilian starliners were far away, and getting farther. But something about them piqued her interest. Ekk had pointed out that it was foolish for the starliners to be going deep into the system without armed escort. Which meant those ships were up to something important enough to justify the risk.

"Can you tell where the civilian liners are going?" she asked.

General Ekk tapped his keyboard, and issued a few orders to some of his subordinates in the command module. After a couple of minutes, one of the junior officers reported back.

"Sir," the woman said, "we haven't tracked the civilian craft long enough to obtain a definitive trajectory. But based on their present course and velocity, it seems they're on a gravity-boost course which will fling them from two of the larger, outer gas-giant worlds toward the smaller terrestrials close to the home star."

"They've found something," Vex declared.

"Madam?" Ekk said, his face confused.

"It's the only rational explanation. Either those liners contain cargo and personnel Constellar wants to keep very far away from us, or this cargo and those personnel *have* to be delivered to the inner system before we can interdict. Our arrival—here—has been anticipated. Your counterpart on the Constellar side is think-ing ahead of you, General. So, we will split our resources. Four ships, then five. *Alliance* will lead the group of four, and pursue the unarmed civilian ships to their final destination—whatever it might be."

"But, Madam Kosmarch," Ekk protested loudly, "even outgun-ning them, five of our destroyers against seven of their smaller ships stand much less of a chance of victory, compared to all nine of us taking the entire Constellar security group in one melee."

"No," Vex said. "Defeating their security group, here, might be moot—if they've got something waiting for us closer to the sun. We'll pursue the starliners, to whatever end. If during our pursuit we detect additional Constellar craft, we can relay that information to General Ticonner, and this can ultimately be communicated back across the Slipway if necessary. Do you doubt General Ticonner's tactical ability to successfully engage the 'slapdash' Constellar effort, as you called it?"

"No, Madam Kosmarch," Ekk said, somewhat abashed. "I have full confidence in my counterpart's abilities."

"Then let us waste no more time, please. Execute as I've instructed."

General Ekk appeared to want to protest further. The words practically trembled on the older man's lips. She could read the thought in his mind: she was no trained battle strategist, but it was insanity to countermand a kosmarch—even when common Nautilan sense told the man that Golsubril Vex was wrong.

She waited, unblinking, and stared at him. He could take his time. Weigh it out, as he must. When finally he said, "At your order, Madam Kosmarch," she smiled slightly. That had taken a bit longer than she'd expected. Which wasn't necessarily a bad thing. Ekk was capable, if not especially creative. He greatly disliked the current plan, as much as he had disliked coming across the Slipway before they had amassed what he considered to be a sufficiently large number of ships.

But she'd won that argument, and intended to keep on winning the arguments. She didn't need people trying to be smart for her on this mission. She was plenty smart herself, assuming her subordinates provided her with quality information.

They merely had to obey.

Within minutes, *Alliance* had split off from the main Nautilan squadron with three other sister destroyers, flanking two to starboard and one to port. Ekk was busy on his headset, calming the fears of some of the other destroyer captains who doubtless objected to the plan as much as Ekk himself did. To the general's credit, he didn't lay it off on the kosmarch. Instead, he issued instructions as if the plan had been his own, so as to reassure those men and women beneath him that they could trust his judgment—even if he himself didn't trust Vex's.

She relaxed into her gee chair, watching the tactical hologram as her pursuit force formed up, then she felt the increase in thrust as *Alliance*'s captain ordered the ship up to full gee, and beyond. Going over full gee would be an uncomfortable experience, Vex knew. Even for experienced spacers. But every second counted, now. And assuming those civilian ships couldn't match against the *Alliance,* Vex would gradually be able to gain ground. Perhaps enough to capture the starliners in flight? Before they reached orbit around whichever world they were in such a hurry to reach?

On that note, Vex ordered the *Alliance*'s sensor module activated, for as extensive a scan of the new system as could be accomplished at such great distance. They were still in the outermost part of the plane of the planetary disc, beyond even the farthest jovian world. It would take many days to get all the way to the big superjovian orbiting very near to the home sun. They ought to be able to determine what might be waiting for them upon their eventual arrival.

Meanwhile, Vex ordered General Ticonner to prepare a hasty brief, so that she could examine his adjusted plan of attack—against the Constellar security group. The DSOD ships had numbers on their side, but Ticonner had mass, as well as weapons. It would take a bit of tactical thinking to devise a plan which might split the security group enough for it to be possible to mass the five assaulting destroyers in a way that they could pick off the Constellar vessels in sequence.

"This is why we win," Vex said to no one in particular, as Ticonner relayed several different courses of action, and asked Vex which one she preferred. She examined the little simulations on her gee chair's flatscreen display. Running each of them in turn. Then, running them once more. And finally, a third time. With percentages for estimated success tallying on every iteration, until one of the simulations showed a higher potential percentage than any of the others.

"Attack plan two," she finally said.

Ticonner relayed his understanding, and then Vex went back to looking at the larger tactical hologram, in which her pursuit force was getting farther and farther away from Ticonner's engagement force.

Oddly, the Constellar security group did not appear to have reacted to this division of opponent assets.

"Is it possible they just haven't noticed yet?" she asked.

"We've got the stealth disruption network powered up," Ekk said, "to try to keep them in the dark as long as possible. Though, if they're using their countermeasures to compete with *our* countermeasures, it won't be too long before they figure out what we're doing. Madam Kosmarch, I feel compelled to point out that if the Constellar security force ignores Ticonner's assault squadron, and tries to interdict *Alliance*'s pursuit squadron instead, we'll actually be at a disadvantage in that fight. Our four against their seven. It won't be the kind of battle for which I can guarantee a victory. Are you ready to take that risk?"

"Of course," Vex said, and meant it. This was hardly the time to get cold feet over a matter as mundane as personal safety. Those starliners were on to something. She could feel it. Whether Ticonner was successful, or had to retreat with a damaged and reduced force, or was even obliterated entirely, finding out what those starliners were on about would be the key to leveraging this new system—to both Vex's and Starstate Nautilan's advantage.

"Very well, Madam Kosmarch," Ekk said. "I will prepare several defensive scenarios for simulation. It will be hours before anyone is shooting at our squadrons anyway. We have time to prepare."

# CHAPTER 20

SPACE BATTLES TENDED TO FOLLOW AN ASYMPTOTIC CURVE: VERY little combat for a very long while until, suddenly, everything was blowing up at once. Even ships pushed to the limit of their crews, at three gees of thrust, or more, took hours or days to intercept their intended targets. And then, engagements would be conducted across thousands, tens of thousands, or even hundreds of thousands of kilometers. Cold, empty space. You could detect your enemy, and your enemy could detect you, well in advance. Missiles thus launched could be detected too. And countermissiles also launched. Precious little was ever a surprise.

Thus ship-to-ship doctrine in any Starstate war college stipulated that the successful commander was the person able to force his target to commit an error in defensive prioritization. No ship could successfully intercept and destroy missiles in every quadrant, at every range. Overwhelm a given target's countermissile and railgun batteries with enough nukes inbound from different directions—at different speeds and distances—and you stood a good chance of landing a hit.

So, a great deal of thought and computer simulation were dedicated to anticipating these scenarios. With the hours of battle flight dedicated to running these simulations again, and again, and again, just as the hardware itself would be checked and run through its paces and firing patterns. To be sure that when the critical moment came, and a defending ship's number was up, all of the hardware performed to expectation, and hopefully nobody aboard had to experience the deafening sound of a ship-to-ship warhead detonating against—or near—the hull.

Of course, some theorists stated that the best defense was a good offense. Waiting for the missiles to come to you was an automatically losing move. So, you sent your missiles to them *before* they could overwhelm your defenses. Which entailed still more readiness drills and even lengthier equipment checks. Such that the amount of time spent merely getting the ships close enough to fire on each other was actually some of the busiest in a crewperson's life. Almost to the point of not having time to get nervous. Especially since the crew almost never saw the enemy. Not up close. If a foe was launching missiles at visual range, your situation was so critical that any hit might lethally damage both the defender *and* the attacker.

So, the visible action was carried out on a reduced scale, with wallscreen and holographic projections shrinking total distance down—and blowing actual ship sizes up—to the point each could be made intelligible for commanders, as well as command staff. All of whom would be intensely fascinated with these displays up through the moment of hostile contact, until the enemy was either destroyed outright, crippled into impotency, or fleeing for their lives.

Unless of course, it was your ship getting crippled, or fleeing.

Wyodreth Antagean had never been aboard a ship on actual battle alert. He'd certainly never anticipated doing so aboard one of his company's own ships. Starliners were big, happy targets for even the most diminutive warships. And Antagean Starlines had, in its history, been canny enough to get its assets *out* of a threatened system long before the shooting started.

He and Captain Loper carefully eyed their separate displays, while the ship's conventional pilot gradually pushed the vehicle toward one-point-five gee thrust—or approximately one and a half times the normal force of gravity, measured according to the ancient scale which had come from Earth.

Wyo felt heavy as a result. Like being on an amusement ride— the kind that did centripetal force, going in a circle—perpetually. He knew from past experience that he'd wind up with a headache soon. All of them would. Gee beyond one-point-oh meant everyone aboard was having to work that much harder to move, and each heart was having to pump blood harder too. If anyone had a preexisting cardiac condition, the ship's surgeon—and DSOD medics—would be hearing about it soon. Especially if Wyo had to push them beyond two gees thrust. That's when things would become truly painful.

Although, not as painful as being blown out of space by a Nautilan nuke.

"She'll hold out, even at three gees," Loper reassured his boss.

"Yeah," Wyo said, fully depressed at forty-five degrees into his gee chair. "But some of the *people* won't. I'm going to hope that our pursuers aren't any more interested in punishing their crews than we are in punishing ours. I still can't figure out why they split their squadron up in the first place. If they can see us, they can see that we're not armed. If I was the squadron commander, I'd want every available ship on the line. To increase my tactical advantage against Admiral Mikton's force."

"They're interested in what we might know," Loper said, also pressed into his forty-five-degree gee chair. "It probably looks odd, just three starliners burning hard toward the inner planets. So, they split up. One bunch intended to intercept us, and the other bunch intended to take out the Task Group proper. Which, judging by the mass of those Nautilan ships that came across the Slipway, they might do. It's too bad we didn't get just one more day to prepare. We'd have an additional twenty-four-hours distance on our pursuers, and Mikton would probably have four or five more ships at her command."

"What do you think our plan ought to be? In case you're right?"

Wyo watched his old mentor chew on his bottom lip.

"If Mikton's Task Group is destroyed, the Waypoint belongs to Nautilan. Mikton still has the Oswight yacht. And the yacht will get shot to pieces before it ever gets close enough to the Waypoint envelope to activate its Key. Which means no more reinforcements from the Oswight side of the Slipway. We'll have to go to ground on the planet *Daffodil* showed us. It's our best—maybe only—shot."

Wyo suddenly had an image in his head of all three Antagean starliners jettisoning every available emergency pod—plus several of the combat drop modules which had been mounted specifically for the purpose of putting DSOD TGO troops and equipment on any given world's surface as quickly as possible. Data from the *Daffodil* indicated the air might be breathable. They'd know for sure once they were down and able to do an atmosphere analysis. Which would go a long way toward increasing their chances for prolonged survival. As would the availability of water, which the planet appeared to have in abundance.

With the TGOs leading the way, Antagean's people might be able to hold out for weeks. Perhaps months? Assuming the Nauties weren't particularly equipped for ground maneuvers.

But he had to assume they were. Both Wyo and Captain Loper had been talking as if their Nautilan opponents were every bit as smart as themselves, with an equal capacity for anticipating contingencies too.

"Damn," Wyo said to himself, feeling entirely too pessimistic. His father's ships carried the best reactors money could buy, but that didn't guarantee he could keep pace with, or outrun, the Nautilan ships. Sooner or later, he'd have critical working-fluid shortages.

The reactors didn't need hydrogen to fuse, nearly as much as the hydrogen itself was the substance which created thrust in the first place. Heat, all by itself, was just energy. That energy didn't move the ship until there was working fluid spewing out the backs of the ships—in long, sun-hot streams of plasma. Once the working fluid ran low, each of the Antagean starliners would be using reaction control thrusters only. Which was enough to maneuver a ship in orbit, but not enough to push them anywhere else in interplanetary space. Much less get them back to, or through, the Waypoint.

And there would be little chance of distilling replacement hydrogen now. That plan got scrapped the moment the Nauties showed up.

So, the real long-term success of the mission depended on Admiral Mikton repelling the Nautilan attack squadron. Then sending the Oswight yacht back over the Slipway to begin bringing additional reinforcements—assuming the Nauties didn't bring their own reinforcements first.

Anything Constellar's people could think up and do, Nautilan's people could think up and do too. Only question was: would they?

"Lady Oswight for you, intraship," Wyo's comms watchman said.

"Lady?" Wyo said to the small image which had just appeared on the tactical net. Her expression was deceptively calm.

"How are we doing?" she asked.

"We're keeping a close eye on the pursuit squadron's relative velocity and distance," Wyo said. "If they speed up, we speed up. We've got almost thirty-six hours on them. That's a lot of space. Too much for them to effectively employ weapons. So, as long as we can remain effectively out of reach, they can't touch us. We'll pick up a gravity boost at the first, and then the second, jovian world. That will give us a good kick in the pants without forcing us to use additional fuel. But the real question is: Do we brake in an attempt to orbit the clement planet? Or just let ourselves coast on by?"

"We *cannot* let the clement world fall into Nautilan hands," the Lady Oswight said. "Those structures we saw on the planet's surface? They belong to us now."

"And that means abandoning my spaceframes in orbit, while we drop to the surface," Wyo said. "Captain Loper and I are planning for this. Though I have to admit, we're basically cutting off our noses to spite our faces if we do that. If Nautilan controls both the Waypoint and the orbital space around the clement world, it'll only be a matter of time before they begin landing troops of their own. And while they'll have a logistics chain stretching all the way back to Nautilan space, we will have nothing. No backup. No way to medically evacuate dead and wounded. They will wait us out."

"Not if I can help it," Admiral Mikton's face said, suddenly blinking to life in a different square on the tactical net.

"Ma'am," Wyo said, acknowledging the Task Group's commander.

"We've analyzed the signatures of those ships," she said, "and while I can tell you they're bigger than anything we've got on this side, we still have numbers. I anticipate that the Nautilan attack squadron commander is going to try to carve our ships away from the task group, one at a time. Like a pack hunt. But two can play that game. This isn't my first time to the dance hall, Lieutenant Commander. I have no intention of letting our Nautilan friends claim this system. It's more important than ever before that you successfully reach the clement planet. Speaking of which, the captain of the *Daffodil* has deferred on naming our prize. He felt that honor ought to go to you, Lady Oswight. It's a hell of a time to ask, but what shall we christen the place?"

Garsina's face showed surprise, then she wrinkled her brow in thought.

"I feel like it ought to be something poetic. But I'll be damned if I can think of anything right at this particular moment."

"Get back to us on that, Lady," Admiral Mikton said. "Meanwhile, you'll have to prepare yourself to join Lieutenant Commander

Antagean on the surface once you arrive. You'll still—hopefully—have a day and half head start. Which means your starliners are going to get captured or destroyed in orbit, Lieutenant Commander. The DSOD is going to owe your father a *lot* of money when we get back."

"Damned right!" Wyo said loudly. "Though, to be honest, Captain Loper and I have been trying to figure a way out of that. Once we've evacuated each of the ships, we could leave skeleton crews aboard—to break orbit and burn for the superjovian. Which could be used for a third gravity assist, sending them back out to you on long trajectory, where they could theoretically rendezvous with... the *Daffodil*? There's no use abandoning them in place. Hell, I'd rather put them on autopilot and try to ram the Nautilan pursuit force. Or rig the reactors to detonate once a Nautilan ship gets close enough. If they want my ships, they're going to get bloody."

"That's the spirit, Lieutenant Commander. We're going to be getting some serious communications lag soon. Light-seconds turning into light-minutes. Be advised that we'll try to keep the *Daffodil* appraised of our status, and that the *Daffodil* will try to keep you appraised in turn. We're doing two things at once now with this mission. And I expect you're going to soon be making a lot of split-second decisions. I support you in whatever calls you have to make, right or wrong. Remember what they taught you at the Reserve command school: A decision, even if it's a poor one, always beats no decision at all. Do what you think is best, when you think it. Am I understood?"

"Perfectly, ma'am," Wyo said.

With that, Mikton's image faded from the tactical network.

"You know, ramming them isn't a half-bad idea," Captain Loper said.

"I was mostly being rhetorical," Wyo admitted.

"But if we started now, we could move all of the people and vital equipment off of one liner onto the remaining two. Program the empty liner to gradually drop back. Eventually the Nauties catch up with her, and she's autopilot-programmed to plow into the first Nautie ship which gets close enough. *Boom.* One less pursuer to worry about."

"Assuming the Nauties don't just blast her to pieces," Wyo countered. "We're thinking they have any interest at all in seizing our ships. They could have orders to kill at the first opportunity.

Then it doesn't matter if we sacrifice one of ours to try to take out one of theirs. We'd simply lose one of ours without having gained any advantage whatsoever. Not like we even *have* an advantage right now, save for the raw distance separating their squadron from ours. I wish to heck we had other options. Some weapons with which we might inflict real damage."

Garsina Oswight suddenly cleared her throat.

"Lady?" asked Captain Loper, observing the tac net.

"If it's weapons the lieutenant commander wants, need I remind him of what I saw up in the secure cargo area under the ship's shield dome? I don't know what the Tactical Ground Operations people plan to do with five-kiloton thermonuclear devices. But it seems to me you could get creative."

Loper and the lieutenant commander raised their eyebrows, looking first at the tactical net, then at each other.

"She's right," Loper said, a tiny smile creeping onto his face.

"But how to deliver them?" Wyo said. He was intrigued by the idea, but skeptical he could put any of the TGO's thermonuclear shells within proximity of their Nautilan pursuers before those pursuers took the shells out—either with antimissiles, or their railgun point-defense systems. Objects, even small objects, hurtling at any of the Nautilan destroyers, would be taken for incoming and wiped from space with extreme prejudice.

Wyo tapped keys on his gee chair keyboard, until the face of the resident TGO company commander appeared.

"Captain Fazal," he said.

"Copy you, Lieutenant Commander. I understand we're running from some Nautilan gunboats? I've got all my people restricted to gee chairs until further notice. I don't want anyone getting hurt before we have to land. We'll need every able hand once we're securing the landing site at the new planet."

"Good work, Fazal. Actually, what I have for you now is a bit of a kludge project. Lady Oswight reminded me that we're carrying a load of TGO nuke shells. Are those proximity fused? Or air burst?"

"Either, sir," the TGO company commander replied.

"How many did you bring aboard?"

"Five thermonukes, sir, as well as about a hundred conventional rounds in the same size. We're carrying one mechanized mortar capable of firing either."

"Think you could cook up some kind of delivery method for using those shells ship to ship? I know you're trained strictly for on-planet work with that kind of weaponry. But right now we've got four Nautilan destroyers trying to eat up the distance between us. I'd like to find some way to slow them down. Perhaps even hurt them bad enough that they think twice?"

Based on the gleeful expression on the captain's face, Wyo knew he'd gotten the infantry officer's attention.

"That . . . is a very intriguing suggestion, sir," Fazal said. "I'll get together with my lieutenants and senior NCOs, and see what we can work out. Are we talking, like, getting in close, sir? Or is this something that's got to deliver shells over thousands of kilometers?"

"The greater the distance, the better," Wyo said. "I have no intention of getting any closer to the enemy—with these unarmed starliners—than necessary. But since we won't have any firepower from the Task Group assisting us, we have to come up with something on our own."

"I might be able to help too," Garsina Oswight volunteered. "Part of my degree on Waymaker technology involved learning astrophysics. If there's a way to build—or repurpose—anything aboard this vessel which might operate as a delivery method, I can set it up."

"Lady," Antagean said, "your assistance in this regard will be most gratefully accepted. How about it, Captain Fazal?"

"We'd be cheered by the Lady's participation," he said, dipping his chin to his chest.

"Okay, it's a plan," Wyo said. "Captain Loper and I will keep the Nauties far enough away that you will have time to work. I am thinking our best times to spring something on them will be when we're doing gravity assist at the two outer jovians. If we can launch something in our wake, or better yet, simply drop the ordnance rigged to seek on a large starship's signature—"

"Consider it done," both Fazal and Lady Oswight said in unison. Then their images blipped off the tac net.

"I have a feeling," Loper said, "that both of them have been positively itching for the chance to get involved."

"I don't blame them," Wyo said. "I just hope whatever they come up with actually works. We're going to need it."

# CHAPTER 21

GENERAL TICONNER HAD NEVER HAD EXCLUSIVE CONTROL OF A squadron before. Mostly, he had served as General Ekk's trusted deputy through several different changes of command. Until now, quite suddenly, Ekk wasn't around to give Ticonner ideas anymore. It left the Nautilan officer feeling rather uneasy, as he filled his hours with continual status checks on the five destroyers at his disposal. Each of the ships' captains were perpetually slaved to Ticonner's tactical comms network so that he could give orders at any moment and expect them to be quickly followed. Once the squadron had closed to firing distance, they were going to use a combat-tested engagement pattern—with Ticonner's destroyer, the *Unity,* acting as the hub of a revolving wheel. Which would expose no single ship to prolonged enemy counterfire, but allow Ticonner's force to deliver almost continual salvos at the designated target.

Once the target was destroyed, they would begin firing on the next target. And then the next target after that. And so on, and so forth. Ticonner estimated that none of the Constellar vessels was sufficiently armed or armored to withstand more than a couple direct hits without being crippled or obliterated.

When the last minutes before contact had finally trickled away, General Ticonner discovered—rather unhappily—that his opponent was mirroring his formation. Two discs approaching each other edge-on. The oversized frigate sat at the center of a slowly revolving circle of combat craft. None of which, individually,

149

posed a significant threat. But in their current formation, which presented a new ship at the front of the line every few minutes... Ticonner's hope of massing two or three destroyers' firepower on any single Constellar ship was dashed. To say nothing of the fact that their flagship was now just as protected from Ticonner's attack as Ticonner's ship had been protected from theirs.

"Sir," said the comms officer, who'd been ensuring that Ticonner's ship-to-ship connection with the other Nautilan destroyers remained stable.

"Is there a problem, Lieutenant?" Ticonner asked.

"I'm not sure, sir. I think we're getting a broadcast directly from the Constellar commander. She's asking to speak to you, General."

Ticonner considered. Kosmarch Vex had not given much thought to parley. Though the protocols of the Nautilan military did entertain it.

Ticonner raised his hand, and pointed a finger at his personal workstation flatscreen.

The signal that came across left an image mildly distorted—a clear lack of clean interfacing between Nautilan comms and Constellar comms. Just the same, Ticonner could see the face of an older female officer, whose rank clusters on her collar identified her as an admiral in Constellar's Deep Space Operations and Defense force. At one time, she might have qualified as pretty. But her hair, which was mostly gray, and shot through with increasing strands of white, had been cropped close to her head.

"What business do you have in this system?" Ticonner demanded. "Per the will of my Kosmarch, Golsubril Vex, we have claimed this star, and all the planets surrounding it, for Starstate Nautilan. You will surrender immediately, or my squadron will be forced to destroy you."

One thing which had survived the Exodus: the universal language of all humans—Mariclesh. Every Nautilan officer knew how to speak it fluently, as did the officers of most of the other Starstates' militaries. Individual planetary dialects existed aplenty, but if you wanted to conduct business at the interplanetary level, or do diplomacy across borders, Mariclesh was the go-to option.

"What business do *you* have in this system, General?" the woman asked—a question for a question. "You cannot claim this system for Nautilan, because *I* have already claimed it. With the expressed blessing of the Lady Oswight, of First Family Oswight, Starstate Constellar. You will withdraw your squadron back to the Waypoint, and depart. Or *I* will be forced to destroy *you*, sir."

Her Mariclesh speech was seamless. Even more practiced than Ticonner's.

He laughed. Harshly.

"Come now, Admiral. We both know neither of us intends to stand down. Why are you making us bother with this impotent overture? You can see my ships. You know that I have you beaten, without ordering a single barrage. Surrender, and I will spare your lives. Perhaps even entertain the possibility of repatriation. All we want is this system, which until recently was uncharted space for both our countries. There doesn't have to be any bloodshed."

"See," the admiral said, "there's the real problem. We both came prepared to fight, because fighting is all our two nations have been doing for as long as either one of us has been alive. There's a little angel on my shoulder who keeps hoping, despite all logic, that one of these days Nautilan and Constellar will solve a dispute without shooting. Alas, I don't think that day has come just yet. So, since you're not interested in retreating like I told you to—and do please remember, I said so *nicely*—there's just one thing left for us to do."

Suddenly the *Unity*'s battle klaxon began to blast from speakers all over the ship's command module.

"We've got several inbound," shouted the countermeasures officer from his workstation.

"Begin deploying your antimissiles," Ticonner ordered, then turned in his gee chair to face the offensive weapons officer.

"I don't care which ship you pick," he said, "just choose one, and start launching our missiles! Make sure to relay your choice to the other four destroyers as well. If our opponent thinks she can be cute with us, and win the day, she's not nearly as experienced an officer as her age suggests."

In the blackness of space, across fifty thousand kilometers, fusion warheads—propelled by expendable fusion thruster motors—raced toward each other. It was a contest to see who would get the most missiles through the enemy's countermeasures first.

For the first thirty minutes, nothing happened. The holographic display over the heads of Ticonner's command module staff showed the wheel of the Constellar squadron approaching the wheel of the Nautilan squadron, with a small cloud of missiles and antimissiles dispersing between them. Even at maximum thrust, it took time for the weapons to cross the midpoint. And then, each nuclear-armed offensive missile was independently programmed with an autoevasive routine which would detect incoming antimissiles. The cloud of weapons quickly turned into a chaotic dance of larger objects dodging a host of smaller objects—while the larger still tried to home on and accelerate toward their designated target. Every few seconds, some of the antimissiles would self-detonate in an attempt to knock out one of the bigger antiship warheads.

Little glowing balls—representing blast radii—blossomed in the holographic tactical space.

"Attrition?" Ticonner asked the two officers crewing the weapons and countermeasures stations.

"Our squadron has fired a total of twenty-five warheads, sir. Looks like . . . seventeen have survived. No, make it sixteen. Correction, fifteen."

"Is point-defense warmed up and ready?"

"Yessir," countermeasures replied confidently.

On the hull of the *Unity* a host of electromagnetic acceleration cannon were alive and actively tracking the Constellar warheads in closest proximity to the ship. No single railgun could hope to take out all of the incoming missiles. But three or four railguns firing into a given quadrant at one time—each hurling a lethal wad of antimissile pellets, like a shotgun shooting at a clay pigeon—would usually do the job. Nothing was done by eye, nor were the turrets manned. Everything was done via computer targeting, using an interlinked battle pattern controlled directly from the command module. If need be, each of the individual railguns could uncouple from the rest, and fire using its own independent targeting system with its own independent sensor unit—with far less range than that of the *Unity*'s main sensors. The only crew on the weapons were engineering staff watching specifically for computerized failures or mechanical problems. Until or unless something went wrong, they simply waited.

The view out the railgun porthole showed nothing but black space, with occasional flashes of light as the swarming missiles and antimissiles gradually diminished in number.

"We've still got three Constellar warheads inbound," counter-measures said. "One thousand kilometers, and closing."

"Railguns," Ticonner ordered.

But the computer was way ahead of him. Bursts of fire—invisible to the naked eye in the dim light of the far away sun—lashed out. Within five minutes, three separate balls of light flared within the three-dimensional hologram. A bit too close for Ticonner's comfort, but still distant enough that *Unity* wouldn't experience any deleterious effects.

In the cold emptiness of space, shredded pieces of missiles, antimissiles, railgun pellets, and obliterated warheads spread in all directions. Any ship plowing through that mess was going to wind up with a pockmarked shield dome. Though both squadrons were already changing trajectory to avoid the debris. Even a small particle, moving at interplanetary speeds, could cause significant damage—if it came in at the right angle.

When the two battle wheels were within thirty thousand kilometers of each other, the melee began anew. More warheads launched. More countermeasures effected. Each ship in Ticonner's squadron had started the day with over a hundred nukes in her magazines, and close to a thousand countermissiles. Given effective employment of the latter, the fight could go on for many, many hours. Both squadrons barraging each other repeatedly, until one or the other began to suffer casualties. If Ticonner's guess was right—that the smaller Constellar ships carried less ordnance overall—the battle might come down to simply outlasting the stores of the enemy. When their antimissile magazines and rail-gun batteries ran dry, the Constellar ships would be defenseless.

In the end, Ticonner's only concern was ensuring that no Constellar ship escaped. Not to the Waypoint. And not to the inner system—trailing the starliners now being pursued by the kosmarch aboard *Alliance*.

# CHAPTER 22

FOR ADMIRAL MIKTON, THERE WAS BUT A SINGLE OBJECTIVE: punch through the Nautilan attack force, and deploy the Oswight Family yacht within close proximity of the Waypoint. Presently, the yacht was mated to one of the security flotilla ships which had come over from Commodore Iakar's bunch. The yacht—and her Key—were the only way to bring additional reinforcements before the Nauties could. But if the yacht were prevented from making the crossing, or destroyed outright...

Zuri thought hard, her brow beetled. The tactical hologram—not very different from that used by her opponent—was a colorful mirage of slowly moving ships mixed with faster moving missiles and antimissiles. Thus far her point-defense network had managed to take out the few Nautilan nukes which had slipped through, and she'd steered her force wide of the ensuing mist of wreckage. Now, the battle was in its second round, and her eyes kept straying to one of her gee chair's flatscreens, which displayed not only *Catapult*'s stores, but also the stores still aboard the other ships as well. Little vertical status bars with little numbers at the bottom, were slowly diminishing.

"If we close to within ten thousand kilometers," Commodore Urrl said, "things could get ugly."

"I'm not sure we have a choice," Zuri replied. "With them square in our path—blocking a clean lane to the Waypoint—our only choice might be to take all of our ships up to three

155

gee acceleration, and hope we can zoom our formation directly through theirs."

"With us launching on each other the whole time," Urrl said, and shook his head. "It's a good way to die. Might cause them to hit some of their own ships with their own warheads. I like that. But we're liable to be shredded in the process."

"We still have more ships in total," Admiral Mikton said. "The trick is going to be getting them to attack all of us at once. We're too far away from any of this system's planets to use the natural real estate for cover."

"Maybe, maybe not," Urrl said, and used his gee chair's controls to temporarily expand the command module's tactical hologram until the battle itself occupied just a tiny fraction of the glowing space. Other objects now appeared—much larger than any ship.

"Kuiper objects," Zuri said, catching her exec's meaning. "The nearest is still pretty far away."

"But reachable, if we divert course now. Look at that trio."

The hologram suddenly zoomed in on a significantly sized cometary body with what appeared to be two smaller cometary bodies captured in orbit.

"Rocky mass, mixed with water and gas ice. Two auxiliary masses. I estimate if we adjust course and push to three gee, we can get there before the Nauties."

Zuri expanded the holographic view even more, until the simulated picture of the Kuiper object and its satellites almost filled the entire command module. Her experience at Cartarrus had involved planetary orbital fighting, as well as fighting in the spaces between the planets. Using the same tactics on a drastically reduced scale *might* work. But it would be almost as much of a gamble as simply running her squadron through the enemy group, with the throttle on full.

Which choice presented the least amount of death? Because that was what she would be doing, she knew—picking who lived, and who died. Some of her ships would make it, and some would not. The point was to ensure that the yacht got back to the Slipway and through to the other side. Not only to bring more ships across, but to also warn Iakar that the enemy was on this side of the Slipway, and could theoretically attempt to cross to Oswight space—if the Nautilan commander assumed that Iakar's security flotilla might be compromised.

*Compromised,* Zuri said to herself, and continued to stare at the Kuiper object. Something about the two little balls of rock and ice circling their much larger, irregularly shaped parent...

Taking control of the hologram, Zuri zoomed back out to interplanetary distance, and set up an autocalculation for the purpose of triangulating between the Waypoint, the jovian world where *Daffodil* orbited, and the Kuiper object. She used her gee chair keyboard to do several calculations regarding thrust, fuel and working-fluid consumption, relative velocity, and time to intercept—assuming the Nauties followed.

"Is there any sign that Nautilan is yet aware of the *Daffodil's* existence?"

"Tough to gage," Urrl replied. "So far we've only seen them react to us splitting our force, with four of them detaching to pursue Antagean's liners. My guess is that they haven't seen *Daffodil* yet, and are unlikely to see her unless she lights up her fusion reactors and breaks orbit. What do you have in mind?"

"I'm not sure yet," Zuri replied, her eyes tracing the little wires of light which connected the many points of interest on the overall strategic scale. Seeing those connections gave her another idea, so that she quickly changed the hologram again—this time to reflect a regional view of the Waywork itself. Oswight's star was a bright point not too far from the home star for the planet Jaalit, from which the Nauties had dispatched their interceptor force. A Slipway line connected Jaalit space and Oswight space, just as new Slipway lines connected the unnamed system to both Oswight and Jaalit.

"Maybe our whole problem is playing to lose, not playing to win," Zuri said, as she zoomed in until only the Slipway line between Jaalit space and their present location glowed in the air over their reclined gee chairs.

"There's nothing to prevent them from sending more assets across their Slipway," Urrl said glumly.

"But what if everything that could be moved, has been moved?" Zuri said. "We're looking at nine destroyer-sized ships, with Keys. This may represent the totality of Jaalit's capital capability. Leaving just their own security flotilla at their Waypoint for protection."

"Just what in the hell are you getting at?" Urrl said, sitting up a bit more in his gee chair—despite the exertion—and giving his boss a skeptical glare.

"I'm still thinking it over," Zuri said, her thoughts chasing each other while she stared at the hologram. Security flotillas tended to be overstrength, for the purpose of warding off would-be invaders. Any ships coming out of the Waypoint, and not immediately broadcasting the correct identification codes on the correct identification frequencies, would be attacked with extreme prejudice. Those codes and frequencies were always changing—for every Starstate—and were second only to the Keys themselves in terms of value. An enemy able to mask itself during Waypoint use could wreak havoc. A lesson which all of the Starstates' militaries had learned the hard way. Thus the ever-changing code and frequency schemes.

"Urrl," Admiral Mikton said, the plan suddenly falling together in her mind's eye. "Get the message laser lined up for *Daffodil*. Tell her to break orbit, and steer wide of the incoming Antagean ships. We're going to meet up with her at that Kuiper object you seem so fond of."

"One more ship for the fight," Urrl said, nodding slightly. "Though she will arrive far too late to help us in battle."

"I don't want her for the fight we'll have there," Zuri said. "I want her for what I've got in mind *after*."

"You assume there will even *be* an 'after,' boss. What are you cooking up?"

"First things first," Zuri said, and rotated her chair to face the *Catapult*'s communications officer. "Broadcast to all Constellar ships. We're disengaging, and pushing all ships to three gee. Target the Kuiper trio—we'll call it Objective Epsilon for the tactical log. This order effective immediately. Tell all captains I am aware of the fact that we're going to have the Nauties on our heels the entire way. Keep the countermeasures hot, and dump nukes in our wake as the opportunity presents itself. Maybe we get lucky, and lose one or two of those destroyers before we're at Objective Epsilon."

Only a few seconds elapsed before *Catapult*'s superstructure audibly complained under the strain of not only being driven at three gees worth of acceleration, but changing course to boot. The ship was using reaction-control thrusters to rotate until the tail was facing in the correct direction to effect the course adjustment. Zuri, Urrl, and everyone else in the command module sagged and swayed to one side as the ship began its trajectory change. Struggling to keep her mind focused—against the physical discomfort of the maneuver—Zuri slowly tapped fingertips at her keyboard, until the hologram showed her entire squadron veering away from their intercept with the Nautilan force.

After a few minutes, the enemy force also began to veer.

It would be close. The Nauties would definitely be inside the ten thousand kilometer radius before Zuri's ships began to rebuild some distance.

"*Daffodil* has confirmed her orders," Urrl said, grunting out his words due to the fact he was being pressed into his gee chair at three times his normal weight.

If they had not already been working in gee chairs, the crew of the command module would have been driven to their knees.

"Good," Zuri said. "Keep an eye on their progress. Meanwhile, group our ships back into wheel formation as soon as possible. We don't want to present the Nauties with a greater target aspect than necessary. To include never leaving the same ship exposed to potential fire for too much time."

"Admiral," said the comms officer, "the captain of the *Gouger* is curious to know why the sudden change in course and velocity, since we're already deeply engaged with the enemy."

Mikton's fingers tapped her keyboard, broadcasting a graphical representation of the current plan to all of the other captains in the Task Group. The biggest concern for all involved would be the estimated point of closest proximity to the Nautilan attack force before the course correction had been fully effected. That's when the wheel formation would be in greatest disarray, with the most vulnerability to enemy attack.

"Can we be reasonably certain which ship is my esteemed peer's flagship?" Zuri asked.

"We can," Urrl said. "Just as they can assume which ship is *Catapult*. For a couple of hours, they're going to get some clear shots at us."

"And we at them," Zuri said. "I just wish we had a way to get in closer. Long enough to be worth it."

"The captain of the *Gouger* is volunteering for just that purpose," Urrl reported, his headset making tiny little noises over the continued complaint of *Catapult*'s spaceframe.

Zuri's eyes widened. "That's a one-way trip," she said matter-of-factly.

Urrl engaged in conversation with the *Gouger*'s commander
for several seconds, then responded, "He knows this, ma'am. He's
also eager for the chance to take out one of them before they
can take out one of us."

"Losing a ship for a ship doesn't effectively change things."

"*Gouger*'s commander is optimistic that if he breaks with us
now, and runs *Gouger* up to four gees deceleration, he will have
sustained enough relative difference—his ship versus the oncoming
Nauties—that their ship-to-ship weaponry will struggle to com-
pensate. He says one of his engineering people says she can stick
a stealth package onto one of the nukes, then he'll deploy it in
passive mode once *Gouger* is dropping back at a sufficient rate."

"We've tried that," Zuri said, speaking about Constellar
experimentation with stealth technology, regarding its application
to drones. "Stealthing will mess up the nuke's internal targeting
ability. Here, let me talk to the man. *Gouger*? This is Admiral
Mikton on the alternate battle channel. Yes. . . . Yes, Commodore
Urrl informed me of your plans, Captain Hebrides. I can't autho-
rize it. It sounds like a great idea from a tactical standpoint,
except I think you'd be throwing yourself and your ship away
with little guarantee of success. . . . I know you have faith in your
engineers. Don't we all? . . . No, I don't think there's something
dramatically original your people can come up with, in the next
thirty minutes, which hasn't already been devised by the best
engineers and scientists back at DSOD. . . . No, you can't disobey
a direct order. . . . Look, Captain Hebrides, if you . . . dammit, he
broke the connection."

"*Gouger* already beginning relative deceleration maneuver,"
Urrl reported, shaking his head. "The bastard was in position
before he talked to you."

"I'll drag him out of the captain's chair myself," Zuri said
angrily—then her voice softened. "Assuming there is anything
left of him when this is all over."

"Not much we can do about it now," Commodore Urrl said
dryly. "I don't know if you remember Hebrides from the last
Oswight system defense conference? Big guy. Lots of scars. Spent
most of his career with TGO before going mustang and earning a commission for DSOD space ops. He told me he likes to
use the same methods, out here, that he used on the ground. A
veteran's veteran."

"May God favor the bold and the free," Zuri whispered to no one in particular, as she readjusted the main holographic image to show the single signature of *Gouger* falling out of the reforming Constellar combat wheel into which all the other ships had been previously ordered. Urrl was talking into his headset, ordering all the other ships to ignore *Gouger* and focus on the wheel, with attention being paid to countermeasures—as a new wave of Nautilan incoming would be expected any moment.

All eyes—even those of the command module crew with better things to do—kept straying to the overhead hologram. *Gouger* looked more and more vulnerable as she fell farther and farther back. When the salvo of fresh Nautilan nukes launched, they were homing almost exclusively on Captain Hebrides' ship.

"Cover the man," Zuri said forcefully. "Throw everything we've got in his defense."

Antimissiles raced out from every single Constellar ship, charging ahead at the very limit of their internal structural capability—tens of gees acceleration. Many minutes advanced, until those antimissiles overtook *Gouger* and began tail-chasing with the incoming Nautie nukes. But, of course, antimissiles hadn't been the only thing Zuri's Task Group deployed. Their own nukes zipped ahead of the antimissiles, and suddenly the Nautilan attack force was busy trying to eliminate the oncoming threat—having done a much less successful job reforming their battle wheel compared to Zuri's people.

"Come on, come on," Zuri said, feeling the sweat pooling along the small of her back—as both the physical toll of prolonged three-gee acceleration, and the drama of the moment, was felt.

Blooming spheres of light began to pop up all around the *Gouger.* But her slaved ship-to-ship status told Zuri all of *Gouger's* systems remained operational. If Hebrides was getting rocked and rolled, nothing had turned critical. Yet.

Eventually, the holo signature for *Gouger* was right in the middle of the Nautilan signatures. Nukes and antimissiles were popping like mad.

Almost simultaneously, one of the Nautilan ships flared into an especially bright, very large circle, along with *Gouger* herself.

The slaved status didn't just go red, it went black—total loss of signal.

"Dammit!" Zuri swore, practically leaping out of her gee

chair, then collapsing back into it. "Talk to me, Commodore. Was Captain Hebrides successful?"

"Not sure yet, ma'am," her exec said. "We're still getting some interference from . . . wait, now it's coming in. Looks like . . . he did it. One of their destroyers is in pieces."

"Was it their flag vessel?"

"Hard to say, since they're all identical, and their battle wheel has not reformed. But the damaged ship is combat ineffective, based on the large number of individual small contacts I'm now seeing—where once there used to be just one big one."

"And the *Gouger*?"

"I'm not seeing . . . Admiral, I am not seeing *anything* from Captain Hebrides' command. My gut says she took multiple nuke hits. Total vaporization."

"Except for the Key that *Gouger* had aboard," Zuri said. "I wasn't going to chew Hebrides out for it, but he wasn't thinking about the one truly finite resource aboard his scout. Constellar's loss of his Key is almost as bad as us losing him, his ship, and his people."

"Keys can be recovered," Urrl said.

"At this rate, both *Gouger*'s Key, and the Key employed by the enemy destroyer, are floating free—and hurtling through deep space. If the Nauties don't salvage them both, they could wind up in some cockeyed solar orbit. Which means practical invisibility out here with all the other Kuiper and Oort material. It will be almost impossible to find them."

"The cost of doing business," Urrl reminded her.

"I know," Zuri said. "It's just . . . Damn. To hell with it. First things first. What's the status of the rest of the Nautie force?"

"None of our nukes got through their point-defense, though they don't seem to be thrusting up to match our new course. We've gained on them, and continue to gain. We're now at sixty-five thousand kilometers distance, and adding a thousand kilometers each minute."

"Do you think his stealth gimmick did the job?" Zuri asked.

"Tough to say," Urrl replied. "Either that, or they were in such deadly proximity to each other, it was impossible to miss with a direct strike. That was a whites-of-their-eyeballs engagement."

Zuri imagined the crew of the *Gouger*—loyal, frightened, yet matching the determination of their commander. She may have been just a long-range scout, but she'd given Mikton's Task Group the cushion they required to reach Objective Epsilon. Now, Zuri hoped that her plan—not shared yet, even with Urrl—would make the sacrifice of *Gouger* worth the expense. Dying in space could look like many things. For the *Gouger*, Zuri hoped, it was as Urrl predicted. No chance to feel the end.

The same could not be said for the crew of the destroyed Nautilan ship. A wrecked craft—drifting in bits—might still harbor life. Desperate people in space suits. Huddled in emergency ejection pods. All hoping that the rest of the Nautilan fleet would spare enough attention from the chase to recover them. Assuming such recovery could be conducted before air supplies—among the survivors—ran out.

Dying inside a suit or pod from lack of oxygen wasn't much different from being buried alive.

Chaplain Ortteo came into the command module, taking baby steps under three gees of weight. His movements were careful, and he gratefully slumped into an unoccupied gee chair before asking, "We lost one of ours?"

"That is correct," Zuri replied. "The *Gouger*, with all of her crew."

Chaplain Ortteo bowed his chin to his chest, raised his arms over his head with the palms facing up, and said, "Lord of space and time, who is God above all others, accept into your mighty care the souls of our brave war dead. May they take rest in the shade of your eternal protection, and be at peace." Then he clapped his hands together once, and brought his fists—one closed around the other—slowly down in front of his chest, until they stopped at his sternum.

"Thank you," Commodore Urrl said.

"It's the least I can do," the chaplain said. Then he asked, "Are any of the civilian ships in danger? Are we going to lose one of them too?"

"Not as long as Lieutenant Commander Antagean can maintain the lead he's got," Commodore Urrl replied.

"I don't like the fact that we can't help them," Ortteo said.

"None of us do," Zuri said.

"I mentioned before, in the Eighteenth Prophecy, about how a doorway would be opened in the loneliest wall of heaven? There's another passage in that same Prophecy you might want to know about. And I quote, 'The merchant with his wagons will be driven before the chariots of battle.' I know you look askance at these words, Admiral, but I have to say again that I am convinced we're all part of something larger—a higher strategy which goes beyond merely trying to fight Starstate Nautilan."

"I'd feel better if you could just cut to the end, and tell us all we get to escape with our skins," Commodore Urrl groused.

"If the Eighteenth Prophecy makes anything clear, it's that the final outcome is not certain. Wickedness and righteousness will vie for supremacy. The word 'worthy' is mentioned again and again. We are being *judged,* Commodore."

Urrl looked around the command module, his mouth curled in an expression of mild contempt. "Would it help if I ordered all hands to chapel service?"

Chaplain Ortteo sighed. "If only it were that easy. But this isn't about slapping a bandage on a gushing wound. Starstate Constellar itself is on trial. Right here. Right now. We tell ourselves we stand for justice. We pride ourselves on our freedom. Yet, what have we done with these things? And if we're so sure that we're standing on the right side of God, why have we been *losing* this war for so long? You'd think God would intervene on our behalf, wouldn't you? I'm here to tell you I think God *won't* intervene. Because His people have always been forced to endure terrible things. Men are not made worthy in comfort and ease. Men are made worthy in hardship and suffering. This is a big part of what the Word is all about, as it was passed to us from the Exodus."

"If this is supposed to be a pep talk, it's not helping," Zuri said.

"I'm sorry, Admiral. I don't mean to be a morale buster. It's just that... everyone aboard *Catapult,* and in this Task Group, needs to be aware of the higher ramifications. My job is to comfort and assuage, yes. But there are times when I can't help shaking my stick at you all too. *Gouger*'s captain and her crew clearly felt there was something worth dying for. Is each of you ready to do the same?"

# CHAPTER 23

FOR THE SECOND TIME IN AS MANY DAYS, WYODRETH ANTAGEAN took the lift up the spine of his ship to the sensitive cargo space under the shield dome. Upon arrival, he found the cargo area swarming with TGO personnel, as well as Lady Oswight and her majordomo, Elvin Axabrast. The old veteran had eschewed his formal house attire for a stained work coverall borrowed from somebody on the crew. He was helping some of the TGO enlisted personnel lift one of the TGO low-yield nuclear weapons out of its gee crate—a feat which took double the ordinary number, just because of the additional weight everyone experienced while the ship was under unusually high thrust. Wyo himself felt heavy with each footfall, and was careful to watch himself—using half strides lest he stumble and hit the deck. With this much gee, even a modest fall could break something.

"Aye, lads, be gentle with this wee lovely," Axabrast wheezed, as they carefully maneuvered the weapon's case out of the crate, and set it on the deck.

Then the old man puffed out his cheeks—bent over—with one hand braced on the open gee crate's exposed lip.

"There are younger horses for that work," Wyo said as he came to stand beside Axabrast.

"We couldn't beat him away with sticks," Captain Fazal remarked, smiling, while he too took a breather.

"Nor should ye try," the old man said between breaths.

The Lady Oswight was sweaty too, though not from having

assisted unloading the crate. The mere fact that she was enduring double her normal body weight was causing significant strain. Her shoulders were hunched and she took every opportunity to brace herself on a nearby object or person. Her steps were baby-like and gingerly.

"What's the plan?" Wyo asked, doing his best to effect a positive attitude despite their predicament.

"The trick is going to be getting something through their antimissile and point-defense screen," Captain Fazal said. "We can install the warhead, as is, into an emergency ejection pod, and program the pod's computer to proximity-detect on anything over a certain mass. Then the reaction-control thrusters will do the rest. Once the pod gets close enough, the warhead—wired to the pod's computer—goes off. But it's moot if the pod gets blasted from space before it can come close enough to its intended target."

"Aye," Axabrast said, slowly regaining an erect posture. "'Tis a tough nut to crack."

"Lady?" Wyo asked the Oswight heir.

"I've been looking at some DSOD data that Captain Fazal extracted from the DSOD's intelligence files regarding Nautilan sensor capability. Their technology is about on par with ours, which means for the ejection pod to come anywhere near the intended target, it can't be taken for anything except naturally occurring space matter. A chip off an asteroid or comet. Something a pilot might steer clear of, but not go so far out of his way to avoid that we'll miss our shot. So, it's going to take three things.

"First, when we drop the pod, we have to be incredibly accurate about where we're sending the thing. We can't be so much as a thousand kilometers off before the pod's reaction-control system will be incapable of effecting the maneuver in time."

"That's impossible, given how much distance we have between us and them," Wyo said.

"Maybe, maybe not," the Lady Oswight said. "Assuming their navigators are trying to be as fuel conscious as we are, they will try to remain on as similar a trajectory—to us—as can be man-aged. Once we come off the first gravity assist from the outer-most jovian world, we can be relatively certain that our pursuers will come out of their gravity assist with the goal of eventually matching with us. We can already tell that they're pushing to three gees thrust, while we're remaining at a modest two. This actually works to our advantage between the two jovians, because we'll be able to calculate to a relative certainty where they will be, and when, in relation to entering the second gravity-assist maneuver around the second jovian. If we can predict them being at a specific relative spot, at a specific moment, we can try to make it so that our rigged ejection pod is in that place at that moment too."

"Pods," corrected Captain Fazal. "We're going to dump our entire supply of field nukes. Hope you don't mind using up five pods per starliner, sir. I've been in contact with the other TGO company commanders, and they're following our lead. Whatever we build here, they can build there."

"Throw a gee toilet at them, for all I care," Wyo said. "Anything that works, *works*. Expense—at this point—doesn't matter. So okay, we try to thread the needle with the initial toss. What're the other two concerns?"

"Cloaking," Lady Oswight said. "Exposed to space, the ejection pod will read as man-made. But if we freeze it in a casing of ice, then wrap the ice in a shell of slush hydrogen, the pod won't be so easy to detect—as a pod. And in fact, the sublimating slush hydrogen will make the pod appear like nothing so much as a nugget of comet, drifting into the inner system. Again, something for any pilot to avoid, but not by so much that reaction-control thrusters and proximity-detonation won't work."

"How long is that going to take? And where can you do it?"

"The ejection pods' own launch tubes will suffice. We just have to connect hoses from this starliner's water supply, dump the liquid into the tubes, and turn off each tube's launch preheaters. Let it all freeze for about a day, then do the same, only with a cryo hose from the hydrogen fuel storage. Which ought to also take another day.

"When we eject, we turn on the preheaters *just enough* to make sure there is a slippery layer between the inner insulation of the ejection tube, and the pod proper. Then, we *nudge* the pod into space. Using men in suits, versus the rockets. The pod should drift far enough that it's not an impact danger to our ships, but remain on course with us overall."

"Once all three starliners have dispersed all five pods," Lady Oswight said, having taken a deep breath, "we gradually dial up our thrust to three gees. This puts enough distance between us and the pods that we're not endangered, but the Nautilan pursuit force—already doing three gees, plus whatever they gain from gravity assist—will eventually overtake the pods."

"What's the third thing?" Wyo asked.

"A bloody helping of good luck," Axabrast said. To which both Fazal and Lady Oswight nodded vigorously.

Wyo considered, as he eyed the nuclear shell resting in its insulated case. Amazing that something smaller than a person could be enough to destroy an entire ship. The fusion warhead was scaled so that it could be used during ground campaigns. Five kilotons was quite modest, where hydrogen bombs were concerned. But it was plenty to wreck even a large spaceframe, if detonated within a few hundred meters or less.

"So, we've got the time and the resources, but only barely," Wyo said. "We're going to be making our slingshot around the outer jovian within ninety-six hours. If this is going to work, it'll have to be ready by then. Fifteen nukes, free-falling toward four warships—in the hope that at least *one* of our nukes connects. Still, it sounds better than anything I could have come up with. Lady—and gentlemen—you have my thanks."

"It's all our lives at stake together," Axabrast said. "And I'll admit I'm happy to be working with the lads again. Been far too long since I got my hands dirty handling things that go boom."

It was the least-grouchy attitude Wyo had yet seen from the majordomo.

"How about our plan to arrive safely at Uxmal?" Lady Oswight asked.

"Ook-*what*?" the Lieutenant Commander stuttered.

"She named the new clement planet," Captain Fazal said. "Per Admiral Mikton's request."

"Oh," Wyo replied. "I am not familiar with the word. Doesn't sound like anything out of Mariclesh, nor the other dialects I've encountered."

"Not much real data came down to us from the Exodus," Lady Oswight said, "but we do know there were pyramids built on Earth. Almost all of them were constructed long before men ever went into space. By civilizations which were often extinct by the time modern record keeping had begun. One of them was a pyramid called the Pyramid of the Magician at a place called

Uxmal. I can't tell you what Uxmal was like, but if we're looking at a Waymaker artifact on the new world—and I am *certain* that we are—then the magician reference seems apt to me."

"Ook-shmall," Wyo said, testing the word. "Okay, sounds as good as anything else."

"Well?" she pressed.

"Captain Loper and I have been going over the math," Wyo said. "In order to slow down for orbit—after burning at higher than normal gee—we're going to be using up a lot of our hydrogen. The good part is, the Nautilan pursuit force will be slowing too, and also using their hydrogen. My intent is to drop a landing force sufficient to secure the pyramid site—and the remains of the ship that's on the beach—without losing these liners. If our calculations are correct, we can actually skip orbit, and use the planet—excuse me, *Uxmal*—for yet another gravity assist. This time launching the liners toward their final destination."

"Which is?" Captain Fazal asked.

"The largest jovian, near the sun. I anticipate there will be several moons, at least. Maybe even some trojan-point asteroids? Places these liners can *hide*. Until such time that we need them again."

"What about the landing force?" Elvin Axabrast said, suddenly getting grumpy again. "I may not be schooled to my Lady's level, but I've done a few combat deorbit drops in my time. If the ships are coming in too fast, anything they try to put on the ground will burn up during atmospheric entry. Didja think of that, lad?"

"We did," Wyo said. "Or, rather, Captain Loper did. Ejection pods don't have sufficient retro rockets for the job, but the military drop modules can run their retros at up to one hundred and forty percent max thrust—at least per the manufacturer's guidelines. We'll need to pull retros off some of the modules, and use them to augment the modules which remain. Between them, it will make for a hell of a ride. We estimate the period of worst deceleration will last about two minutes, during which the occupants of the modules will experience seven gee or more. Enough so that even gee chairs might not be enough to keep people from passing out. But assuming the drop modules can handle the strain—structurally—we can put troops and equipment on the ground safely, without sacrificing so much starliner speed that we can't effect the slingshot to the big jovian farther in."

"Billiards," Axabrast said gruffly. "Never thought I'd see my Lady behind the cue ball like this, nossir. Well, if that's the best we've got, it'll have to do. But, lad, them kludged drop modules can't take all of us. Who goes down to Uxmal, and who stays aboard?"

"That's Captain Fazal's next chore," Wyo announced, eyeing the infantry officer. "We have to be choosy about who and what we take down."

"Right, sir," Captain Fazal said. "Once we get this first nuke rigged and ready, I can devote some time to parsing my company roster, as well as assets. We're probably going to have to skip the heavy stuff. All these conventional explosive shells, and the mechanized mortar? Nope. We'll want a varied concentration of personnel—by pertinent skill set—as well as plenty of consumables. Even if there is water to drink and air to breathe, we have to feed ourselves. Possibly, for a long time?"

"That's my thought as well," Wyo said.

"Elvin and myself can make do with half rations," Lady Oswight said confidently.

"Me too," Wyo agreed.

The captain, the majordomo, and the Lady all stared at him.

"You're dropping with us?" they said in unison.

"Of course," Wyo said. "Why wouldn't I?"

"Well, sir, it's just," Captain Fazal stammered, "I think we all assumed you'd want to stay with your ships. I mean, you're not TGO after all. And while Lady Oswight has a vested interest in seeing that pyramid, what's in it for you?"

"The detachment *flag* goes where Lady Oswight goes," Wyo said, "and that's where I go too. Captain Loper can handle my ships—he does anyway."

Their mutual expression of surprise remained.

"All things being equal, I'd choose otherwise," Wyo said. "But then again, what else is new? Look, if you're worried about me being underfoot, Captain, I won't be. You, the other TGO company leaders, and your battalion commander? You'll have the run of the place once we're on dry land. I'm just doing what Admiral Mikton told me to do."

"Right," Axabrast said, seeming unconvinced.

"Like you said, Mister Axabrast," Wyo quoted, "we all share the danger. Since it's my decision, with Captain Loper, to risk atmospheric entry at higher than normal speed, it's me who's going to stick his neck out with the rest of you. And believe me, Lady Oswight, if you decide to *not* go down to the planet—"

"I would not miss it for anything," she said, cutting Wyo off. "The whole point of this detachment is to get to Uxmal—and its potential secrets—first. I intend to be involved in the effort every step of the way, regardless of the hazard."

"I will make the drop as well," said a high voice from behind Wyo.

Every head turned to observe Zoam Kalbi laboring up to stand beside the lieutenant commander.

"For you," Wyo said, "the risk is wholly unnecessary."

"You're not going to get rid of me that easily, Lieutenant Commander Antagean. Like I said before, Article Thirty-six covers a lot of things. And whatever you may think of me, I am not averse to risk when the potential for a story is so great. Many of the veteran informationalists of our time have gone into danger alongside Constellar's military personnel. And as the Lady said, the whole point of the detachment is to claim the planet. I want to be the first informationalist on Uxmal. Even though I deeply regret that we're going to be fighting Nautilan forces long before we get there."

"No choice on *that* piece of business," Wyo grunted.

"Oh?" Kalbi said. "I'm not so sure. Have any of you spent any time considering the possibility of negotiations? Instead of racing against the expedition from Starstate Nautilan, we could forget about hostile action and try to work *with* them for a change. I mean, no shot has been fired in anger just yet. We're making all kinds of assumptions about their motives, based simply on past history. Has it occurred to any of you that they may be as afraid of us as we are of them?"

"From your mouth to God's ears," Lady Oswight said.

"Mister Kalbi," Axabrast said, "yer givin' the Nauties credit they nae deserve. Take it from a man who's lost friends on several worlds. Starstate Nautilan only understands taking things by force. Uxmal will be no different. Why d'yae think they sent warships in the first place?"

"We have warships with us," Zoam interjected.

"Aye, and civ craft too. Think any 'o them Nautie ships is civ? No, sir. Not a civilian in the bunch. They will conquer this system, as they have conquered all else in my lifetime. Be sure of it."

Zoam Kalbi's expression was doubtful. "It just seems like such a waste," he said. "We actually have much more in common with Starstate Nautilan than we like to admit."

Axabrast made a scoffing sound.

"Wait," Lady Oswight said, before her majordomo would get profane. "I know you didn't say that to be insulting. Can you clarify what you mean? Starstate Nautilan has been Constellar's enemy for as long as any of us has been alive. Their way of being is so foreign to us, as free people, we can hardly imagine it."

"That's what the First Families insist," Zoam opined, "but when you're an informationalist, you have to be able to see the other fellow's point of view. Even people you may be inclined to dislike. There is an international league of informationalists—spanning all of the Starstates—and we exchange as much data on Nautilan as we can. Granted, it's not easy obtaining an accurate picture of life inside Nautilan. They go out of their way to protect their people from outside influence, and this makes it hard to know what's happening for the average Nautilan citizen on a given world."

"You mean, average Nautilan *serf*," Wyo commented.

"Serf? No, Mister Antagean. That word has much more applicability to Constellar, if you care to see our own country through an informationalist's eyes. Nautilan does not, after all, have anything like the First Families. Consider the fact that *none* of the extant Starstates allow the common person to partake in governmental decisions. But Nautilan's leadership—so far as I understand it—speaks directly for the people. Not the monied corporate class. Nor the privileged royalty of First Family estates."

"Amazing," Axabrast snarled, "we're fixin' to fight the damned Nauties to the last man on Uxmal, and the wee infotainer's got Nautie sympathies!"

"*All* of humanity has my sympathy," Zoam corrected, his posture—in the double gee—remaining defiantly erect. "Not just the people who walk beneath Constellar's banner."

"Okay, okay," Wyo said, stepping between the informationalist and the former colour sergeant. "We can talk politics some other time. Mister Kalbi, I think that's a very generous attitude you have, albeit somewhat misplaced at this particular time. If the expedition from Nautilan had come in a primarily civilian capacity, maybe you'd be on to something worthwhile. But even I know—and I am not full-time DSOD, just to remind you—that nine identical warships spell hostile intent. I think Mister

Axabrast has it: Nautilan intends to conquer. Our mission now is to frustrate them, in any way possible, and to hopefully learn as much as we can about the artifacts remaining on Uxmal's surface. Before those artifacts are seized or destroyed."

"All the more reason I need to be there," the short man said. "If there is to be a proper record of this, the Waywork's first known voyage to Uxmal, I intend to produce it. Article Thirty-six guarantees my rights in this way. Again, informationalists have been present for almost every major Constellar military action in our era. This is no different. So, you can't keep me off the drop, Lieutenant Commander."

"Fine," Wyo said, throwing up his hands in resignation. "But if things get dire, don't say you weren't warned."

"I would never blame anyone for anything over which I have full control," Zoam said sniffily. Then he turned to Captain Fazal and said, "Please inform me how I may best fit into your drop-module plans, Captain. As you can see, I don't take up much room."

"Loper to boss," said a voice over the cargo module's internal speaker.

"Copy, Captain Loper," Wyo said. "Is there a problem?"

"Not with us, sir. But I thought you should know, Admiral Mikton's Task Group has closed with and engaged the Nautilan squadron near the Waypoint."

"What's the news?" Wyo asked, as every person in the compartment stopped what he or she was doing, and listened intently.

"So far, one of ours has been destroyed. The *Gouger*. For the sake of destroying one of theirs. Admiral Mikton has ordered the *Daffodil* to rendezvous with her at a Kuiper belt object she's dubbed Objective Epsilon. That's all the *Daffodil* relayed to us before they got underway. They're going to go wide of us, so as to avoid the Nautilan pursuit force on our tail."

"Thanks, Captain Loper. I appreciate the update. Antagean out."

The speakers went silent.

Everyone looked at each other.

"So much for Mister Kalbi's desire for dialogue," Lady Oswight said, somewhat sadly. "Now there's no question."

Kalbi's attitude was hard to read. The expression on his face—in those eyes—had become void of outward emotion. He simply turned around, and slowly walked out of the cargo compartment, maintaining the same posture as when he'd entered it.

# CHAPTER 24

GOLSUBRIL VEX WAS DINING ALONE WHEN WORD CAME REGARDING the engagement against Constellar's armed squadron. It had been a draw. A loss for a loss, with General Ticonner reporting that he was maintaining pursuit, following the Constellar squadron's diverting toward what appeared to be a large comet. Live fire had ceased, as the distance between the two forces had grown too great for the finite fusion motors on Ticonner's nuclear missiles to manage the distance—and still be able to successfully track and engage their targets. Also, another Constellar ship had manifested. Similar in design to the Constellar long-range scouts—one of which had been successfully destroyed—but with less armament. It appeared to be on course for the same comet which had attracted the Constellar admiral's attention. Ticonner promised to relay further details as he had them, and remained confident of success.

Vex set her gee bottle back in its cradle on the arm of her private gee chair in her quarters. Thrusting at three times ordinary capacity had made even the simplest chores remarkably difficult. She'd been slowly sporking bits of cooked, spiced beef—with rice and vegetables—into her mouth. Even raising her arm for a few moments made the muscles in her shoulder complain. And she'd dropped enough bites in her lap to realize that even with gee chair support, the best way to ensure the food got to its destination was to go slow, and use her alternate hand to guide the wrist of the hand which held her utensil.

The appearance of another enemy ship was concerning, only because it indicated that Constellar had been far enough ahead of Nautilan to be able to move even more assets than had first been assumed. Was there more waiting for Vex's pursuit force the closer they got to the clement planet in the inner system? Had she been foolish to follow her instincts, and divert four ships to handle the civilian starliners? With Ticonner's squadron now down one destroyer, it was becoming evident that Constellar wouldn't let Vex have the new system without significant resistance.

Still, not everything about the voyage was proving problematic. The data her ships were collecting about this new system was remarkable, considering the fact that it was the first time any Starstate Nautilan expedition had been able to reconnoiter a foreign system without having collected a wealth of data via espionage first. Everything ahead of them was literally brand new. And while telescope imagery of the clement world was still difficult to resolve at this great distance, every day took them a step closer to their prize. A world with a nitrogen-oxygen atmosphere was worth every life in Vex's expeditionary force. Such a world—properly harnessed, and seeded with human life—would transform the fabric of Starstate Nautilan for generations to come. It was the kind of thing Vex could never have dreamed of. Because there simply were no new worlds within the Waywork, much less clement worlds. And while lifeless, airless terrestrials always offered the possibility of mining and manufacturing resources, they took a lot of time and energy to develop. A lifetime's effort, for limited immediate results.

But now, a world which might have air to breathe, and water to run through her fingers...Vex's standing as Jaalit's kosmarch was going to be increased dramatically. In time—perhaps even within her life?—Starstate Nautilan might enjoy two capitals, versus one. With Vex herself on the new capital's throne. Assuring herself a high place in the annals of the Starstate, if not the Waywork as a whole.

Still, her eyes remained focused above even this possibility. Because the mystery of how or why a new Waypoint had appeared—where none had been before—still needed to be solved. And this spoke of yet more potential power, just out of reach at the moment. Assuming such power could be comprehended by human minds, and used for human purposes.

"Madam Kosmarch," General Ekk's voice announced through the little speaker at her door.

"Enter," she said.

The old officer used a walker, sliding himself in slowly under three gees worth of downward force. He gratefully collapsed into a gee chair across the table from Vex, and waved away her offer of food.

"I am getting too old for this," he said dryly, wiping at the perspiration on his forehead with one of Vex's napkins.

"When this expedition reaches its successful conclusion, General, your retirement will be abundantly generous, I can assure you," Vex said.

"Assuming my heart doesn't quit on me first," he said, then laughed weakly at his own joke.

"What's our pursuit status?" she asked.

"The same as it's been. We will very soon be following the Constellar starliners through their slingshot maneuver at the outer gas giant."

"Is that going to be dangerous?"

"Madam Kosmarch, I have made such maneuvers dozens of times in my career. They are an essential tool of all planetary travel, both military and civilian. You use the gravity of one world to hurl you onward to the next. With no additional expenditure of hydrogen. In our case—assuming the starliners are still heading to the clement terrestrial in the inner system—I anticipate two gas giant planetary gravity-assist maneuvers. If we'd arrived at a different time during this system's solar year, we wouldn't be so lucky. But it just so happens we can use the first big jovian in our path to throw us toward the second big jovian, which will send us careening into the inner system at tremendous speed. So much so, I've got my officers figuring out how much hydrogen we'll use braking to mere orbital velocity when the time comes."

"Will it be too much to prevent us from going back out to the Waypoint?"

"So far, the calculations I am seeing do not pose a problem in this regard."

"Be sure, General."

"Madam Kosmarch, I always am."

"Once we *are* in orbit, what resources do we have for a ground fight?"

"Not nearly as much as I'd like, Madam. But we should be able to land a significantly armed force, capable of dealing with the Constellar expedition on our own terms."

"What about your colonel," she asked. "The one who keeps daring me to strip him of his rank—for his flagrant informality in the presence of a kosmarch?"

"He's ready to go, Madam. I know you don't think much of Jun's military bearing. To be honest, I don't think much of his military bearing either. But I've known the man for many years. And despite the fact that he's been sick, he's hearty enough to plumb the mysteries of whatever Waymaker artifacts may await us when we arrive—if they're even there at all."

"They're there," Vex said firmly. "It's the only explanation for the rapidity with which the Constellar admiral dispatched her starliners. They want to be first. Assuming there is not already a Constellar expedition on site."

"We've seen zero indication that there are any ships in orbit around any of the planets of the inner system," Ekk said.

"Which may or may not mean anything," she said.

"If Ticonner's loss is bothering you, Madam, I think it's not too late for all of us to regroup, and forge a different strategy."

"Absolutely not," she said sternly. "Speculation about what's to come does not mean I have wavering faith in *my* choice to split our squadron. We lost one of ours to one of theirs. We still have them outgunned. And, I am willing to bet, we will have reinforcements arriving before they do. There have been no new arrivals through the Waywork from Constellar space. This tells me that whatever they were using to ferry security ships across the Slipway is now within our grasp. Probably a Key-operational ship small enough it can mate with other ships, acting as a Waywork piggyback? Once we seize or destroy *that* vessel, the only Constellar assets moving across will have to come from elsewhere beyond Oswight space. We know enough about that system to realize that their interstellar footprint is limited, even before recent events unfolded. And by the time Constellar's DSOD can put additional starships into play, our second wave from Jaalit should be arriving."

"True," Ekk said. "Assuming there are no complications."

Vex ate in silence for several bites, then placed her spork carefully on her empty plate, and laced her fingers behind her head.

"Aside from the war, General, how does it feel to be in uncharted territory?"

"Are you asking me from a purely academic standpoint, Madam Kosmarch? Or is this a personal inquiry?"

"Both," she said.

The old officer's eyes got a faraway look in them.

"When I was a boy," he said, "I used to go out in my father's buggy—the kind with fuel cells, so you can drive for hundreds of kilometers on an airless surface without needing to recharge—and stare up into space. I'm originally from Dau-Lat, you see. Everything is built underground there. We've got more people than most terrestrials in the Waywork. We were one of the first to be settled after the Exodus. But it does present a crowding problem. So, when a teenager wants to be alone, he takes his father's buggy and spends a few days wandering around the craters and in the mountain valleys. Thinking about his future. And whether or not he'll get a chance to go anywhere. Be somebody."

"That doesn't tell me anything you haven't told me before," she said.

"My apologies. I frame the following statement by emphasizing that I had more than a little wanderlust in me when I joined our military. And though I've traveled to dozens of stars and seen the many worlds circling them, I've always had a yearning to see what the universe *beyond* the Waywork offers. Up close, I mean. We've been studying the systems outside the Waywork for centuries. They've become objects of academic curiosity, until now. But what if we can finally explore them in person? What if the Waywork no longer contains us, the way it's contained us from the beginning? How might this change our universe as we've known it up until now?"

"You speak as if you believe there is much in *need* of changing, General," she said, with just the right amount of tonal warning in her voice to remind Ekk that he was speaking to a superior.

He cleared his throat, and attempted to pivot his meaning.

"I speak purely in terms of Starstate Nautilan being able to expand its efforts to virgin territory, Madam Kosmarch. Instead of liberating the other systems from the other Starstates, we could launch a whole new expansion effort. Especially if there are more clement worlds to be found! That alone is cause for much excitement. With new planets adaptable for Earth organisms, Starstate

Nautilan would have no need for costly and protracted campaigns within the Waywork. We could grow above, under, and around the rest of the Starstates. Become a cocoon of control. With an unlimited number of fresh systems at our disposal, meaning virtually limitless resources!"

"Yes," Vex said, eyeing him. "That would be a very attractive scenario, would it not? I myself foresee a great many possibilities opening before us in the months ahead. Having claimed this new system for us, I am not limiting my ambition. This new system is the fulcrum on which an ever-larger set of plans will tilt. But it won't just be me working alone. I need men and women I can trust. Not just for their competence at what they do. But for their personal loyalty to me in particular. The other kosmarchs...will each react differently to news that I've expanded my domain. I will, in fact, be devoting a great deal of Jaalit's resources to aggressively developing this clement world. Regardless of how my peers may feel about it."

Ekk stared at her as he seemed to consider the deeper, more subtle implication of what she was saying.

"I serve Starstate Nautilan," he said firmly. "And all of the men and women who fall under me serve Starstate Nautilan as well. If your leadership is going to be the future of the Starstate, then I will happily devote my services—indeed, the remainder of my life—to carrying out your orders. Even if there is some... ah, might I say, *resistance,* to a reorganization in the hierarchy of kosmarchs."

Vex's smile was wolfish. "Very good, General Ekk."

"I have served other kosmarchs, Madam. Given your age, and mine, you are liable to be the last for me. My legacy is therefore tied to yours. I would see you achieve all that you desire, because I trust that what you desire for yourself will also be of benefit to the Starstate as a whole."

"I am grateful for your service, General. Nautilan is also grateful. I am a careful student of Waywork history. I believe very much that we've been overdue for a dramatic shakeup. I think people who can keep their heads in the midst of profound change are needed to ensure that we take full advantage of the path going forward. Once we've secured this system and its potential for Nautilan, I think there will be a lot more work for you to do. Can you handle that?"

"Again, Madam, my legacy is now intertwined with yours. I will exert myself toward the accomplishment of any objective, provided you make the objective clear."

"And if even our own people—some of whom are quite foolish—stand in the way of that objective?"

Now the air between them had turned deadly cold. But Ekk was not a fresh-faced ensign. She could tell he'd had these kinds of conversations before. And had been forced to follow through on his commitments too.

"It's the good of Starstate Nautilan before all individual concerns," he said carefully.

"That's precisely what I want to hear. Thank you for visiting me for dinner, General. I am sorry three gees doesn't agree with you."

"In my youth," the man said, carefully pulling himself back up with the handles on his walker. Then he shuffled for the compartment door.

# CHAPTER 25

THE OUTERMOST JOVIAN WORLD WAS A SIGHT TO BEHOLD. GARSINA Oswight watched through the porthole next to the ejection pod. Multicolored bands belted the planet at different latitudes, with whorls of storms disrupting and distorting the bands—like the eyes of a massive potato. Little satellite moons drifted here and there, some of them casting shadows against the tops of the jovian cloud patterns. If the Constellar detachment had more time, she'd insist that they remain in orbit for a few days, so that a proper survey could be conducted: the satellites catalogued and a wealth of video footage obtained.

As it was, they were only entering the jovian's significant gravity long enough to be pulled in a relatively tight curve around the planet's orbital circumference, at which point the ship would thrust out and away into space—having attained additional velocity which would carry the starliner onward to its next destination.

She checked the rigged-up coupling to the ejection pod. For several hours, slush hydrogen had been pumped through the cryogenic hose that snaked along the deck, slowly filling what little space was left in the ejection pod's tubular silo. When all was said and done, the pod itself would be a deep-frozen popsicle, encased in ice, then encased in a layer of frozen hydrogen. Dumped into the void, the hydrogen would begin to sublimate almost immediately, throwing off a small, thin trail of gas mixed with tiny water ice particles, much like a microsized comet.

They wouldn't begin dumping the pods until they were well

clear of the slingshot maneuver. Until then, the ship was momentarily on reaction control only. The pressing weight of two-gee acceleration was mercifully lifted. And everybody aboard seemed to be thankful for the reprieve.

Though, to be honest, Garsina felt embarrassed by the fact that a mere two gees had almost crippled her. She was a woman used to pursuing intellectual effort, not physical effort. And while the DSOD troops and some of Antagean's more seasoned people had borne the brunt of the increased gees without complaint, for Garsina it had been an exquisitely uncomfortable experience—with the added promise that things would get much worse once they had dumped their nuclear payload, and were pushing at three gees for the next jovian.

Minute by minute, the gas giant world got larger in the porthole. Until it had filled most of the black sky.

An alert sounded across the ship's speakers, notifying everyone aboard that the starliner had officially entered the first phase of the slingshot. Presently, the gas giant's tremendous gravity was pulling the starliner into the planet, but at an angle sufficient that the vessel would circle the planet's waist, and break orbit on the other side.

Using the controls on the porthole, Garsina ordered the tiny camera mounted in the porthole frame to take as much high-resolution imagery as could be fed into memory. This was a world not too different from many others in the Waywork, but Garsina was struck by the fact that no humans—in Waywork history, at least—had ever seen this world up close before. There was an awe-inspiring thrill of discovery while passing over the gorgeously banded face of the jovian planet, with its swirling streams of gas tinged by the complex molecules boiling up from underneath. If the world had been half again as large as it was, it might have undergone fusion at its core. But like so many brown dwarfs in the Waywork, this gas world was a star that never happened.

Before Garsina knew it, they were out of the maneuver, and the ship's speakers broadcast a new message, ordering everyone into their nearest gee chair—time to burn out of the planet's gravitational embrace.

Garsina settled into the single gee chair near the ejection pod's main hatch. Inside the pod, one of the TGO's five-kiloton nukes had been neatly wired to the pod's computer system, with the nuke's detonation sequence tied to the pod's proximity detectors.

If a mass roughly on par with a Nautilan destroyer came within five hundred kilometers, the pod's reaction-control thrusters would pop on, and push the pod in the direction of the mass. When the pod got within one kilometer, the detonation process would begin, and the pod would explode with enough force to obliterate even a very large dome habitat.

Similar devices had been used all over the Waywork since the very beginning. Both for war, and for peace. A lot of mining and excavation was assisted by thermonuclear means. Even the countless number of individual power generators which ran the lights, computers, heating, and cooling, and much else that made life possible on every world, were just sustainable forms of fusion weaponry—harnessed in a perpetual state of not-yet-going-critical. Just like the starliner's own reactors, which powered the ship and provided it with interplanetary propulsion.

In the case of a weapon like the one inside the ejection pod, there would be precious little fallout. Not enough to notice, considering the already harsh conditions of deep space, where radiation was a way of life. Every ship, no matter how small, had to deal with it. A solar flare could be significantly more dangerous than a nuke, if the flare was not detected in time to evacuate the crew to those modules which had been specifically hardened against increased radiation. Almost all of the electronics onboard were hardened as well, so a ship near a nuclear blast—without being caught in the event itself—would not be adversely affected. Though the crew, lacking time to seek shelter, would receive a higher than usual dose. Which just upped the chances for cancer, which plagued much of the Waywork's population to one degree or another.

Would Uxmal be different? What little was known of Earth suggested a planet with an active magma core—which had generated a substantial electromagnetic field. Planets with cool cores were typically devoid of such fields, leaving the occupants wide open for radiation. But a clement world with a strong field would have a built-in shield against all but the worst solar activity. Which again spoke of the potential for millions who could thrive happily without domes, suits, filters, hydroponics, water electrolysis for making hydrogen to power the generators, and air to circulate in the ventilation systems...a life unlike anything in which Garsina had grown up. Where even a First Family member could not escape the mundane necessities of space living.

Resting in her gee chair—not crushed, yet—Garsina imagined walking in an open field, like the kind her brothers said existed at the Constellar capital. Far skies as blue as a swimming pool, with lovely white clouds and breezes that brought delicious scents to one's nostrils. The biosphere on the capital's surface was, after a couple of centuries of Starstate coaxing, self-sustaining. Pumping huge quantities of oxygen into the nitrogen sky, where it freely mingled with carbon dioxide from the people, animals, and a few specific kinds of equipment. Which in turn benefitted the plants. All of which had been grown from seeds passed down from the ark-borne refugees who'd fled Earth so long ago.

Elvin Axabrast appeared, and knelt at his Lady's side—interrupting her reverie.

"Think ye best be returning to the executive suite," he said. "Once we're clear of the nukes, we're goin' to be pushing hard for several days. It'll be easier to bear there than anywhere else."

"I wanted to watch," she said, and then added, "but I appreciate the consideration, Elvin. I really do. In fact, I intend to make sure you're accorded extra compensation when we get back, for all the work you've put in with Captain Fazal's people. You didn't have to do any of that. Lieutenant Commander Antagean is correct. They are much younger than you are. But you sweated with them all the way. And seemed to enjoy yourself doing it too."

"Like I told Antagean," Elvin said sheepishly, "it was good to be working with the lads again."

She smiled at the old man, and ran an affectionate finger across his military-trimmed beard. Once, his hair had been pure brown. But now? He was silver to white everywhere.

His hand touched hers, ever so gently, and his cheeks—not covered by hair—turned a brighter color of pink.

She noticed the faded tattoo on his hand. The same one Antagean had noticed at the start of their trip. She hadn't thought much of it over the years. Family Oswight didn't devote a lot of time to rehashing finished business. The Dissenter problem was buried back in Family Oswight's past. That particular squabble belonged to another time, when there had been virgin territory to carve out of new worlds—not all of whom had been settled by populations amenable to Family management.

"Why *did* you get so upset with the lieutenant commander?" she asked.

"Beg pardon?" Elvin replied.

"Back in the galley, the first day we came aboard this ship. He noticed your hand"—she ran a fingertip gently over the tattoo for emphasis—"and you got upset about it."

"Complicated business, Lady," Elvin said, demurring.

"But I've known you since I was a little girl. Surely there are things you couldn't share with a stranger that you might share with me? I only know of the Dissenters based on what my father instructed my tutors to tell me. And the details often seemed glossed over. 'We are past that now,' the tutors would say. And then we'd move on to more recent history, and the immediate problem of Starstate Nautilan camped on our doorstep. But that doesn't erase what happened. Elvin, how *did* you come to serve my family so loyally?"

The old man sighed. "Can we please return to the suite?"

Garsina said yes, and reluctantly left the ejection pod behind. For several minutes, they endured life under increasing thrust, until finally they walked—gingerly, with steps made wise to the nature of thrust-induced gravity—into their suite. The gee chairs were even more plush and comfortable than those used in other parts of the ship. Garsina settled into hers, and Axabrast his. They turned to face each other, their chins aimed at one another across the distance, while the vibrations and ambient noise of the starliner changed to reflect the fact that more thrust was being applied every minute.

"Just wanted you to know, we're punching 'em out, now," said a speaker voice—it had been Captain Fazal.

"Thank you," Garsina said. "Let's hope we get a strike. Or two!"

"Yes, ma'am," Captain Fazal said enthusiastically. Then the speaker went dead.

"Now, please, tell me," she said to her old friend and protector.

Elvin closed his eyes, and chewed at his lower lip, before speaking.

"It's like this, Lady. A long, long time ago, my people—God, it's almost a joke to say that, since we haven't been our own thing in centuries—settled the system that is now Oswight's. Depending on which one of us you ask, he may or may not agree with the idea that Family Oswight's appearance was a positive development. My personal opinion—and this comes down to me from my sire—is that the original Dissenters were a lousy lot.

Unhappy, prone to quarreling amongst themselves, and unable to do much with any of the real estate around them, except waste it. We didn't even call ourselves Dissenters then. We were just *us*. Ill-tempered refugees from the arks that settled the Waywork. No allegiance to any Starstate, because no Starstate could yet touch us. We *became* Dissenters the moment Family Oswight moved in, and suddenly this sorry bunch of dysfunctional complainers had a *cause*—something to push against, or fight for, depending on which way you saw it.

"But the point is, we Dissenters never had a chance. We were poor, because we could barely take care of ourselves and our own needs, and we never managed to cooperate amongst ourselves long enough to make a sustained stand against outside encroachment.

"So, Family Oswight came in, set up shop, and brought Starstate Constellar with them. The Dissenters fought, and died, and fought some more, and died some more, until the sane among my folk who were left realized they were dyin' for literally *nothing*. Bein' a Dissenter is not an identity. It's a bloody joke."

"But the tattoo—" Garsina said.

"Put there when I was too young to understand, by a grandfather who wanted his grandchildren to have at least *some* kind of connection to the past. Which caused me a fair bit of grief being a Dissenter kid livin' in Oswight system, surrounded by his betters. When I was old enough, I saw my way out."

"The military," she said.

"Right. DSOD didn't give a damn who you were or where you were from. They didn't even give a damn about the First Families, if you asked some of the training cadre. It was all about Constellar proper—and the need for able young men to go fight against a *real* enemy who was fixing to make us all miserable, such that it would have set my Dissenter ancestors howling. Makes ye wonder why every world in Nautie space isn't eruptin' in civil war every hour? But then again, you keep a person down long enough, he gets used to it. His eyes never see a bigger horizon. So why get angry?"

"Were *you* angry?" she asked. "Did you ever…hate any of us?"

"Hate you, lass?" Elvin said, his facial expression becoming incredulous. "You were the sweetest little one I ever did see! How could I hate you? Besides, I could be proud of the fact that I had a place in this universe. And a war record to match any man's.

If I first left home confused about where I fit, I came back to Oswight space knowing who I was, and what I was capable of doin'. To include servin' your family. Who gave me a title, and a comfortable living, and never expected me to be anything other than what I was. Which is more than I can say for the few Dissenter rabble-rousers who occasionally try to make trouble, even to this day. Miserable idiots. Stuck in a past that never existed— when they oughta be looking *forward,* like I ultimately done."

A few moments of silence passed between them, as Garsina mentally metabolized what she'd heard. Like Wyodreth Antagean, and Garsina herself, Elvin had worked to build his own identity, apart from his heritage. Not an easy thing to do, when you didn't have much in the way of resources. But DSOD had given Elvin a home, and he'd clearly embraced military life so thoroughly that the military state of mind went with him when he left the service. She could still remember him dressing up in his old DSOD formals—on Constellar Founders Day—proudly puffing out a chest decorated with numerous medals, while he waved the Constellar flag more enthusiastically than any Oswight Family member ever had.

"Anyway," he said, "you know what happened to my little family. When that all went to hell, and there was no way of getting back into the service, Family Oswight made a place for me. And gave me people I could *care* about. Not like I was an equal, mind you, there was a never a day when I wasn't fully aware of the fact that Oswight *employed* me. But there are far worse jobs in the Waywork, with far less reward. I may not show it sometimes, but I'm a happy man for havin' a home, Garsina. And when that Antagean fellow brought up my Dissenter heritage—like it oughta be a wedge between you, me, your father, your brothers—I got so angry, I wanted to put him on the deck. Ain't no officer in any service who's got the right to suggest I'm part of something I don't *want* to be part of. Through my own choice. Does that make sense?"

"Yes," she said, smiling, with tears rapidly dropping down her face.

"Now don't go spreadin' any of that to outsiders," Elvin pleaded. "I can't let any of these people think I'm *soft,* you see."

"Secret happily kept," Garsina said, and allowed herself to laugh.

"That's music to my ears, lass," he said, and grinned warmly.

# CHAPTER 26

ONE BY ONE, THE ANTAGEAN STARLINERS PUFFED THEIR JURY-RIGGED ejection pods into the void. Nothing spectacular, per design. The pods were gently pushed out of their tubes. Like ice cubes being dropped from a dispenser, they floated slowly away from their respective ships, at the same time those ships dialed their thrust up slowly past two gees, and into three-gee territory. Leaving the ejection pods to drift in a small but expanding sphere of space—looking for all the universe like a collection of comet nibblets, shaved from the hulk of some larger, much more impressive body.

It was days before the slumbering weapons crossed the Nautilan pursuit force's path. At which time some of the ejection pods had dispersed very widely indeed. Too wide to be of any use.

But a few were within the desired activation envelope, which brought their small attitude-control computers to life. The computers quickly identified where the nearest, largest masses were, and activated their respective reaction-control thrusters. Ice and hydrogen blasted away from the thruster nozzles, and formerly drifting bits of interplanetary junk suddenly became accelerating projectiles.

At first, the threat-detection matrix being used by the Nautilan pursuit force did not recognize the pods. They were moving too slowly, and not giving off the right signatures for the kinds of missiles the matrix was programmed to recognize. But when the other detection system—the one designed to help with conventional collision avoidance—began to *bwoop* painfully at the Nautilan crews, they knew something was seriously wrong.

Of the four ejection pods within reach of a warship, only one of them found its mark. The other three went off prematurely, providing their prey with a trio of very bright, very disturbing explosions. The fourth got to within one hundred meters of its intended target, blowing away half of the ship's fuel tanks, and cracking the superstructure like a man might bend dry sticks between his hands—before tossing the kindling on an open fire.

Golsubril Vex was sleeping when it happened. One moment, she was nestled securely in her gee hammock. The next, she was rolling out of the hammock and almost smashing her face into the deck, on account of three gees pulling her much more quickly to the floor than her reflexes could remember. The threat klaxon was very loud in her ears, and when she called for her compartment's lights to come on, she got just the dull orange of the emergency lanterns, which popped out of the ceiling near the door.

Vex pulled a zipsuit from the wall locker where she kept her emergency-readiness supplies, and struggled into it. Once she had it secured at the collar, she made her way out into the corridors of the *Alliance,* intent on reaching the lift shaft, which would take her to the command module. Crew bustled past—if one could call struggling in three gees *bustling*—and Vex had to make way several times for space-suited security personnel who clomped past her. Each with beads of sweat on their foreheads, visible through the transparent face bowls of their space helmets. If she thought it was tough carrying just her own weight around, trying to move in a full vacuum suit seemed much, much worse.

Finally, the kosmarch emerged through the hatch to the command module.

"What happened?" she demanded of the watch officer.

"We're not sure yet, Madam Kosmarch," the young woman said. "It looks like the *Destiny* has been catastrophically damaged. Except there are no enemy ships close enough to fire upon us."

"Constellar forces?" Vex said, sliding into the gee chair next to where Ekk normally sat. The old man was conspicuously absent.

"Too far away," the watch officer said. "This is something else."

"What does your tactical readout tell us? Give me the three-dimensional visual."

The air over their heads came to life. Three of the four Nautilan destroyers, remained in formation. But a fourth was now drifting out of line—in what appeared to be fragments.

"Any response from the *Destiny*'s captain?" Vex asked.

"No, Madam Kosmarch," the watch officer said. "I've notified our own captain, who should be here any moment."

"Those," Vex said, stabbing her finger at the tiny little lights forming a halo on the pursuit force's three-sixty perimeter.

"Looks like bits of cometary debris," the watch officer said. "We were steering past them when the *Destiny* broke up."

"Those aren't massive enough to cause catastrophic failure, even if a ship hits them at interplanetary speed," Vex said.

"I agree, Madam Kosmarch," said the watch officer.

Ekk appeared, laboring hurriedly with his walker.

"What the hell is going on?" he demanded. The watch officer quickly relayed to him everything she'd been telling to Vex up to that point.

Again, Vex pointed at the little, drifting lights.

"Weapons," she said. "It's got to be."

"But what kind?" Ekk said, peering into the hologram. "There are no ships nearby to deploy them. Looks like . . . well, if the spectrographic evidence is any clue, those are little hunks of comet."

"Destroy them!" Vex ordered.

The watch officer merely stared.

"Do it now!" Vex practically screamed.

"Y-yes, Madam Kosmarch," the watch officer said, and relayed the order to the countermeasures officer, who had to manually identify each of the little lights—on his own display—before the antimissile system would launch. Three ships deployed over a hundred antimissiles, which streaked out and found their targets. One by one, the supposed cometary slivers vanished from the tactical display.

"Wait," said the countermeasures officer. "We're getting a fresh look with the spectrograph. There's more to those targets than we first thought. Picking up traces of steel, copper, aluminum, carbon . . . and plutonium."

"Plutonium!" Ekk roared, slapping his fist onto the arm of his gee chair.

"Our quarry sent us welcome notes," Vex said coolly.

"I don't understand how," Ekk said, rubbing a shaking hand over his scalp. "Those starliners aren't armed with ship-to-ship weaponry."

"How big are the smallest tactical thermonuclear devices in Nautilan service?" Vex asked.

Ekk thought about it for a moment.

"Smaller than you, Madam Kosmarch," he said.

"So, small enough to fit onboard any civilian ship of any size, correct?"

"Apparently so," he said, slightly embarrassed.

"But we never saw them coming, because they didn't look like missiles—to our computers. Do I have that correct?"

"Madam Kosmarch, we'll have to go back over the computer logs. We don't have enough data at this time to draw a conclusion."

"Of course we do," Vex said, exasperated. "We're following the trail left by the Constellar squadron—and following it so exactly, their diffuse hydrogen exhaust is like a beeline vector. So, they dummied up their weapons to look harmless upon initial sensor detection. We're lucky more ships didn't suffer damage. General Ekk, take us *off* the wake of those starliners. We don't need a repeat of what happened tonight. Is there anything left of the *Destiny* worth salvaging?"

"We're doing an initial sensor sweep for survivors," he said, tapping fingers at his gee chair keyboard.

"Damn the survivors," Vex said angrily, "was there anything aboard that ship we *need*, once we arrive at our destination?"

Ekk stopped typing, and gave the kosmarch a bleary eye.

"Nothing we don't have with us on the *Alliance*, or any of the other two destroyers. Beyond personnel, of course. Who will require rescue, assuming there is anyone still alive *to* be rescued. Watch officer, order our sister ships to match with us as we stick close to the *Destiny* and try to determine what we can do to help them."

"Belay that, pilot," Vex said. "Follow my original instructions, and take us away from the trajectory we were on when the *Destiny* got hit. As in, several thousand kilometers away. And get the countermeasures computer programmed so that it treats anything—even something that looks like it might be natural—as a potential threat. Those starliners played us once. We cannot let them do it again. As for the *Destiny* and her crew . . . we can't waste time poking through the rubble. We've got to get out of harm's way, and continue the pursuit. Do I make myself clear to everyone in this command module?"

A small chorus of *Yes, Madam Kosmarch* went through the place, save for General Ekk, who simply stared up at the splintering remains of his former destroyer, now diverging from the rest of the pursuit force. His eyes didn't blink. He merely watched for several minutes, then made a sour expression with his mouth, and changed the tactical view to a larger, system-wide strategic view.

"Trajectory altered," the pilot reported.

"We're still behind them," Ekk said to Vex. "We can try to push ourselves to four gees, but that's going to be almost unbearable for everyone aboard. And it won't allow us to catch up completely, Madam Kosmarch. One way or another, they're going to reach the next gas giant, and do a second slingshot maneuver. I'd say their rear-guard attack was their way to try to delay us."

"Which is precisely why we can't waver," she said. And then added, "Even if it was the *Alliance* which had been hit, I'd expect the remaining three ships in our formation to keep after the Constellar ships."

"But what about *Destiny*'s Key?" Ekk protested.

"We'll track the wreck. A salvage expedition can be deployed later."

"Doesn't make it any easier to leave them," Ekk said softly, almost for nobody's ears but Vex's.

She chose not to upbraid him in front of the rest of the command module. She knew that he was still a spaceman first, in his bones. Abandoning a wreck without doing everything possible to assist survivors was contrary to the tacit spaceman's code.

Vex stayed at her station for the rest of the night, and well into the next morning, monitoring their progress. When the time came to make the second gravity-assist maneuver at the second jovian world, she ignored the beautiful exterior camera feeds sending back gorgeous imagery of a chocolate-milky striped world, swirled with white cream. The moons, the thin ring, none of it interested her. She had a mind only for completing the slingshot, and staying parallel to the Constellar starliners' trajectory—which now appeared to be dead on for the small terrestrial with the oxygen-nitrogen atmosphere.

# PART THREE

# CHAPTER 27

OBJECTIVE EPSILON WAS A COLD, DARK PLACE. THAT FAR FROM the home star, the comet's surface remained a wilderness of shadows. Gravitational pull was minor, but present, so that *Catapult's* pilot had to spend some time maneuvering into a stable orbital position which did not conflict with the orbit of the comet's small satellite, nor the tiny flake of rock which in turn served as the satellite's satellite. From a purely exploratory standpoint, the place was no different from countless other Kuiper bodies orbiting in almost every system. What made Objective Epsilon special was the fact it was the only Kuiper body Admiral Mikton could reach before having to risk another full engagement with the Nautilan attack squadron which was hot on her heels.

"We made it," Commodore Urrl said, floating out of his gee chair while stretching his arms and chest. "Now what?"

"How long before *Daffodil* arrives?" she asked, still seated, staring into her flatscreen.

"About a day, at best," he replied.

"Then we'll have to be done with it before they arrive."

"Care to tell me what 'it' actually is, ma'am?" Urrl asked—an edge of annoyance in his voice.

"I said it before. Our whole problem up until now has been playing to lose, not playing to win. Now that we're in this system, and *they* know it, we can't say we're really holding ground until we stop them from bringing their ships over. They're obviously confident in their ability to cut the Task Group apart, one ship at a time. And Antagean is on his own for the duration—though I give our detachment commander credit for taking out one of the destroyers dogging him. I doubt he'll manage the same trick again before he's landing people on the clement planet."

"Uxmal, according to Lady Oswight," Urrl said.

"Right. They'll be extremely vulnerable as long as Nautilan controls the space around Uxmal. Just as we're extremely vulnerable while Nautilan can potentially push a second squadron across from the Jaalit Waypoint. What we need to do is neutralize their Waypoint on *their* side. Bottleneck their relief effort. Which buys us the time we need to redouble *our* effort on the Oswight side."

"It will take many more ships—and a *lot* more firepower—to tangle with their security flotilla in the Jaalit system."

"If it's a stand-up brawl, sure," Admiral Mikton said, punching keys on her keyboard—until the command module holographic projector displayed Objective Epsilon, and all of the Constellar ships currently surrounding it.

"But what if we could pass *as* Nautilan in origin? Cross through and emerge in Jaalit system space while sending the right codes to keep their security flotilla happy? Even if it was just one ship, by the time that ship got close enough to launch weapons, their security flotilla might not be able to respond before several ships are destroyed or disabled. More to the point, it rocks them back on their heels. I know Nautilan doctrine well enough to realize that an offensive operation *against* them, in their own backyard, will shake them up a lot. Constellar hasn't done a counterstrike of that kind in years. I am betting they will immediately shift their effort to rebuilding the defense at Jaalit—under the assumption that we're using resources in the Oswight system to hit them with their pants around their ankles. And while they spend days or weeks getting fresh ships moved to Jaalit—from across Nautilan space—we can get the rest of Iakar's flotilla moved to Uxmal territory."

"That's one hell of a gamble, ma'am," Urrl said. "What if you're wrong? What if their assumption that we're striking from Oswight merely causes them to hit Oswight system in reply? Without Iakar's ships to guard the Waypoint, the system is more or less wide open for a Nautilan Task Group to go in, surgically knock out the defensive planetary stations, and then begin a siege of Planet Oswight proper."

"We'll just have to find out if I understand their thinking as well as I suspect I do," she said.

Urrl's face held an expression of skepticism, while his mouth curled slightly.

"And…how are we supposed to *get* their codes, Admiral?" he asked.

"That's what I need to figure out in the next few minutes," she said, staring intently at the hologram of Objective Epsilon. "Out in deep space we'd never get close enough. But this comet gives us something to work with."

"Work with for *what*? In order to have their codes, you'd actually need the physical item—the computer installed in their communications array, which carries the codes, and automatically syncs with other, similar computers of Nautilan manufacture. And *our* version can self-destruct. To prevent somebody else from doing to us, what you're proposing we do to the security flotilla in Jaalit space. Is there something you suddenly know about the Nautilan code machines which I don't?"

"No," Zuri said, her eyes still fixated on the hologram. "But sometimes the best way to surprise an enemy is to do the exact thing he himself believes is too crazy to try. So, this is what I propose. We've got four destroyers to deal with. They'll arrive within half a day. We only need to isolate one of them long enough for a boarding action."

Now, it wasn't just Commodore Urrl with an expression of incredulity on his face. The entire command module staff had stopped what they were doing, and were staring at the admiral with their mouths hanging half-open.

"Sure," Urrl said. "Too easy. We just match course and speed with one of them, snake out the ship-to-ship dock, and *walk* over."

"Don't be facetious," the admiral snapped. "Lieutenant Commander Antagean was on to something. If the report he sent is correct, his ships used ejection pods encased in water and hydrogen ice—to mask the pods from enemy detection. I don't think we'll be able to do the same—Nautilan knows the jig at this point—except we have a whole comet to work with, plus its tiny companions. So…we *soft-land* the Task Group on the big comet, then break up the satellites for the sake of the debris field they'll form: tens of thousands of drifting bits of ice and rock, some of them larger than a man, some of them less."

"If I were your opponent," Urrl said, "I'd simply stand off a hundred thousand kilometers, and pummel Objective Epsilon into rubble."

"Right," she said. "This is why we need bait. They'll shoot on sight at a warship. But they may hold their fire and come in for a closer look if it's the *Hallibrand* hanging in cluttered space, broadcasting distress signals."

"The *yacht*?" Urrl said.

"I already told the Nauties we're here under the auspices of Lady Oswight. Capturing a First Families heir would be . . . well, it would be too good of an opportunity for any Nautilan officer to pass up. Hell, they'll want *Hallibrand*'s Key, if nothing else. So, they pull in for the chance to capture the *Hallibrand* and her crew intact. We put a team of our people—in zipsuits and armor—on some of the debris near the *Hallibrand*. With Manned Maneuvering Units. When the enemy ship is close enough, our team uses the MMUs to move on the destroyer. Conventional demolition charges can punch into the destroyer's comm module. And at that range, the other three destroyers won't dare launch on the *Hallibrand* without risking their companion. Once the boarding party has secured the code computer, they bail out of the comm module on MMUs and head for *Hallibrand*, while the ships *we've* previously soft-landed, fire up their engines . . . and given the Nauties something else to think about."

"Preposterous," Urrl said. "Utterly preposterous. Too many variables, ma'am. Too much that can go wrong. Besides, nobody even knows what a Nautie code computer looks like."

"I do," Zuri replied. "At Cartarrus—before the eventual retreat—I was able to board the wreck of a destroyed Nautilan cruiser. We went to their comm module explicitly for the purpose of finding the code mechanism, which we did. It was a doorstop by the time we got to it, but I *do* know what to look for."

"And what's to prevent the Nauties from junking their code box again, this time?"

"The main thing will be keeping them focused on securing *Hallibrand* while our team moves in. With all that debris floating about, the potential for detection is reduced. If the team can latch onto the comm module, blow a good hole in it, and enter, within about two minutes, we might be able to pull it off."

"But if you're the only one who knows...wait, boss, *no*. This plan has gone from preposterous, to *stupidly* preposterous."

"Which is exactly why it might work," she said. "No sane Nautilan officer will expect it, because no sane Nautilan officer would ever attempt anything like it himself."

"You describe the computer to me," Urrl demanded. "And *I* will go."

"Negative," she said. "In the heat of the moment, you might grab the wrong thing. I've held the actual device in my hands. The internals were fried, sure, but I'll know exactly what we're after when we get to it."

"And when something goes wrong? Because something *will* go wrong."

"Take command in my stead," she said. "Like any good exec should."

Urrl's expression told her he was not convinced.

"But we have to start *now*," Zuri said. "Otherwise there won't be time."

"Okay, boss. We'll do it your way. But I am filing an explicit protest in my log."

"Fine," she said. "And you can owe me explicit drinks if we get back to Oswight space, so you *can* file your damned log."

With that, the matter was closed.

Soft-landing a starship on the surface of a comet was no easy feat. Though the relative gravity was almost nil, it was still strong enough to cause significant damage if care wasn't taken to land the ship in a specific way. The process would be similar to docking at a shipyard built into an asteroid. Aim the shield dome down toward the surface, and use the reaction-control thrusters to gently brake as gravity gradually tugged the dome into contact. Do it carelessly, and the extremely strong dome might crack. Even against the relatively mushy surface of a comet. But with attention paid to precise piloting, the ship could theoretically come to rest dome-down on the surface without significantly stressing either the dome or the superstructure itself.

The ships from the security flotilla—though not starships—would be similarly soft-landed. So that all of them would be spread out in a line across the comet's kilometers of dirty-snowball surface.

First ship down was the *Tarinock*. Smaller than the *Catapult*, she still massed something like a small office building, and used a painful amount of fuel for the constant firing of the reaction-control thrusters as she descended. When her shield dome touched the surface, Admiral Mikton held her breath—while she waited for the scout to settle in. Irregularities in the density and composition of the comet's surface might cause the scout to topple. If that began to happen, *Tarinock*'s captain was going to have to go to full retro on the thrusters to try to right the ship before she settled onto her side—potentially crushing one half of the huge shield by the main engines, not to mention damaging the modules coming into contact with the comet's surface.

But, the *Tarinock* held. And held. And held. After that, it was just a matter of repeating the process.

Chaplain Ortteo paid the command module another visit.

"How can we help you?" Commodore Urrl asked, busy with his landing instructions to the other ships.

"Is it true that the admiral intends to leave the ship?" Ortteo asked.

"It is," Mikton said, also busy.

"Then you might want to know about the 'coldest hell' passage," the chaplain said.

"More prognostications from the Prophecies?" Zuri asked.

"It's what they are there for, Admiral."

"Fine. What's the Word got to say about things now?"

"The text is, 'To coldest hell goes the strongest heart, whose courage will seem like folly.' Later on it talks about how the strongest heart will eventually beat alone. In the darkness."

"That sounds more like a tragic love ballad than scripture," Commodore Urrl remarked.

"Only when taken out of context, Commodore," the chaplain said. Then he turned his attention back to the Admiral. "Ma'am, if I thought I'd be any good to you, I'd demand to go too. But I am old. Older than anyone else aboard this ship. And I am realizing that my chances for physical valor faded long ago. So I will pray for you. And for the safety of your team. And that you are successful in achieving your goal."

"For what it's worth, Chaplain, my team will appreciate it."

Ortteo accompanied Zuri to the lift hatchway, which took them both to the *Catapult*'s shuttle pod dock. Several of the four-person shuttles were already fueled. Zuri didn't need a pilot. Running a

shuttle pod was just about the only time she got to do any flying
at her rank. She climbed aboard, and Ortteo climbed in after
her. The few minutes it took to depressurize the dock, lift off on
reaction-control thrusters, then cross space to the *Hallibrand*'s
tiny dock, were spent in concentrated silence. At the other side,
Ortteo cupped his palms together so that one fist overlapped the
other, and pressed them to Zuri's forehead.

"May God's power and vision be granted to you, in this our
hour of need."

When the *Hallibrand*'s dock had repressurized, and Zuri
departed, Ortteo closed the pod's hatch, and readied the little
shuttle for its return trip to the *Catapult*.

Zuri—now in command aboard the *Hallibrand*—prepared her
boarding team. The lieutenant in charge of the TGO squad was
extremely dubious about having Admiral Mikton along. But he
didn't dare argue with her. All of them spent time double- and
triple-checking their zipsuits, the armor which went over the
zipsuits, their demolitions ordnance, and their small arms. The
submachine guns used for shipboarding were compact in design,
with a powerful cartridge—able to be discharged in all manner
of gaseous or liquid environments, or even vacuum itself. Each
TGO squad member carried one of these, plus a smaller pistol-
sized sidearm, and magazines with several hundred rounds of
ammunition.

Zuri herself hadn't touched such weapons since before her
transfer to the Oswight system. She held her submachine gun
in both hands, carefully testing the charging handle, the magazine spring-release button, the pencil-laser aiming aid under the
barrel—with her helmet on, it would be extremely difficult to
effectively use iron sights, or scopes—and fitting a magazine into
the magazine well itself. Like a lot of other technology which had
survived from the time of the Exodus, the basic functionality of a
firearm had not changed much. Size and style were various. But in
the end, it was all about putting a soft-metal casing—containing
propellant behind a bullet—into a firing chamber, and hitting
the casing's rear-mounted primer with a firing pin. *Boom.* The
propellant would combust, creating pressure sending the bullet
down the length of the barrel at tremendous speed, hopefully to
connect with a target.

Zuri had killed, but never face-to-face. While the squad

continued to ready themselves—now focusing on their backpack MMUs—she wondered if she had the fortitude to pull the trigger on a human being directly in her line of sight. Very different from launching nukes across space, and watching the results in a tactical hologram. It was easy to attack and destroy electronic blips in an electronically simulated representation of reality. It was *not* easy to imagine gunning down some crewman who just happened to be in the Nautie comm module at the time of the breach. Assuming vacuum decompression didn't kill the occupants first. If the destroyer was built anything like a Constellar ship of similar role, the different modules of the ship were all self-sealing against atmospheric loss. This too might aid Zuri's team in their attempt—since there would be no security force barging through the central hatchway the moment Zuri and her people were inside. If there was to be a manned Nautilan response, it would come in the form of suited Nautilan security coming in from *outside* the hole.

But Zuri intended to be long gone before then. It would take them minutes to respond. Minutes during which her team would duck in, grab what was needed, then get the hell away from the destroyer. *Hallibrand* would be waiting. And if the timing—with Urrl's attack from the surface—was right, when the Nauties got around to directing weapons against *Hallibrand*, the little yacht would be rocketing away from the comet at five gees.

Part of Zuri agreed with her exec. The whole thing *was* too contrived. But what other choice did they have? The civilian pilot of the *Hallibrand* had protested Admiral Mikton's explicit use of the Oswight yacht for a dangerous military operation, but Zuri was confident that *Hallibrand* would be too tempting a morsel for the Nautilan commander to resist.

Now, the fallback plan...Zuri had to admit she was still working on it as they went. Much to her TGO lieutenant's chagrin.

"Ma'am," the young man said, as he adjusted his zipsuit's helmet, testing both the seal and wireless voice communication with the other squad members, "assuming we can't get close enough to use the demo charges before the Nauties are aware of us, what do we do?"

"Even if they do detect us," Zuri said, "they can't exactly shoot at us when we're that close. Their point-defense system will be neutralized inside of a kilometer, because railguns triangulating on us will be programmed to *not* fire into an arc which might include other pieces of their own ship. They're also not going to fire on the *Hallibrand* as long as it's not clear that the threat is coming from the yacht. Which is why we're going outside immediately after Commodore Urrl has executed my instructions to blow up the comet's little satellites."

"Debris can puncture and wound as badly as a bullet," the lieutenant said.

"Copy," Zuri replied, her helmet sealing around the neck collar, and her ears filling with the familiar noise of her nitrogen-oxygen circulating system. "But the debris is going to be our cover. We need all those random, natural signatures occupying the battle space. It will make us far harder to identify, and will provide *Hallibrand*'s captain with his cover story as well."

Urrl's voice came across the helmet speakers—sounding small, and distant.

"Commodore Urrl to boarding squad," he said.

"We copy you," Zuri said. "Admiral Mikton and Lieutenant Eolo commanding, with Colour Sergeant Mertul bossing the squad proper."

"You ready for egress yet?"

"Getting there, sir," Colour Sergeant Mertul said, then added with emphasis for the rest of her people, "Get it fastened and tight, you barge rats! The commodore and the admiral are on a timeline!"

The rest of the squad redoubled their effort to finish, with every free piece of equipment tied back to its respective owner via stretch cording. In the microgravity of space, anything left to drift would either get lost or become a hazard.

"Any sign from the Nautilan attack force that they're aware of what we're doing?" Zuri asked her exec.

"Negative. All four destroyers are still in a relatively compact battle wheel, closing on Objective Epsilon. I estimate they will arrive within two hours."

"Better light up the satellites now," Zuri said.

"Affirmative, ma'am," Urrl said.

Down on the comet's surface, *Catapult*, with her cold stern facing up into space, deployed two groups of three nuclear missiles—one targeting the larger satellite, and the other targeting the satellite's smaller, rocky companion. With the *Hallibrand* circling on the comet's opposite side, the missiles slow-burned their way up into cometary orbit before slow-burning to within detonation proximity of the targets. Urrl waited until his ships were also on the opposite side—from the satellites and the nukes—before he ordered the weapons to blow.

For a split second, space became brighter than the sun. Then, what was left of the comet's former satellites dispersed in all directions. Some of the debris pelted off into deep space. Other pieces immediately crashed down into the comet's bald surface. Still others became part of a new cloud of gas and dust.

Taking great care to avoid the largest pieces—when the *Hallibrand* orbited back around again—her captain guided her into the thick of the cloud. Bits of rock and ore rolled off the *Hallibrand*'s shield dome. When the captain was satisfied with his stable position, he began sending the dummied distress signal he'd worked up earlier.

"We're going out now," Zuri reported on the encrypted tactical wireless network.

"Be careful, please," Commodore Urrl asked.

"We're way too late for that," Zuri said, laughing at the irony of his caution.

The bay doors for the *Hallibrand*'s smallish cargo hold clamshelled open. Outside, the murky cloud presented an almost opaque, hazy appearance—with occasional, dim glints as pieces of ice floated or spun past.

"Captain," Zuri called to the civilian pilot of the *Hallibrand*, "what's ship's status at this time?"

"We're getting a few bumps from all that crud out there," he said unhappily, "but nothing's been damaged yet."

"Good," she said. "Keep the distress signal going continuously. As soon as the Nauties get within range, they're going to try to talk to you. It will be threats. Agree to everything they demand. Make as if you're scared."

"Not hard to do," the pilot replied. "Between the potential for puncture and air loss—amidst all this junk—and those destroyers closing in on us, I think I speak for all of the Oswight employees on this ship when I tell you that we're half freaked out of our minds, Admiral."

Zuri felt a small twinge of guilt. Having experienced space combat before, she knew how to tamp down the fear—for the sake of the mission. But none of these civilians were combat ready. Nor had any of them taken oaths in front of the Constellar flag while a ceremonial dirk sliced a line of blood across their palms. Zuri could still remember standing in formation with the other teenagers in her DSOD accessions group—their arms raised while little trickles of blood ran from their palms down into their sleeves. It had been a bit of a shock, feeling that warm fluid pooling along her cuff, as she recited the words of death and allegiance. Afterward, every wound had been properly bandaged to eventually leave barely a hair's width of scarring. But the emotional impact had been forever. Never would Zuri go back to being the girl she had been before standing in that group, pledging her soul in service to the country.

"Steady," Zuri said, trying to reassure the pilot. "As long as Nautilan doesn't see you as a threat, they won't launch on you. So, stick to the script—and if you have to improvise, be as submissive and meek as possible. Make no move—utter no sound—which might give them cause to launch. And you should be fine."

"I hope you're right, Admiral. *Hallibrand* standing by for your egress. Good luck."

Two dozen MMUs began thrusting out into space. They went slow, using their tieback to the *Hallibrand*'s sensors to find their way in the cloud. Rocks and lumps of ice smaller than a man, were ignored. What they wanted were the bigger pieces, to which two or three troops could cling and appear as if they were part of the whole—at least to a cursory sensor sweep. An in-depth examination would give them away. But Zuri was depending on the Nauties to have all eyes on *Hallibrand* over the next ninety minutes. Giving the admiral a chance to slip in quiet, and do what Commodore Urrl thought could not be done.

# CHAPTER 28

GARSINA OSWIGHT STIRRED AWAKE WITH A SHOCK. THOUGH HER gee hammock was comfortable, she felt a distinct desire to throw herself out of it. The nights since they'd rounded the second jovian planet—and begun their journey to the terrestrial worlds of the inner system—had been rough on her. Too many times, she'd startled herself out of sleep, her heart pounding furiously at the feeling of sudden, imminent destruction.

Unlike the majordomo, Garsina had never faced battle. Nor death. Until joining the expedition to Uxmal's system, she'd never confronted any significant danger of which she was aware. Her father—and Axabrast—had seen to that. But now? Whatever Garsina and her allies could do to Nautilan's forces, so too could Nautilan's forces do to Garsina. There was nothing magical about being a member of a First Family. As her father had said so well, he had been lucky to avoid the fates of his siblings—both of whom had died in war.

Would Garsina join their ranks? A memory in the Oswight Family tapestry? Such morose questions kept her increasingly occupied as the detachment neared its objective.

Preparations for landing on Uxmal were proceeding according to Lieutenant Commander Antagean's and Captain Fazal's plans. Roughly half of the drop modules on each starliner had been stripped of their descent retros, so that those retros could be jury-fitted to the drop modules which remained. It wasn't exactly a designer-approved modification, but the DSOD and

TGO personnel working on the problem had assured her that with double the number of descent thrust pods—outboard of the module proper—each module could be dropped toward Uxmal without its parent starliner needing to decelerate to orbital-insertion velocity. The modules themselves would perform the deceleration, while the starliners did one more slingshot around Uxmal, and headed to the heart of Uxmal's system.

By the time both sets of outboard descent thrusters had been used up, each module would theoretically be going slow enough for the inboard planetary-descent rockets to kick in, braking them from reentry speeds down to a gentle meter-per-second rate, which would allow the modules' landing bags—already inflated—to absorb the impact on dry land.

Assuming all of the drop modules *did* fall over dry land. Being sure of their deceleration sequence—and the potential for mathematical error—kept Antagean's DSOD aerospace personnel, and the TGO drop specialists, very busy. Even a minor variation in thrust, speed, or trajectory could have disastrous consequences. Drop modules landing far out to sea would have no way of reaching shore. They were dependent on someone else to come tow them in. Drop modules landing too far inland would be separated from their companions by hundreds of kilometers—with no way to quickly make up the distance. It would take days or even weeks of marching to regroup with those personnel who arrived successfully at the target.

Drop modules which experienced a thruster failure...

No, Garsina didn't want to think about that. Imagining her drop module falling helplessly at hundreds or even thousands of kilometers per hour, to smash flat on contact, merely sent her shivering back to her suite, with a renewed feeling of doom in her heart.

"I don't have any magic cures for the jitters," Axabrast said one morning, as he watched her come weary eyed into the starliner's galley. She barely poked at her food, while Elvin pounded down two full gee trays worth of hot breakfast, followed by a full gee mug of hot coffee.

"I know," she said glumly. "Elvin, how did... how did you just *make* yourself forget about it, in the days and hours before you had to do something dangerous?"

"TGO and DSOD training usually keeps a young lad too busy

to fret," the majordomo said, pausing between sips. "When you're up to your ass in battle prep and drop planning, you literally can't slow down long enough to think about any of it. And by the time you do slow down, you're already strapped into your drop module with your mates, all of whom are every bit as scared as you are, so you make fun of yourselves. Laughter can make anything seem easier."

"Not much to laugh about right now, I guess," Garsina said, mentally trying to make the spork-sized bites of fruit and sausage seem more appetizing than they were. Intellectually, she knew she needed sustenance. But emotionally? Her appetite fled when she became depressed or nervous. How ironic that she should be experiencing this much dread on the eve of finally being able to walk Uxmal's surface. She'd been so excited to come here. It was everything she'd ever wanted since she'd been a teenager. But now that she had to endure the uncertainty of the actual process of getting down to the planet—to say nothing of the danger posed by Starstate Nautilan—she found herself silently regretting the fact that she had been so eager to leave home.

"There, lass," Elvin said, reaching across the tiny galley table, to put his hand reassuringly on her forearm—her spork poised indecisively over her tray. "Think of it this way. You're experiencing something just like what I've experienced, and it didn't kill me, right? And you're not alone, either. Look around at the faces in this mess compartment. The lieutenant commander? He looks nervous as hell. And that Zoam Kalbi fellow? Even he's letting the mask slip—now that things are getting real."

"I guess that's all true," Garsina said. "But there's something else, Elvin. I participated in the ad hoc weapons project Antagean gave us. You and Captain Fazal seem fine about what we did. But ever since it happened—ever since we destroyed one of the Nautilan ships—I can't help but wonder about the people who died. What was it like? Did they feel anything? Was it quick? Was it slow? Were any of them really *bad* people, who deserved to die? Who am I to be their executioner?"

"'Tweren't your hand alone in the matter," Elvin said, squeezing her forearm, then leaning back in his seat—grip boots keeping him firmly attached where he was.

"I don't think that makes it any less complicated," she said.

"Sure it does," the older man said, pleasantly disagreeing.

"War is war. And war makes even decent folk do terrible things to others, who maybe also are decent? It's not for them to decide the rightness or the wrongness of it. Oh, there's personal honor at stake, and I am not suggestin' ye set aside all notion of proper conduct. There's things I'd never do in a fight—malicious, sadistic— even if I am fixin' to kill another man. But the killin' itself? Like a law of nature, really. All our lives, Starstate Nautilan has been murderin' Starstate Constellar, in a slow strangle. A bit here, and a bit there, they close their hands over our throats. What choice is there, then, but for us to put a knife in their belly? Might not be enough to force them off us, before the end, but by God we can make sure they *hurt* for the evil that they do. Even if their little people—down at the baseline—aren't evil in their hearts. I am quite sure some of the men and women who died in the battles I've been through, and who were on the other side, were just like me. Doin' a job that needs doin'. And they paid for it with their lives."

"You say that like it's all so simple," Garsina said, looking intently into her majordomo's eyes. "As if the whole thing is a kind of game!"

"Well, lass, like my cadre sergeant screamed at me when I was new, war *is* a game. And everyone in it should play to *win*. You're seeing the war now, lass. For the first time, up close, in your young life. It's the kind of thing I'd not willingly show you, but now that we're up to our necks—hint: when passing through hell, do not under any circumstances *stop*—the best thing to do, is just push through. Gut it out. Maybe you die? Maybe you live. I know a lot of men who thought they'd live, and didn't. And I know a lot of men who thought they wouldn't, and did. It's not anything you can control. Other than you just keep doin' the best job you can do, in that moment, and if you're walking and breathing in the next moment, you keep *on* doin' the best job you can. Until the war gets you, and it's over. Or you emerge on the other side—a real veteran. Whether you're military, or not. Nobody's going to be able to take any of this from you, lass, when you get back home. And if you keep your mind right, it's only gonna make you stronger. See?"

Garsina considered. The older man's firm hand remained on her forearm. The look in his unblinking blue eyes—contrasting with her eyes, which were so brown they were almost black—was as serious as she'd ever seen it. Almost too serious. But there was a small smile on his lips too. As if to say that even in the midst of the most critical moments, there was sufficient levity in the universe to maintain the candle flame of a person's humanity.

Garsina grinned in spite of herself.

"I guess I've been gazing much too much at my own belly button," she confessed, and suddenly felt her appetite swell up from the depths of her stomach. She attacked her tray with the kind of enthusiasm she had not felt since leaving Planet Oswight.

Elvin's teeth showed happily.

"That's my girl," he said. And took a healthy mouthful of coffee from his gee mug.

Packing occupied the remainder of their morning, though in truth there wasn't much to take. Not when it came to individual luxuries. If it wasn't food, or a tool, or a weapon, it stayed behind. Including the vast majority of the contents of Garsina's gee chests, which remained in the starliner suite. She felt a moment of panic, when she realized that all of her many comforts—her hair brushes, combs, skin lotions, special soaps, custom blankets and pajamas, scented oils, and all the rest of it—were going away. Then she steeled herself, and pushed such thoughts from her mind. Focusing instead on the chore of loading what could be taken into her specific drop module, where Elvin, the lieutenant commander, Captain Fazal, and Zoam Kalbi were also stowing their equipment.

The drop module itself was a large, cone-shaped spacecraft, with the top of the cone mated to a docking collar which held two other cones at the waist of the starliner. There was a second collar, also with three cones attached, for a total of six on the ship. And only two of them would be detaching for deceleration. When those drop modules used up their first set of outboard thrusters—perched on the tips of pylons jutting from the cone's sides—the second set would kick in. And when the second set had finished, all of the thrusters and their pylons would be jettisoned, so that the drop modules could enter the atmosphere with no disruption in streamlining. It was crucial for each module to remain belly-first into the blast wave of friction heat.

At a certain altitude, the ablative reentry shields on the modules' bellies would drop away, then the inboard set of deceleration thrusters would kick in, and the landing bag would inflate—making each cone appear as if it had a huge rubber skirt sprouting from the bottom.

If at any point the drop module were to be up-ended before the heat shield could be jettisoned, it would be death for all thirty people inside.

But, having successfully landed on its bag, the module's computer would reassure itself that the module was on solid ground, then automatically blow the sides off, with slide ramps deploying for the people on the second and third decks. In the hands of an experienced TGO platoon, a drop module could be evacuated—with all of the necessary combat stores and equipment—within five minutes.

Elvin seemed almost gleeful, as he took his seat in the narrow gee chair next to Garsina's assigned location.

"It's been quite a while," he said, smiling, as he worked the buckle on the straps, clicking them into place, then releasing them, clicking them back into place, and releasing them once again.

"You are entirely too eager for what I am assured will be a bone-jarring experience," Zoam Kalbi muttered before taking his own seat, and testing his own straps and buckle.

"Life is for living!" Elvin said proudly. "If ye can't handle gettin' yer blood pumpin' now and again, why bother?"

The infotainer—whose video and audio recording glasses seldom left his face—merely stared at the majordomo before he shook his head in disbelief, puffed his cheeks out, and leaned his head back to stare at the ceiling above. Each of the three decks in the drop module was stripped of all superfluous bulkheading. Bare tubes and wiring snaked all over the place, kept immobile by metal or plastic tie-downs. The lamps were not soft either. They glared down from above with the kind of harsh, utilitarian light that was seldom used on the civilian starliner—except in crawlspaces or utility closets. The air in the module smelled different too. Aboard the starliner, the atmosphere plant had ensured that any odor from oils, fluids, machinery, or electronics was minimized. The drop module made no such accommodation. Garsina could almost taste the steel surrounding her, as well as the plastic, the rubber, and the mesh netting which secured most of their stores and equipment.

The lieutenant commander seemed awkward with the bulky armor for his zipsuit attached. Unlike Captain Fazal, who effortlessly glided about the drop module—with several of his sergeants, all checking to be sure their people and equipment were secured. This was definitely *not* Antagean's area of expertise. His eyes darted about as he tried to avoid running into people, or things, and his fingers clenched the handrails as he moved.

"Fish out of water," Elvin muttered in her ear, when he noticed.

"He's in good company," she said. "We're not exactly taking a clipper down, are we? Once the drop module is in the atmosphere, there's no turning back."

"Aye," Elvin said, and nodded his head once. "Which reminds me..."

The old man suddenly produced a gun. It was two-handled, with a grip on the barrel and a grip back by the collapsible stock. A well for magazines was apparent, as was a tubular scope for sighting. He pressed it into Garsina's hands, with the shoulder strap floating free.

"I'm not experienced in how to use it," she said.

"You've fired target rifles back home," Elvin said. "This isn't much different. Except, when the magazine's inserted *here*, you can take up to forty shots. See that little button *there*? Safety. Red means fire, black means no-fire. That little lever by the *thumb* will allow you to pick between one shot each time the trigger is pulled, and shooting ten rounds per second for as long as the trigger is pulled. I'd recommend against that. The kick will make it so that you're firing wild. Here's some magazines. I already loaded them."

Garsina tugged the bandolier from Elvin's hands—it was heavy, based on the mass she could feel being exchanged between them.

"I don't know that it'll do any of us much good," she said, "I'm probably more useful carrying things than I am fighting."

"Just a precaution," Elvin said. "I am sorry we don't have more time, or I'd have put you through your paces with that weapon. Before departure. As it is, we'll have you give it a go, once we're down. I borrowed the rifle from one of the female TGO troops, about your size. She's not coming on the drop with us. But this weapon should suit you."

Elvin himself had reequipped—with his customary sidearm, which had not seen the light of day since leaving Planet Oswight. His zipsuit was much larger than Garsina's, to contain a person who had many kilos and centimeters on her, but the sidearm's gunbelt was clipped neatly into place, as were two bandoliers of ammunition.

"Also for precaution?" she asked.

"Aye," he said.

"Why not a snubby rifle like mine?"

"I can one-handed quick-draw this beastie"—he placed a hand on the sidearm's grip for emphasis—"faster than anyone on this ship. If there's to be shootin', I'm going to need to keep arm one pointed at the enemy, and the other arm free to protect you, Lady Oswight."

Garsina blushed slightly.

"How do you know it won't be *me* protecting *you*?" she asked, only half-jesting.

"It might come to that," Elvin said, "but I'm gonna do my damnedest to ensure things aren't so dire that you're shootin' at Nauties, with my corpse as a sandbag."

"Sir," Captain Fazal reported to Lieutenant Commander Antagean, "I think we're about done here. We should take our seats too."

"Right," Antagean said, and got himself buckled in tight. All of them were facing in toward the center of the circular deck. Cargo-netted equipment was bunched in stacks in front of them, and they could hear activity over their heads, as the other sergeants returned to their designated gee chairs.

Once he was all strapped in, Antagean used a set of switches on his gee chair's arm to activate intraship communications.

"Antagean to Loper," he said.

"Copy you, sir," the older man replied.

"We're ready to go here. How much longer?"

"About twenty minutes from drop," he said. "Once we've disengaged, you'll be on your own reaction-control system. The module's guidance computers should begin deceleration almost immediately, so we're going to pull away from you fast. I'll keep the line open until you hit the reentry blackout, sir. Hopefully all goes well."

"Agreed," the lieutenant commander said. Then seemed to become aware—for the first time—that Garsina had been watching him.

"Any questions about what happens from here on out, Lady?" he asked.

"No," she said. "Mister Axabrast and Captain Fazal briefed me well ahead of schedule. Though I can't say I am too sure how my stomach is going to handle this."

"It shouldn't be too much different from being on a clipper," Wyodreth said.

Elvin grunted, smiled, and shook his head.

If Lieutenant Commander Antagean was offended, he didn't show it. The expression on his face merely remained nervous. He was fully aware of the fact that he was doing something dangerous, and for the first time as well. It wasn't a position Garsina enjoyed any more than he did, though he seemed to be managing his discomfort by asking each of his other deckmates in turn if they had any questions or problems before the drop module disembarked.

"We'll go in waves," Antagean said, returning his attention to Garsina. "Two, then two, then two. Each of the starliners will be putting its pair of drop modules into rough atmospheric entry alignment. The computers aboard the modules will do the rest of the work from there. Assuming nobody has a thruster failure, we should have a third of the TGO battalion deployed on the ground within two hours. At which point Captain Loper and the liners will be long gone. Captain Fazal will coordinate with his commander, Major Goodlin, who will be the nominal TGO authority on Uxmal. Overall mission command stays with me, and all civilian and First Family personnel will stay with me too."

Zoam Kalbi's eyes looked this way and that. Axabrast's merely stared forward, as if he were looking at nothing. Some of the other, much younger TGO troops appeared to be doing the same. Garsina wondered: Was it something they'd all learned in training?

"Five minutes," Captain Loper's voice said over the drop module speakers.

Helmets came on. Garsina had to fumble with hers a bit—her hair tied back in a very tight bun—before she got it secured, and the neck ring sealed. There was a mild hissing sound, then the regular, gentle *whir* of the zipsuit's atmosphere processor. An invigoratingly fresh feeling of icy cold suddenly sprouted out along Garsina's body as the zipsuit's internal temperature control system automatically boosted coolant circulation.

"Two minutes," Loper announced—this time through the speakers in Garsina's helmet.

The gee chair beneath her felt reassuring, but didn't stop the tiny little butterflies which began to fill her stomach.

"Thirty seconds—" Then came an audible *thunk-clunk* as the docking mechanisms which held their drop module in place released. Now it was simply the magnetic lock of the drop module itself that kept the module joined to the starliner.

"DROP!" Loper said loudly.

And for about forty-five additional seconds, nothing seemed to happen. There was no change in the sensation of microgravity. Everyone inside remained perfectly still. But then, Garsina felt the entire module being spun forcefully by its reaction-control thrusters, followed by a seat-of-the-pants thrumming through the entire vehicle, as the deceleration thrusters kicked in. Each thruster was an oversized, finite-fueled version of the reaction-control thrusters used to maneuver the module. As a combined group, the initial set began to take the drop module down from interplanetary speed to relative orbital speed. At first, the gee was negligible. But then Garsina felt herself being pressed into her gee chair.

Looking around the drop module's main deck, she could see everyone else visibly being pressed into their gee chairs as well. Some of the cargo contained within the netting shifted slightly, but did not move again.

"One gee," Captain Fazal announced, this time on the drop module's internal comm circuit, which included all of the suit helmets aboard.

Then, "Two gee."

"Three."

By the time Captain Fazal announced four, his voice was wavering, and Garsina thought she could hear some grunting and cursing from some of the other people aboard. She herself could only liken the experience to what she'd dealt with before, aboard the starliner proper. Until Captain Fazal ultimately announced five gee, at which point Garsina was panting and clenching her eyes shut, trying to not think about the immense sensation of being pulled down into her gee chair. Almost as if the universe were going to shove her *through* the gee chair, and into the deck.

"Six!" Captain Fazal shouted.

"Dear God," Garsina said through clenched teeth. An intestinally strained groan came from Elvin sitting next to her.

"Are you okay?" she said, putting her hand out to grab Elvin's through the sealed gloves on their zipsuits. Her arm felt like a solid block of cement.

"I'm...not...as...young...as...last...time...I...did...this."

"Just a bit more," Lieutenant Commander Antagean announced, also panting. "The first set of...thrusters, will burn out and then...we'll use the second set...for a more gentle...ride."

The spaceframe of the drop module itself was now groaning, and Garsina regretted having the rifle slung across her lap, because it was digging into her thighs quite painfully. In fact, everything about her—the rifle, the bandolier, the zipsuit itself, even the buckle of her harness—felt almost lethally heavy. Her sense of balance began to fail, and suddenly her head was swimming dangerously. She knew that it was quite risky for the human body to endure over five gees. Garsina opened her eyes only to see her view of the drop module tunneling into blackness. She shrieked, and pushed—almost as if constipated—trying to fight losing consciousness.

And then, the weight was gone.

Everyone aboard was gasping.

There was a moment when Garsina could feel something through the gee chair. A kind of buzzing, followed by several noticeable, jarring *clanks*, and the sensation of heaviness returned. Albeit greatly reduced from before.

"Two-point-five, heading to three," Captain Fazal said, his voice cracking.

Garsina risked lifting her head up, and looking to her left and her right. All the occupants of the drop module were weakly trying to do the same.

"We won't do more than three," Lieutenant Commander Antagean said, "until we're in atmospheric entry proper. For now, we've got at least an hour or more at this deceleration, while the computer lines us up on our precise corridor."

Antagean labored to hit some more switches on his gee chair.

"Captain Loper, this is Antagean," he said.

"Good copy, sir," replied the older civilian officer. "How was it?"

"I wouldn't do that over again by choice," Antagean wheezed. "But I think we're okay in here. Captain?"

Fazal called for a round-robin check with every trooper, and then gave Antagean a thumbs-up sign.

"Yup, we're nominal," Antagean said. "How about the other drop modules?"

"There've been some problems," Loper replied.

Garsina's hand clenched reflexively on Elvin's.

"How bad?" she asked into her helmet, before anyone else could speak.

"Lady," Loper's voice reported, "two of your six drop modules had misfires on the first set of deceleration thrusters. The module flight computers failsafed, taking those two out of their trajectory for atmospheric entry. We're dropping a starliner back to pick 'em up. But I am afraid that means Major Goodlin *and* his company commander won't be joining you on Uxmal. We'll have to take them with us—and their equipment."

"Damn," Lieutenant Commander Antagean said, and slammed a gloved fist onto his knee. He looked up and across at Captain Fazal—who held the lieutenant commander's gaze for a moment, the two of them simply staring at each other through the transparent surfaces of their face bowls—then dropped his head back into forty-five-degree position, lest the prolonged strain of three gees prove too much for the muscles in his neck.

"Anyone else having issues?" Antagean asked.

"The rest of your drop modules are sending solid metrics," Loper said. "We're well past you now. Once we've resecured the two which misfired, we'll begin our own burn for the gravity assist. I know you can't see it from inside, but Uxmal is getting mighty beautiful out the porthole."

"I hope Uxmal is worth it," Antagean said. "Thanks."

Garsina felt the sudden urge to urinate, and realized she was going to have to use her zipsuit's waste handling protocol for the very first time. There wasn't much to it, save for using her fingers to depress a few raised patches on her stomach and thighs, which activated the correct mechanisms riding next to her skin. But then she realized she was sitting in a room filled almost entirely with men, and the last time Garsina had gone to the bathroom with *anyone* watching she had been all of two years old.

Her expression on her face must have given away her discomfort.

"Problem, lass?" Elvin asked.

"Big problem," she said.

"Anything I can do to help?"

"You can fetch me a privacy curtain," she muttered.

Elvin's face—through his helmet—appeared mystified for a moment. Then he roared with a belly laugh that seemed like it would make them all deaf.

"There's nothing to it, Lady," he said. "Half the troops in this drop module have already pissed themselves. Hell, I've done it twice. Just close your eyes and think of how much better you'll feel when it's over."

There was laughter from some of the other TGO people, and even Lieutenant Commander Antagean.

"I . . . I don't know if I can," Garsina squeaked.

"Hush, lads," Elvin barked. "A moment, please."

Garsina's bladder warred with her brain until finally her bladder won, and there was a curiously euphoric moment of warm release—urine passing out of her body, gratefully, and into the zipsuit's catch membrane, where it was promptly absorbed and passed into the feeder tube that dumped the urine down to a holding bag on her right calf.

"Better," Garsina finally announced, and was greeted with hoots and laughter, as all the TGO personnel—who'd endured such things many more times than Garsina—enjoyed the notion of Lady Oswight, of the First Family Oswight, wetting herself.

"That's enough," Lieutenant Commander Antagean said. "Captain Fazal, what does losing Major Goodlin do to us?"

"Sir," the captain replied, "we'll have to shorten up the command structure once we land. With both Major Goodlin and Captain Chuq derailed from the landing, there's just you, me, some lieutenants, and the colour sergeants to lead the battalion. Which is now going to be more like a big company."

"No critical hardware aboard those two modules?"

"I won't know for sure until we're down," Captain Fazal said.

"Okay," Lieutenant Commander Antagean said. "Let's just pray nothing goes wrong at entry. Losing two modules on the initial burn didn't kill anybody."

"Copy, sir," Captain Fazal said.

Much of the rest of the time passed in silence. Until the module entered yet another momentary period of microgravity, during which the second set of deceleration thrusters and their pylons were shed. Then it was the drama of entry. Which proved to be far more nerve-wracking than anything Garsina had ever endured while riding a clipper. Especially in Planet Oswight's thin atmosphere, where the clipper's engines did the bulk of the work, and there wasn't a deafening roar of superheated plasma passing below and around the spacecraft. The drop module began to vibrate and shake, with netted cargo shifting noticeably, and people once again dropping down into the padding and protection of their gee chairs. Fazal called off the gee numbers, and when he hit six once more, Garsina was back to groaning through clenched teeth, her eyes clamped shut, as she tried desperately to keep from passing out. The reclined gee chairs were reclined for a reason—positioning the human body at a forty-five-degree, seated angle greatly relieved the work done by the body to keep circulation going. But it was still a fight with an elephant on her chest.

Garsina thought she heard Fazal call out another gee number, but then she experienced a blank moment during which it seemed like absolutely nothing had happened at all.

When she came to—her lungs heaving—the drop module was vibrating even more noticeably than before, but the force of deceleration was much, much less.

"We're through the worst of it," Elvin gasped, his hand still clutching hers. "Only part now, is the landing."

Which did not take long. Gee ramped back up momentarily, and then everyone aboard grunted as the drop module slammed down on its landing bag. The world seemed to tilt and sway, falling over to one side. And then the whole module *was* rolling, which meant everyone aboard was left dangling practically upside down from their gee chair straps.

"Bloody hell," Elvin said.

"Won't the module right itself eventually?" Garsina asked.

"Unless the module came down on something preventing it from righting itself," Captain Fazal said.

"We'll know once we're outside. Blow the number one and number four bulkheads *only*," Lieutenant Commander Antagean ordered.

Half the walls of the drop module suddenly ceased to exist, and a bright, brilliant light flooded into the decks, earning gasps from virtually everyone aboard.

Garsina was not surprised to see sunlight. But this sunlight had been filtered through a nitrogen-oxygen atmosphere. Craning her neck to get a better view—along with everyone else—she gazed out through the empty space between decks, at an upside-down-at-an-angle landscape that seemed to be heaped sand and jutting rocks rising into a gorgeously magnificent blue sky. The kind of blue that seemed to go on forever. Like a perfect blue, stretching off to meet a horizon made entirely of water.

"Lord above all!" Garsina heard Elvin exclaim with reverence.

TGO troops began to carefully unlatch themselves, dropping temporarily to the ceiling, before they crawled to the edge, and carefully began helping each other—often with crates or equipment in tow—down out of the drop module.

Garsina herself waited, at Axabrast's behest, until at least half the module had been vacated. Then she—and Zoam Kalbi, with TGO assistance—were being carefully let down out of the module, and onto the surface of . . . well, Garsina had only ever seen pictures of it in school. Like on the Constellar capital. But this time in virgin form.

The drop module had landed on the edge of a shallow, sandy bluff, overlooking a wide, long beach. The sand and gravel were an identical light gray color, but some of the rocks sticking out of the shallow bluff were covered in what appeared to be green moss, which snaked tendrils down the stone until touching the damp sand at the bluff's bottom. Directly across from the bluff lay the ocean, which rolled lazy combers toward them at regular intervals. The sound of the waves was muffled through Garsina's helmet. She reached up to begin taking the helmet off, but was stopped when Elvin grabbed her hand.

"Not yet," he said, and pointed to some of the TGO people who'd set up a little atmospheric sensing station on a tripod. The tubes on top of the sensing station were tasting the atmosphere, and giving the sergeant at the controls a determination regarding Uxmal's regional atmospheric content.

The sergeant began to nod his head vigorously, then he gave Captain Fazal the thumbs-up.

"Remarkable," Lieutenant Antagean said over Garsina's helmet speakers.

Almost at once, every single human began to rapidly uncouple his or her helmet from the collar of his or her zipsuit.

Garsina almost threw her helmet off, and held her breath for a few seconds, letting her skin feel the intense warmth of the sun as its rays fell on her cheeks. The air itself felt humid, but not so humid as to be unpleasant. And there was a breeze blowing somewhat parallel to the shoreline, which seemed to carry the scent of...

Garsina exhaled once, then inhaled deeply, and gasped. The atmosphere had a pungent quality—the scents of plant decomposition, mixed with wet clay, and a very mild brine. But *fresh.* Fresher than anything Garsina had ever breathed outside of a hydroponics bay. Not machine-conditioned for comfort, nor sanitized against bacteria. It was the air of the world as humans must have first experienced it, when they'd dropped from the arks of the Exodus—onto the five clement planets which had eventually formed the cores of the extant Starstates.

Now, there was a sixth Earth world within the Waywork.

Garsina almost felt like singing, she was so thrilled.

"It's beyond beautiful," she said, enthusiastically rubbing a hand along Elvin's shoulder.

"Wait until you see the bones of the ship, though," said Wyodreth Antagean. Garsina turned to see where the lieutenant commander's arm and finger were pointing. Zoam Kalbi—his recording glasses placed back onto his face after the removal of his helmet—intently stared at the huge, arching spires which sprouted out of the beach perhaps three kilometers distant. They had been the skeleton of a vessel once. Anyone who'd been around a Waywork shipyard—as Garsina had—could tell. What boggled the imagination was the scale of that skeleton. It was bigger by far than anything the Oswight yards had ever produced. The metal curved up, and up, and up, until it almost met itself from both sides, but had crumbled from corrosion. The interior could have contained dozens of starliners, and held many thousands of people—greater than the greatest surface dome to have ever been built, on any terrestrial world anywhere.

"We saw it in the imagery *Daffodil* sent," she whispered to no one in particular. "But now that we're here, I can't wrap my mind around it. It's...it's inconceivable."

"Sir," Captain Fazal said, "we're having trouble reaching Captain Loper."

"What about the other drop modules?" Wyodreth Antagean asked.

"That's just it, sir. We're having trouble reaching them, too."

Suddenly, Antagean stopped staring up at the astounding picture of the beached, mammoth ship, and charged up the slope of the shallow bluff—past the deflated landing bag of the drop module—and stood at the bluff's rim. He swiveled on a heel, while he used the blade of his palm to shield his eyes from the very bright Uxmal sun.

"Nothing," he shouted down at them. "I can't see another goddamned drop module in any direction!"

# CHAPTER 29

*UNITY* AND HER THREE COMPANIONS BRAKED HARD UNTIL THEY were in a roughly matched solar orbit two hundred thousand kilometers distant from the Kuiper object. If the Constellar squadron was still in the vicinity, they weren't showing up on *Unity*'s sensors. Of course, the blizzard of small debris which expanded outward from the comet made accurate sensor readings difficult. Indications were that one or more nuclear detonations had recently occurred in the comet's immediate vicinity. Plus, there was the repeating distress call from the small Constellar craft, which identified itself as the private property of none other than Lady Oswight, of the First Family Oswight. The repeating message—from the ship's pilot—indicated that something had gone seriously wrong within the past day. The yacht was damaged, suffering failing reactors and life support. Immediate assistance was requested, from anyone able to respond.

General Ticonner examined the tactical situation, and was continually annoyed with the fact that his holographic projector couldn't keep up with the number of moving objects in the comet's vicinity. A constant, sparkling shower of tiny dots flitted about like fireflies. But nothing other than the comet—and the Oswight yacht—were readily identifiable. What had happened? And why had the Oswight yacht been left behind?

The General floated through *Unity*'s command module, examining the overhead hologram from different angles. So far as *Unity*'s sensors were concerned, the comet itself was approximately ten kilometers in diameter, give or take a hundred meters in various directions—on account of the comet's uneven surface. Its gravity barely registered, but the Kuiper object had enough of a local field to retain the penumbra of gas, particles, and clutter which presently made sensor readings difficult.

"What's your opinion?" Ticonner asked *Unity*'s captain.

"I'd really like to know how that civilian ship was disabled," the captain said. "Last we saw of the Constellar squadron, the yacht did not exist as a separate entity. It must have been mated to one of the larger ships. But what happened to separate them, and where's the rest of the Constellar expeditionary group?"

"Still no contacts registering at long range?" Ticonner asked the *Unity*'s strategic overwatch officer, who had an up-to-the-minute status report on the entire system.

"None, sir, save for the three remaining ships in the kosmarch's pursuit force. And they're braking right now, to enter orbit around the clement terrestrial. The three civilian starliners appear to have used that planet for another gravity assist, which has launched them on a trajectory which will intersect the system's largest jovian, close to the sun."

"I wonder why Ekk didn't press the pursuit?" Ticonner asked out loud.

"The kosmarch's eye is fixed on that clement world," said the captain. "I doubt very much that General Ekk had any choice."

"True. But those starliners cannot be allowed to escape. If there wasn't such a great distance now separating us, I'd be tempted to pursue."

"There's also the single Constellar long-range patrol ship that is slowly closing on our position. It went well wide of Ekk's force, but would seem to be homing in on the Oswight yacht at this time."

"A rescue attempt?" Ticonner speculated.

"Possibly," the captain said.

General Ticonner rubbed his eyes. There were too many unanswered questions. The Constellar order of battle was in apparent disarray. Had they come to the new system so unprepared that their admiral eschewed all known Constellar fighting doctrine? Starstate Nautilan had learned that doctrine thoroughly. This time, however, there didn't seem to be much rhyme or reason to the Constellar flag officer's plan. She'd sacrificed a scout to kill one of Ticonner's destroyers. A reckless move, which she could not repeat without depleting more of her available vessels. The captains under Ticonner's command were also not so foolish as to allow themselves to fall prey to the same rear-guard attack twice.

"See if you can get live communication with the Constellar civilian vessel," Ticonner ordered. "Before we do anything, I'd like to talk to them."

*Unity*'s comm officer acknowledged, and began setting up the response to *Hallibrand*'s emergency transmission.

Within ninety seconds, the comm officer reported, "There's a reply, sir. Audio only. It's somewhat broken up. Male voice, using standard Mariclesh. Do you want to hear it?"

"Yes," Ticonner said. "Main command module speakers, please."

The comm officer typed at his keyboard until the crackling, distorted sound of the *Hallibrand*'s audio channel came through.

"...have been requesting assistance for the better part of two...unable to use sensors to get a fix on...please send help... Lady Oswight willing to discuss terms..."

"Terms," Ticonner said, his eyebrow over his left eye raising. He chuckled softly as he looked at *Unity*'s captain. Then he cleared his throat, and hand signaled for the comm officer to put Ticonner through.

"This is General Ticonner, speaking for Starstate Nautilan," he said. "To whomever remains aboard the Constellar ship calling itself *Hallibrand* I offer greeting. Having already lost one of my destroyers to your expeditionary fleet, I would like to understand why it is you assume I won't attack and destroy you?"

"...Lady Oswight recommending...possible loss of life support before the day...unable to reach other Constellar ships...no threat being made against...repeat, Lady Oswight recommending face-to-face talks..."

Ticonner considered. A member of a First Family would make for a prestigious prisoner when returning to Nautilan space. If Lady Oswight could be used as a bargaining chip, the Oswight system might fall into Nautilan hands without so much as a shot fired. Which did not make Ticonner feel any better about sending any of his remaining destroyers to assist the yacht. With the rest of the Constellar fleet unaccounted for, the yacht—all by itself—felt too much like a lure. But did Ticonner dare resist?

"Take us to within one hundred thousand kilometers," Ticonner ordered. "Maintain the battle wheel, and perform vigorous sensor sweeps."

Ticonner's force proceeded cautiously. At one hundred thousand kilometers, the visual telescopes began to make out detail, despite the low light levels. The little Oswight yacht was drifting in a stew of randomly moving bits of rock and ice. Ambient gas and dust turned the yacht into little more than a smudgy shadow amongst the debris.

"Have we detected *anything* that looks like another ship," Ticonner asked, "waiting for us amidst all that rubble?"

"Just the yacht, sir," the tactical officer reported. "Though our ability to get an accurate reading on all of the surrounding space is still poor. There's just too much junk out there for the computer to make sense of it all."

"But we can see *Hallibrand* plainly," Ticonner said. "Wouldn't we see her companions likewise?"

"Again, I can't account for it, sir," the tactical officer replied.

Ticonner hovered—hands gripped tightly to the rails which ran around the perimeter of the command module—while he considered his options.

Waiting meant risking the lives of the *Hallibrand*'s crew, and possibly the Lady Oswight with them. Sending one or more destroyers to perform a close inspection meant exposing them to potential attack. According to Ekk's own report, his squadron had lost a destroyer when the point-defense network failed to recognize incoming low-yield tactical nukes. The weapons had been gimmicked to look like something other than what they were. But would the Constellar admiral risk using a similar sneak attack on Nautilan ships if they were in such close proximity to the Oswight yacht?

Finally, Ticonner said, "Send this to the captain of the *Enforcer*. Break from battle wheel formation, and proceed to within fifty thousand kilometers of the Oswight yacht. Go very, very slowly. Maximum sensor activity the entire time. If nothing happens at fifty, then close to within twenty-five. If nothing happens at twenty-five, then close to within ten. If nothing happens at ten, *Enforcer* is to proceed to rendezvous with the Constellar civilian ship. We'll form an attack wedge with *Unity* at the tip, and follow *Enforcer* at a distance of thirty thousand kilometers. Anyone or anything attacking the *Enforcer* should reveal direction and distance, at which time the attack wedge can concentrate its missile fire, and hopefully disable or destroy more of the Constellar ships—if they're even here."

The tactical officer relayed instructions on the encrypted Nautilan battle network. Soon, the *Enforcer* was leaving her cousins behind, as she moved well ahead of the rest of Ticonner's squadron. The remaining two ships, now riding at *Unity*'s starboard and port flank, were sweeping with sensors, trying to detect anything unusual. *Enforcer* herself gradually entered the cloud of gas and particles which surrounded the comet, pausing occasionally to do a detailed inspection of surrounding space, as well as the civilian craft itself, before proceeding again.

"*Enforcer* now within rendezvous range," the tactical officer reported.

"What's the catch?" Ticonner muttered under his breath, as he watched the hologram hovering over the heads of the command module crew.

"*Enforcer*'s captain reports that he's within five hundred kilometers now, sir. He's got limited visual on the comet and *Hallibrand* both. Debris continues to make maneuvering tricky. *Enforcer* is proceeding at minimal thrust to avoid damage."

"Very good," Ticonner said. "Any new contacts?"

"None, sir," said the tactical officer.

"Hold us here, then. While *Enforcer* performs a full inspection. Maybe the captain of the yacht is telling the truth? We'll have to extract answers from prisoners, once we've got them. Tell *Enforcer*'s captain that his boarding party is to use lethal force only as a last resort. The more of them we can get alive, the better our chances of obtaining information that could be useful. Be especially careful about the Oswight heir. If she is onboard, I don't want her harmed or molested in any way. Her usefulness to the kosmarch can be best determined if she's delivered to Golsubril Vex alive and well."

"*Enforcer*'s captain has acknowledged the instructions," the tactical officer replied.

Ticonner returned to his gee chair, and settled in. For now, his wedge of destroyers held position. If they had to, they could obliterate everything in their forward arc. It would be suicide for *Hallibrand* to do anything foolish.

# CHAPTER 30

ADMIRAL MIKTON HAD ATTACHED HERSELF TO A CLUMP OF WATER ice. The clump drifted about half a kilometer from *Hallibrand*'s hull, which was slowly turning end over end, like a good derelict ship should. The *Hallibrand*'s captain was playing the part to perfection, even engaging in a little tearful pleading on behalf of Lady Oswight, who was in severe distress, he said, as her ship's functions gradually deteriorated around her.

Not far off, a Nautilan destroyer was approaching. Zuri had been eavesdropping on the conversation between the yacht and the warship. Her team was spread across several dozen small objects, each drifting harmlessly in the general vicinity of *Hallibrand*. Light levels remained poor, but the little tactical display Zuri had brought with her was tied into *Hallibrand*'s passive sensor network. Everything the yacht saw, Zuri saw too, including the slow-motion storm of debris, and the hulk of the Nautilan destroyer as it approached on minimum reactor thrust.

The Nautilan captain was smart to proceed with caution. It wouldn't take very many hits from random pieces of rock and ice to do significant damage to his ship. The shield dome on the bow would absorb the bulk of it—provided the captain didn't make any sudden course changes, nor begin using the reaction-control system to effect drastic yaw and pitch adjustments.

"Ma'am," Lieutenant Eolo said, "exactly how close do we want to let this thing come before we move in?"

"About as far from us as *Hallibrand* is now," Zuri replied.

"And you're sure you know what to grab, assuming we can get inside?"

"*When* we get inside," Zuri said firmly, "we'll only have a couple of minutes—at best—before the Nautilan captain figures out what might be happening. That's when there won't be any time for hesitation or guesswork. We go in, we cut the code box out of their network, and then we haul ass for the *Hallibrand*."

"I'm looking forward to some live-fire exercise," Colour Sergeant Mertul said. Zuri could hear the smile behind the statement.

"You'll get it," Admiral Mikton said. "Anyone who survives the decompression of the comm module, whether they're zipsuited or not, is a fair target. In fact, you'll be doing the ones *not* in zipsuits a favor. Vacuum death is ugly. Trust me. Just make sure you don't begin putting holes in friendlies, Colour Sergeant."

"Affirmative, ma'am," Mertul replied. "We'll be deadly, but careful."

"I think I see them coming," Eolo said.

Zuri turned her attention away from her tactical display—switching it off with the touch of a thumb control—to the space near *Hallibrand*. A monstrous black shadow was moving into position near the revolving yacht. Small flashes of light along the sides of the shadow were her reaction-control thrusters gently firing, so as to maneuver the destroyer with as much delicacy as possible. On the secure channel, Zuri could overhear the captain of the *Hallibrand* conversing with the captain of the destroyer. The yacht's decoyed comm situation was fooling them so far, or so it seemed. Though the captain of the destroyer was demanding to speak to Lady Oswight personally now. Which was not a situation the captain of the *Hallibrand* was prepared to handle.

"Suggestions?" said the captain's voice, through Zuri's encrypted tactical net.

"You've got to keep stalling," she said. "I want them to get closer."

"I don't think they're coming any closer until they have Lady Oswight visually confirmed aboard."

"That's not hard to do," Zuri said. "Do they know what she looks like? Have they ever heard her voice before?"

"We know they have spies in Constellar—"

"Right, but can we be certain this specific destroyer captain, or his command module crew, have *ever* heard or seen Lady

Oswight before? No. Just throw one of her helpers on the channel. One of the women who stayed aboard while Lady Oswight went with Antagean. Doesn't have to be anyone important. Our actor just has to be young, and able to talk the royal lingo well enough to pull it off. Can you produce such a person?"

"Yes," the *Hallibrand*'s captain said.

"Make it fast. My team can't move until the destroyer is practically parallel with you."

Several minutes passed in silence. Then a young woman's voice came over the crackling emergency channel. She spoke eloquently, assuring the destroyer's commander of *Hallibrand*'s unconditional surrender. The Oswight Family name was invoked several times, assuring the commander of "Lady" Oswight's good intent. She merely wished to see her crew survive, since the premature detonation of several Constellar sleeper bombs—blamed on Admiral Mikton—had disabled the *Hallibrand* in flight. Leaving "Lady" Oswight to express her deep unhappiness with Admiral Mikton, and indeed, the entirety of the DSOD as a whole.

"Laying it on a bit thick, isn't she?" Colour Sergeant Mertul said sarcastically on the tac net.

"The thicker the better," Lieutenant Eolo said.

Zuri waited. After a few more moments of back-and-forth talk, she saw the destroyer's reaction control thrusters light up again. The big ship began to move alongside the *Hallibrand*, which continued its gentle, aimless tumble.

"Almost," Zuri said breathlessly. She flicked the tactical display back on, and got a superimposed look at the angles and lines of the Nautilan ship, as revealed by the passive sensors. She was a warship all right, not too different from *Catapult*. The different modules of the ship were shaped according to function, again like a Constellar ship of similar role. The big difference being the destroyer had more missile and antimissile clusters, plus greater magazine capacity. With thicker armor at the critical points—especially the command module, which was one of the smallest parts of the ship.

The communications module revealed itself by way of the big radio dishes and message lasers, mounted on telescoping bases. Those devices were all retracted now, to avoid damage from the debris in the vicinity. Zuri used the tactical display to zero in on a spot on the hull, which was roughly ten meters below the largest radio dish. Then she put a big red target reticle on that location, and sent the same image to the rest of the team, who were also checking their tactical displays.

"Activate your MMUs on my mark," Zuri said. Waited a few seconds. Then announced, "Mark!"

The team's Manned Maneuvering Units all came to life at once. Zipsuited and armor-plated bodies dropped free from the bits of ice and rock they'd been sheltering behind, and began to descend on the Nautilan destroyer. Zuri felt a thrill run through her—having committed themselves out in the open—but didn't see any indication from the destroyer that her team had been detected. The destroyer's conversation with the *Hallibrand* was still ongoing, as "Lady" Oswight dragged out the diplomatic talk.

"Almost there," Zuri whispered, as the team made the distance to the enemy ship. Then, they braked in unison, careful not to slam directly into the hull. Instead, they formed up in two stacked lines, and hovered over the hull of the ship, toward the point Zuri had identified. There were no egress hatches on the communications module, save for the larger pod-capable bay doors, which allowed maintenance crews to exit the ship and inspect the comm module's dishes and lasers. The spot Zuri had picked was near a porthole, through which a small bit of light streamed. The admiral motioned for her team to stay behind her as she floated up to the porthole's edge, and peered over.

A dozen different Nautilan military personnel, wearing flight coveralls, were either seated in gee chairs, working at their workstations, or pulling themselves through the module via handrails. Grip boots occasionally touched surfaces, and were used to either latch on, or push off toward some other location inside.

Nobody seemed to be giving the porthole any notice. This far from the home star, what was there to see?

"Here," Zuri hissed, using her finger to draw a wide oval around the porthole. "Ring the charges, like that. When they blow, we'll wait ten seconds for the interior atmosphere to clear, then we go in shooting."

Each member of the team detached a small brick of vacuum-proof plastic explosive from his MMU, and gently touched it to the hull's surface. The bricks held, and were quickly daisy-chained together with spiral-wound detonation cord. When the job looked complete, the team backed off, and waited for Admiral Mikton's signal.

"Blow it," she ordered.

Lieutenant Eolo used a small det box attached to the end of the det wire, to set off the charges. At once, there was a bright, noiseless flash, and a huge hole opened in the hull of the ship. Pieces of metal—and several people—went gushing out into space. Zuri thought she saw terrible surprise manifesting on the Nautilan faces. How many of her own people had died in a similar fashion, back at Cartarrus? She steeled herself, and ordered her team to move in.

Laser dots flashed out, and pinpointed flailing bodies. Noiseless rifle rounds thudded into skulls and ribs. Zuri was over the edge of the hole and into the module. She ignored the violence surrounding her and kept her eyes open for the code box. Ordinary ship lighting had been replaced with flashing yellow warning lights. Zuri popped on her hand lamp, and played it around the comm module's innards, seeking the object of her desire. When Lieutenant Eolo began yelling about how the Nautilan captain had suddenly cut off communications with *Hallibrand*—the jig being up—Zuri switched off the tactical net, and allowed silence to fill her helmet as she kept looking.

A body floated between herself and one of the comm module's now-vacant workstations. Zuri shoved the dead woman aside.

"Where is it, goddammit," Zuri said through gritted teeth. They were running out of time.

Suddenly—*there!*

She found it. The overall design of the casing hadn't changed much, and the little lights dancing on the code computer's control screen indicated a unit in good electronic health. Zuri turned the tactical net back on, and hollered for Colour Sergeant Mertul's attention.

"This is it!" Zuri announced, as Mertul and a few others drew near.

Suddenly, the ship began to move. With all of the boarding team floating free, it meant they were unceremoniously slammed into the deck. Bodies and pieces of metal fell around them.

"The destroyer's lit her reactors!" Lieutenant Eolo said, his voice almost cracking.

Zuri struggled to her hands and knees, feeling the sudden gee.

"No," she muttered. "Not yet, for godsakes!"

The rest of the team were fighting to reorient themselves

in relation to the thrust of the ship. Fore was up, and aft was down, with the decks running perpendicular to the plane of acceleration—just like on a Constellar vessel.

Zuri only had eyes for the code box. She fought her way over to where it still blinked happily at her—its internal memory not yet destroyed. Zuri used her gloved fingers to find the little latches on the box's side, then she forced her fingertips past the red safety tape, and pried with all the strength she could manage. The code box broke free, sending Zuri toppling backward with the box clutched to her chest. She slammed onto her back—her attached MMU sending a *bloop-bloop-bloop* impact alarm through her helmet speakers.

The hole into space was so near, and yet so far. With acceleration climbing toward what felt like three gees, Zuri could barely move.

Strong pairs of hands grabbed both of her shoulders.

Lieutenant Eolo and Colour Sergeant Mertul practically dragged her across the deck. How either of them could stand, under their own mass and the mass of their MMUs, was a mystery. But they hustled Zuri to the hole, and unceremoniously flung her out. At once, she kicked in her own MMU—well past its safety threshold—and clutched the code box for dear life as she rocketed perpendicular to the destroyer. Which silently roared past, and away.

Zuri didn't even want to think about the potential radiation she was catching. She kept her back to the glare of the plasma wake, and allowed her MMU to burn up the last of its fuel before she tried to get onto the Constellar encrypted net, and ask for a status report.

But all Zuri got was the crackle of static in her ears.

The lieutenant, the colour sergeant, and the team were long gone. If any of them had tried to jump out after Zuri, she didn't know it. Somewhere down on the comet's surface, Urrl would be launching nukes—if he hadn't started launching them already. Likewise, as soon as the destroyer was at minimum safe distance from the *Hallibrand,* the Nauties would begin launching nukes too. Though *Hallibrand* had doubtless fired up her own main thruster, too.

Zuri still kept her back to the blinding light of the receding destroyer's plasma wake. If the ship turned away from her, she'd be vaporized. Though she wouldn't have time to know it. Her lateral motion—unimpeded by resistance—kept building distance between herself and the column of clear space where the destroyer had once been.

Still nothing on the encrypted net.

In the distance, a bright fireball strobed into existence, and then began to fade—its brilliance made gauzy by all the gas and dust between Zuri and the nuke's point of detonation. Within moments, a few more fireballs erupted, and then faded, each at a different distance. Where either the Constellar or Nautilan ships were was impossible to tell. And Zuri didn't have the heart to let go of the code box long enough to check her little tactical display—assuming the display still worked, since it had lost the uplink with *Hallibrand*'s sensors.

"Angels of space and time protect me," Zuri whispered, as still another nuke flashed brilliantly—and much closer than any of the others. If it was too close, Zuri would be crushed by the shockwave. But nothing happened. She merely kept moving through cluttered space, unsure of whether or not she'd smack chest-first into a floating hill of ice, or get clipped by a bit of rock.

# CHAPTER 31

COMMODORE URRL SHOOK HIS HEAD AND SAID, "I KNEW IT." THE instant the Nautilan destroyer ignited its primary fusion reactor, it became obvious to him Admiral Mikton's plan had gone very, very wrong. Neither she nor her team had cleared the destroyer's communications module. They didn't have the code box, and now they wouldn't be able to get back to the *Hallibrand* either.

"All Constellar ships," Urrl said into the microphone on his headset—wired into the tactical net, "this is the exec. Prepare to launch warheads on my command. I say again, prepare to launch warheads on my command."

"Sir," the captain of the *Catapult* said, "*Hallibrand* is requesting immediate instructions."

Urrl pounded a couple of keys on his gee chair's keyboard, then replied, "*Hallibrand,* the situation's gone critical. They won't shoot at you until you're far enough away that their own nukes won't hurt them at the same time they're trying to hurt you. I'm going to get their attention here pretty quick, though. As soon as those destroyers turn their focus on us, that'll be your chance to escape. Get back to the Waypoint. Pull as many gees as you can stand."

The *Hallibrand* acknowledged—her captain's voice filled with fear.

"We're ready to fire," said the officer at *Catapult*'s weapons station.

Urrl pounded two more keys, and switched back to his squadron.

"Launch at will," he said, "and push your retros hard!"

On the surface of the comet, flashes of light turned into streaking missiles. At first the warheads rocketed parallel to the surface, then they turned sharply away from their points of origin, and lanced upward at the escaping destroyer. Almost immediately, the same ship deployed a flurry of antimissiles, and within a few seconds the cloud of gas and dust surrounding the comet came alive with explosions. There was no sound. Each bright flash made a noiseless pocket of superheated molecules within the cloud, followed by a shockwave like an expanding soap bubble. Bits of ice and rock, already smashed, were further pulverized to nothingness.

Urrl watched the tactical hologram suspended over the heads of the *Catapult*'s command module crew. *Hallibrand* was streaking hard away from the fight. The other destroyers—which had been hanging off earlier—were moving closer, and deploying nukes of their own.

"Countermissiles," Urrl ordered, then turned his attention to *Catapult*'s pilot and ordered, "Thrusters to max. Lift us off this berg!"

At once, everyone in the command module flopped upward into his gee chair's straps. Urrl groaned as he felt blood rushing to his head and arms, which flailed helplessly in front of him. The ship was pushing with her reaction-control system to thrust away from the surface of Objective Epsilon. Gee was now felt going the *wrong* way—if there was such a thing as a wrong way in deep space—and Urrl had to fight to keep his eyes on the tactical hologram, where the bright icons of his squadron were gradually separating themselves from the comet itself. The icy Kuiper body didn't have enough gravity to overwhelm the thrusters, so each ship quickly pivoted on its axis until the main reactor faced toward the surface. Then, Urrl and his command module staff were slammed down into their seats as the *Catapult*'s reactor took over, and his entire squadron moved aggressively toward the enemy.

"Keep them off the *Hallibrand*," Urrl ordered.

The space between the destroyers and Urrl's Task Group erupted with missiles and antimissiles annihilating each other. The total tactical picture remained muddled—that much ice and rock played hell with Constellar sensors, to the same degree it played hell with Nautilan sensors—but there were so many rockets being launched, they couldn't help but find each other.

"The *Laborer*'s been hit," reported the tactical officer. "They say it was a grazing explosion. They're now...wait, sir. No. *Laborer* is gone. Two more detonations on her hull, directly amidships."

The icon for the security craft flared in the hologram above Urrl's head, and winked out.

Then, a second security ship was gone.

"Talk to me, *Tarinock*," Urrl commanded through his headset.

The captain of the long-range scout reported that she was having a problem with one of her antimissile clusters, which had been damaged by debris during liftoff from the comet's surface.

*Hallibrand* was still going like a bat out of hell, but two of the Nautilan destroyers, which had been standing off at first contact, now appeared to be angling for an intercept.

"Weapons," Urrl said, "dump everything you have on those specific destroyers."

Urrl used a cursor to highlight the ships in question.

*Catapult*, now pulling close to four gees, spat nuclear missiles into space. They leapt ahead of the ship, pushed at gee rates far beyond anything a living person could withstand. And though some of them were picked off by the destroyer's antimissile system, two of *Catapult*'s shots successfully got within lethal distance, and proximity detonated. The icons for the destroyers flared brightly, then died.

"A double kill, sir!" the tactical officer shouted.

A cheer erupted across the command module, with the entire staff smiling and pumping their fists in the air, despite the gees weighing them down.

Even Urrl allowed himself a small moment of celebration—clapping his hands together enthusiastically. It had been a long time since he'd managed to draw Nautilan blood. He had too many friends with names on the memorial at the Constellar capital who had waited too long for payback. And though Urrl would no doubt be putting Admiral Mikton's name on that wall eventually too, he was glad to have at least hurt the enemy who'd done Mikton in.

The remaining Nautilan destroyer focused its attacks on *Catapult* now. Urrl watched the status bar for his antimissile magazines drop lower and lower. *Catapult* was burning antimissiles at a catastrophic rate. But what else could they do? Engaging the enemy at this close range didn't leave *Catapult* or the other ships much choice.

"*Tarinock*'s been damaged," reported the tactical officer.

"How serious?" Urrl asked.

"They've taken casualties, and are losing atmosphere. The captain...sir, *Tarinock* is aligning for a ramming maneuver."

Urrl could see it in the hologram. The *Tarinock*'s icon was almost directly between two of the Nautilan ships now. She veered sharply—pulling entirely too many gees—and suddenly both *Tarinock*'s icon and the Nautilan destroyer she'd been nearest to flared, and went out.

Like Captain Hebrides before her, the commander of the *Tarinock* had chosen to make the ultimate sacrifice.

There was no cheering in the command module of the *Catapult* this time. Just silent respect. Especially on the part of Chaplain Ortteo, who'd entered unannounced—per his habit—and taken a seat in the gee chair ordinarily occupied by Admiral Mikton.

*Hallibrand* continued to put distance between herself and the battle. Though she wasn't out of danger yet. If even one Nautilan destroyer remained operational, the little civilian yacht would be in peril all the way back to the Waypoint.

The status bar for *Catapult*'s antimissile magazines had dropped so low, it flashed critically red.

"The *Forager* just went up," reported the tactical officer.

Urrl was out of security ships, which were built to overwhelm an enemy en masse—like hornets attacking somebody who's stumbled into their nest. But they were not true capital ships, any more than *Catapult* was a battlecruiser. Gun to gun, the Nautilan destroyers bested them all.

Urrl exchanged a long glance with the chaplain. "Any good words for us?"

The religious officer merely looked hard at Urrl, and said, "Be *worthy*."

Urrl stared at the man for a few more seconds, then reluctantly ordered, "Pilot, put us on an intercept course. Then take us up to five gees."

All eyes and heads turned to face the boss.

"You heard me!" Urrl said forcefully. "And dump the last of

our nukes, along with what's left of the antimissiles. We won't be needing either of them in a few more moments."

If any of the staff had objections to Urrl's decision, none of them showed it. Though there was definitely fear in their eyes.

A chorus of *yessirs* went around the command module, then Urrl felt himself being crushed into his gee chair as the pilot opened up the throttle.

"Unnnnngggggggggggrrrrrrrrr," Urrl growled through clenched teeth, as *Catapult* shot like a firebolt toward the final enemy destroyer—missiles and antimissiles eliminating each other all along the way. Until the two ships were so close their point-defense railguns engaged, and suddenly the staff started hollering about secondary damage from packets of electromagnetically hyper-accelerated metal pellets, shredding their way through different modules on *Catapult*'s spine. Armored as she was, the frigate wasn't designed to go toe-to-toe with bigger, more robust ships. And though *Catapult*'s railguns might be causing damage too, the real coup de grace was yet to come.

A proximity countdown on Urrl's gee chair flatscreen showed the kilometers vanishing between himself and his intended target. When the number hit zero, he didn't even have time to blink. *Catapult*'s shield dome—already damaged during the rapid burn away from Objective Epsilon—bashed its way through the destroyer's point-defense network like a cowbell through a swarm of horseflies, making contact with the destroyer's spaceframe itself.

The two distinct ships suddenly exploded into fragments. Splintered steel, cracked insulation, and the bodies of men and women went spinning into the void. Rather than going critical, the two fusion reactors simply choked off, having been robbed of fuel. Hydrogen tanks—now hopelessly ruptured—spewed massive quantities of sublimating slush into the darkness of space.

The two ships' Keys were the only objects to survive the ramming unscathed.

# CHAPTER 32

THE FLASHES OF NUCLEAR EXPLOSIONS RECEDED. THEN STOPPED. Zuri, her head becoming light with fatigue—or lack of oxygen, she hadn't checked—could barely keep her thoughts composed. She had enough sense to use a grappler from the side of her MMU to attach herself to the code box, its little control panel still showing flashing lights, then she allowed herself to zone out. With the MMU's fuel reservoir depleted, she couldn't do much more than wait. If there were any Constellar ships still capable of searching for her, she'd have to let her MMU's encrypted distress beacon do the talking.

Admiral Mikton closed her eyes.

Some indeterminate time later, Zuri fluttered them open, to see a zipsuited and armored soldier peering at her through a helmet's face bowl.

The woman's mouth was making sounds, but Zuri couldn't hear anything. Her head felt far too light for comfort, and there was a nasty tingling in her extremities. Oxygen starvation did strange things to a person. Her zipsuit's atmosphere processor could go until literally every last drop of liquid oxygen in its cryo tank had been used up. But it wouldn't be a hard stop. More a petering out over time, as the carbon dioxide scrubber kept the nitrogen clean, but less and less oxygen flowed from the regulator.

How long had Zuri been out? Her helmet speakers continued to crackle with static while the other woman spoke. Zuri wondered— perhaps deliriously—if maybe her zipsuit's communications had been damaged? It would explain why she'd had no luck reaching the tac net. Maybe passing so near the plasma exhaust of the destroyer had damaged some of the suit's more delicate electronics? She still had no idea how much radiation she'd taken, between the fusion exhaust and the nukes. Zipsuits were radiologically resistant, but not proofed against an unlimited amount.

The woman grabbed hold of Zuri's arm, and Zuri saw herself being guided through an open bay door in the side of a different ship. Her peripheral vision caught what seemed to be a Constellar symbol on the side of a gee crate, then Zuri was laid flat on her back, and people were using the emergency releases on her helmet to pry the thing off.

Fresh air—with plenty of oxygen—flooded into her nostrils.

Zuri began to cough spastically, and rolled over, almost vomiting. Then she crouched on her knees, savoring the cool feeling of the deck on her damp cheek.

"Ma'am?" asked a stranger's voice. "Ma'am??"

Zuri wanted to say something, but didn't yet have the strength to speak.

"Admiral?!" asked the voice a third time. "Are you all right?"

"I think so," Zuri whispered, and then felt herself being moved into a sitting position, with her head between her knees. The MMU was taken off her back, and the attached code box along with it. There was gee, but not much. Maybe twenty-five percent? Modest thrust. Though where in the universe the ship might be going, Zuri could not guess.

"What ship is this?" Zuri asked, finally lifting her head. She was surrounded by half a dozen Constellar DSOD personnel in zipsuits. A seventh—with medical insignia on his jumpsuit uniform—rushed into the compartment from an adjoining corridor. He was followed by two others, toting small medical chests.

"You're aboard the *Daffodil*, Admiral," the medical officer said, stooping over to have a look at her. "And you're damned lucky to be alive."

"What happened to Commodore Urrl? The *Hallibrand*?"

"Gone, ma'am," the medical officer said, propping Zuri's chin on his palm while he peered into both of her eyes with a pen flashlight.

"Gone?" Zuri asked, her senses suddenly coming back to her in a hurry.

"Destroyed," the medical officer said, snapping his light off. "Or at least that's all we can tell. We were conducting a search for both *Tarinock*'s and *Catapult*'s Keys when we discovered your MMU broadcasting on the encrypted emergency wireless."

Zuri blinked several times, and looked carefully around her, until she saw the code computer sitting safely in its protective case.

"If that's been wiped or damaged," she said, aiming a finger weakly in the code machine's direction, "none of it matters."

Zuri closed her eyes, and fought back tears. She and Commodore Urrl had become friends during her time in Oswight system. They'd previously seen different battles, across different parts of the Waywork, but their outlook had been very similar. Of the several executive officers who'd come under Zuri's command, Urrl had been the best. In her mind, she said a silent *I'm sorry* to Urrl's memory, then immediately pushed that memory out of her conscious awareness. The job wasn't done until Zuri did what she'd initially set out to do.

"Any luck locating those Keys?" she asked.

"Not yet," the medical officer said.

"Save it for another time, then," she said. "*Daffodil* has a new mission."

# CHAPTER 33

WYODRETH ANTAGEAN RESISTED THE URGE TO VOMIT. HE'D KEPT his composure all through deceleration and atmospheric entry. But the disappearance of the rest of the drop modules was too much for his nerves to take. It had been bad enough landing with the knowledge that they'd all remain planetside until Admiral Mikton could find a way to get rid of the Nautilan pursuit squadron. But now? There was no way a small platoon's worth of people could hope to fend off whatever ground force Nautilan deployed upon arrival. Wherever the other drop modules had gone, they'd not landed anywhere near the objective. And without additional personnel, weapons, and equipment, the little group which had landed with Wyo on the beach was in grave danger.

Wyo turned and walked back down to where the rest of his people were clustered around their overturned drop module. All the crates of gear which they'd brought with them from the starliner had been pulled out, and were being carried in two- or four-person teams. Though nobody seemed to know where. There was a mixture of both fear and indecision on every face. Wyo felt it himself: an acutely insecure sensation of literally not knowing what to do next. But he couldn't show that to his people. Not while there were so few of them left, and they still had so much to do—regardless of how outnumbered they might be.

"Captain Fazal," Wyo said, resisting the sick feeling in his stomach.

"Yessir?" the TGO officer said.

"Do what you can to try to reach the other drop modules via tactical net. Until we learn otherwise, we have to assume they either went long, or fell short. This means we've got people potentially spread out over a wide area. Maybe even in the water? They'll be looking for us at the same time we'll be looking for them."

"Yessir," Fazal said, and beckoned several TGO troops over to him, while he knelt in the sand and began drawing with his finger.

"Lady Oswight," Wyo said, turning his attention to the First Family heir, and her majordomo. "I'm afraid we're more ill prepared than ever before to conduct a proper reconnaissance of Uxmal. It would be best if we postponed your piece of the expedition until we can locate the other drop modules, and formulate a plan to reaggregate Fazal's TGO troops."

"Which will require zero input or effort on my part," Lady Oswight said. "I don't want to sound callous, Lieutenant Commander, because there may be Constellar soldiers in peril. But why postpone the inevitable? Mister Axabrast and myself are perfectly capable of exploring this area on our own."

"Without armed escort?" Wyo said. "I would be derelict in my duty to allow it."

"You've not got many options, lad," Axabrast said. "The Lady's correct. It might be hours, or days, or never, before we find out what happened to the rest of the TGO battalion which dropped with us. For all we know, somethin' about this place is disruptin' our wireless, and they could be on the other side of that wreck. Or beyond the pyramid."

Axabrast's arm was extended, pointing to the metallic peak which projected into the sky—even taller than the ribs of the beached ship. The regular, geometric network of lines cut into the pyramid's surface was even more pronounced when viewed up close. It looked a bit like an old puzzle game Wyo had been familiar with during his boyhood. The objective of the puzzle had been to randomly spin the individually attached pieces of a four-sided tetrahedron, then try to rotate all the pieces back into place, so that one color dominated each side again. Wyo had always struggled with the game. He'd frequently lost patience with it, while his sister had excelled. Something about the puzzle appealed to her personality, which worked similarly well with numbers. But Wyo? He'd never been any good at it.

"You two can't go wandering around this place without some form of protection—no offense, Mister Axabrast, but you're just one man."

"Aye," Axabrast said to Wyo. "So maybe we take a few of the lads with us?"

Wyo considered, then said, "A moment, please," and trotted back up to the top of the bluff. Removing a pair of mechanized binoculars from his tactical pack—which attached to the armor on his back—he scanned a slow three-sixty, to be sure his initial survey was not mistaken. When he still didn't see what he was looking for, he put the binoculars back in their case, then took a knee. All of it had become far too real for his businessman's sensibilities. In the time he'd been running his father's company, the only risks he'd had to take were financial in nature. Now? Men and women were dying. *Had* died. Would continue to die. Was he up for the role assigned to him? Captain Fazal seemed competent enough. As a TGO-trained officer, he had to be. But what good would Wyo be to the group if he turned everything over to the junior officer? He couldn't handle weapons as well as the TGO troops, and he didn't have their tactical land-combat training. DSOD skillset—for Reserve officers—focused more on logistics and space-combat operations than on what to do if you found yourself planetside.

Wyo dipped his chin to his chest, and breathed several deep breaths of the amazingly wonderful Uxmal air. He should have been excited. Instead, he merely felt a cold nugget of dread wedged under his sternum. Because he knew there might not be any way to think his way out of or around their predicament. It wasn't a question of funding, or allocation. It was a question of time, and manpower. Wyo's group didn't have enough of either. Even if they located some or all of the other drop modules, Admiral Mikton *had* to be successful dislodging the Nautilan pursuit force from Uxmal orbit, or Wyo's dilemma remained the same.

When DSOD personnel had first barged into Wyo's father's office, he'd never guessed that it would mean his potential death. Even if DSOD Reserve officer training emphasized the fact that Reserve personnel died in battle right alongside the regulars. It just wasn't a possibility Wyo had ever taken seriously. Until now.

Wyo slowly stood up, went back down to the bottom of the bluff, and asked Captain Fazal if his people were able to get *any* kind of communication going, even if it wasn't with the other drop modules.

"There's still that beacon," Fazal said, nodding his head in the direction of the beached derelict.

"Nothing's changed about the repeating message?" Wyo asked.

"Nossir," Fazal replied. "It's the same as it's been since we entered the system, though obviously a lot clearer and stronger—now that we're so close."

"That would be the obvious place to start," Lady Oswight said. "If we all stick together, the march to the source shouldn't take more than an hour or two."

"Provided we even know what to look for when we get there," Wyo said, eyeing the wreck over his shoulder. "We're not entirely certain what we're getting into."

"It would make a far better place to stage a defense," Elvin Axabrast said.

"He's right," Captain Fazal agreed. "Out here, we don't have any cover. But there? We might be able to set up a hasty fire chart with overlapping wedges. If Nautilan comes, we can at least make ourselves painful for them."

Wyo inwardly boggled at the matter-of-fact way Fazal made such a statement. As if dying in a losing fight still had some kind of moral merit? When negotiating shipping deals, Wyo had never felt any sense of victory emerging from the clinchers having lost more than he'd gained. And he didn't relish the idea of a foot soldier's martyrdom. Especially if Nautilan was going to own Uxmal—and the whole system—eventually. Nobody would be around to carry news of Wyo's passing back to Starstate Constellar. Not even Kalbi the infotainer, who seemed to reflect Wyo's uneasiness.

"Very well," Wyo said. "We'll proceed to the wreck, and hope something good comes from it. Captain Fazal? This is your specialty. You tell us where you want us."

"Modified tactical column," Fazal said, and quickly sketched his concept into the wet sand. "Two rows of people on either side of each other, and spaced at intervals so that nobody is too close to anybody else. We carry our chests and trunks of gear between the two rows. When one set of arms and hands gets tired, they swap out with another set. Lieutenant Commander, Lady Oswight, it would help a lot if you two assisted in this way."

"Of course," Wyo and Lady Oswight both said in unison.

Axabrast had already lined himself up on one side of a chest, his free hand reaching down to grab the handle. He stared at Kalbi long enough for the infotainer to get the hint, then Kalbi reluctantly got on the opposite side, and mimicked Axabrast's movement. When Axabrast said, "Up," he pulled the chest's handle, and Kalbi did the same—except Kalbi struggled mightily to bring the chest to thigh level. And promptly dropped his end back to the ground.

"It's too heavy," he said indignantly.

"Nobody else to do it, Mister Kalbi," Captain Fazal said.

Wyo—sensing the opportunity—got on the other side of the chest, and lifted it to match Axabrast. It was a supremely heavy box in Uxmal's gravity, which felt like it was a small percentage stronger than Planet Oswight's had been. But as hesitant as Wyo was to lead the group, he was man enough to recognize that sometimes you just had to do what needed to be done, and doing something would be much better than doing nothing.

Kalbi eventually teamed with one of the smaller female TGO troops on a much lighter crate, and soon Fazal's modified tactical column was making its way slowly toward the beached wreck. The sand proved to be particularly difficult to walk on, and before long Wyo was panting and sweating profusely under his zipsuit—which could breathe in an oxygen-nitrogen atmosphere, but didn't seem to be helping much.

Eventually, the column found a low part of the bluff, up which the group could successfully switchback, then they were striding across firmer, dryer ground. The land beyond the beach was fairly flat, but occasionally jumbled with boulders. In the very far distance, the crumpled spine of what appeared to be a mountain range disappeared into the horizon. Those mountains had been worn down by time. There didn't appear to be any recent volcanic activity. Nor any tectonic upheaval to thrust fresh pieces of the planet's crust high into the sky.

Which perhaps accounted for why the pyramid had been built in this specific spot to begin with? Geologic stability.

All of the structures between the wreck and the pyramid appeared to have been built from sun-dried brick. Two, and sometimes three, stories tall, the majority of them had crumbled in on themselves. Roads and streets still ran throughout, though they appeared to have been long abandoned. Wyo could not bring himself to think of it as a city. There wasn't a living soul in sight.

"Up here!" Captain Fazal shouted from the head of the column. Wyo—his arms, shoulders, and legs all feeling like they were on fire—gratefully set his end of the chest down. Looking at his elderly counterpart, Wyo was momentarily satisfied to see that Axabrast was also pink faced and puffing, then Wyo jogged as best as he was able to where Captain Fazal was standing at the base of one of the huge ribs which projected high over their heads.

"There are steps up this way," the TGO officer said. He pointed, and Wyo noticed immediately that the steps had been cut into the metal of the rib itself. They ascended steeply for several stories, then curled up and over to a place which could not be seen from the bluff. Wyo tried his luck at the first few steps, then jumped down and said, "We're going to have to be very, very careful, or the people carrying things are liable to get hurt."

"Agreed, sir," Captain Fazal said. "But the signal—from deeper in the wreck—is stronger than ever. And this is the only way I've found up. Unless we want to go farther inland, and try to approach the wreck from a different direction?"

"No," Wyo said, still catching his breath. "This way is as good as any. Though I think it would be smart for us to get up to the top of these stairs and have a look—before we send anyone else up."

Fazal nodded agreement, and began to pick his way up, with Wyo close behind, and Lady Oswight behind him. Wyo had the notion to order her back down, then realized he didn't have the energy to fight with her. Axabrast protectively followed his charge, with Zoam Kalbi following Axabrast. Eventually all of them reached the top of the stairs, and had a proper view into the wreck itself.

The scale was immense. Crumbling sunbaked brick buildings came directly up to the wreck, and mingled between the ribs, so that it was difficult to tell where the ship's internal compartments ended and the newer dwellings began. Everything was clearly sized for human accommodation. Though there was no sign whatsoever that any person had lived there—in the town, or the wreck—for a long time. No skeletons. Nor even loose items, such as abandoned tools. The inhabitants of the place had made a tidy retreat. To where, or for what reason, nobody could tell.

"Lady," Captain Fazal said, "I estimate at least another kilometer of walking, though we're going to have to be more careful than when we left the beach. We don't know the structural integrity retained within. And I wouldn't trust any of the brick dwellings, just because of how obviously vulnerable they've been to the weather."

Lady Oswight gazed out over the wreck, her eyes soaking up the spectacle of her surroundings. Kalbi too, with his infotainer glasses getting still shots and moving imagery. Wyo went after, watching his step, and brought them up short.

"Wait for Fazal to get all of his TGO troops up here," he insisted.

Lady Oswight reluctantly agreed—her eyes continually straying to the arching ribs of the mighty ship, each of which cast a tremendous shadow. Uxmal's rotation lent itself to a natural day and night cycle. Which would or would not be close to the cycles Wyo was used to. Many of the inhabited terrestrials across the Waywork were tidally locked. No day and night cycles at all. Or if there was a day and night cycle, it didn't much matter because living was done in domes, or beneath the surface. Where the rising and setting of the sun didn't matter to those who couldn't live out in the open.

Wyo checked the chronometer on his wrist, and decided that—come dusk—he'd start a timer. Just to see how many hours, minutes, and seconds a local Uxmal rotation might take at this time of the year.

*This time of the year,* Wyo thought, and allowed himself a small smile. Despite his trepidation, he thought it novel that they were on a planet which might actually have seasons. The Constellar capital did, though not as exaggerated as Earth legend. In fact, none of the clement terrestrials in the Waywork had seasonal transitions to match the stories which had passed to them from the Exodus. Earth—the stories said—was a planet of stark contrasts. It was cold and icy in one hemisphere for part of the planet's orbit, then as the axis of the world changed in relation to the sun's rays, the formerly cold hemisphere grew hot, while the formerly hot hemisphere grew cold. And people had *lived* with it. Long before modern fusion power was invented. Humans had been forced to heat themselves with natural fuels, or simply get used to levels of cold, heat, and humidity which most Waywork humans would have considered intolerable.

This particular latitude on Uxmal's surface seemed to be in a mild phase. The overall temperature had been a bit warm, considering the exertion done since leaving the drop module. But not scalding hot, either. Was that the doing of the plants? Wyo had seen moss near the beach, and there was obviously a lot of phytoplankton in the sea. It was theorized—based on what Waywork humans knew of clement terrestrials—that life actually contributed greatly to stabilizing the temperature and precipitation variance of any specific world. Adding complex Earth-based life to the mix stabilized things even more. So that by the current age, all five capitals in the Waywork enjoyed self-sustaining ecologies with comfortable environments. Maybe a little tweaking was occasionally required. But the terraforming projects themselves had each been declared a success long before Wyo was born.

"Thousands upon thousands," Lady Oswight said, snapping Wyo out of his reverie.

"Beg pardon?" Wyo asked.

"You could have put many thousands of people in here, and had plenty of room left over."

"It's an ark," Zoam Kalbi said plainly. "I've studied what we know about the arks which settled the Waywork, and this wreck more or less matches what we know about the originals. They were titanic, because they had to survive centuries traveling between the stars. Practically worlds unto themselves, albeit on a small scale compared to the rest of the cosmos. Obviously the crew—inhabitants?—of this particular ark were attracted to Uxmal by the friendly climate. This world is ripe for seeding with Earth life."

"So why didn't they do it?" Wyo asked.

Everyone slowly looked across the tops of the ruined brick buildings of the town to the pristine shape of the pyramid. The tacit assumption being that whatever had happened, the pyramid was a huge part of it.

"Any hint of a signal from the other drop modules?" Wyo asked.

"Negative," Captain Fazal replied, as some of his people began to join them, while taking their crates up the steps in four- and six-man groups. Once they got a crate to the top, they went back down single file, and brought another up. And then another. And so on, and so forth. Eventually, there was a tidy stack of boxed ammunition, food, and equipment, surrounded on one side by a crescent of people who simply stared at the vastness of the beached ark's interior—hollowed out, over time, by the former inhabitants.

"How about Captain Loper, and the starliners?" Wyo suggested.

"We've tried three times to raise them," Captain Fazal said. "But no luck with that, either. It's not jamming like I'd expect from Nautilan countermeasures. They're just ... sir, it's like they're not *there*."

Wyo swept his hand over his face in frustration.

"Keep trying at regular intervals," he said. "Meanwhile, take a look, and tell us where you want to set up your defensive perimeter."

Captain Fazal used his mechanized binoculars to survey the interior of the wreck, then the town beyond, and the huge ribs which dominated the sky at that range. He suggested keeping the group close to the set of stairs, since they were a funnel point for any enemy trying to come up from the ground. Meanwhile, the interior was a warren of partially dismantled compartments which offered an almost endless number of places in which to hide, or from which to shoot. Fazal theorized as to the possible approaches which might be taken from the town itself, and made hand motions indicating where he wanted his TGO perimeter teams to uncrate their squad weapons, and set up watch.

Lady Oswight, meanwhile, demanded to be able to seek out the source of the ark's transmission.

"It'll be growing dark soon," Wyo said. "We should wait until morning. Besides, none of us has had anything to eat for the better part of a day. Let's get properly camped, allow Captain Fazal to ensure your safety, Lady, and then we can plan for tomorrow."

"Maybe you're right," she said, her shoulders sagging. Then she put her hand to her mouth, and yawned. "I feel like my bones are gaining more weight by the second."

"Aye," Axabrast agreed, his face showing genuine fatigue, for the first time since Wyo had met the man. "The mind is willing, lad, but the body is weak."

For the rest of their daylight time, they set about securing their position, setting up two stoves for heating prepackaged rations, and getting ready to bed down for the night. Unlike their time aboard ship, which was spent in gee hammocks, they'd now be sleeping on hard ground—albeit supported by a thin layer of foam on the bottoms of their sleeping bags.

"Weather?" Zoam Kalbi said at one point.

"What about it?" Axabrast said as he gently stirred a tiny self-contained helping of stew over the hot coils of a stove.

"We have no idea what the patterns on this planet are like. Constellar's capital is known to occasionally have very violent storms, especially along the margins between water and land."

"Not like we can do much about it," Axabrast said. "If a storm comes, lad, we can't exactly fly away, now, can we?"

"He may be right," Wyo said. "We landed in clear air. But that won't last forever. My father used to tell me about a vacation we took—when I was too young to remember—on the Constellar capital. He said we were out on an isthmus, enjoying one of the capital's many waterside resorts, and a squall came up."

"A squall?" Lady Oswight said. "What's that?"

"A kind of sudden, violent weather event," Wyo replied. "Again, I was just a baby when it happened, but my father said he feared for our lives until it was over. The resort suffered a lot of damage. And there were deaths."

"Hard to say where we might ride out a thing like that," Captain Fazal said. "There's nothing in the way of natural shelter here. The land is fairly flat. The wreck itself offers the only protection, and that's assuming the superstructure—what remains of it—is still strong enough to stand against major storms."

"It's held this long," Axabrast grunted. "It'll hold a night longer."

And that seemed to resolve the matter, though Wyo admitted to himself that Kalbi had unsettled him even more than he was already unsettled—by their general predicament. He crawled into his bag, Captain Fazal promising to wake Wyo for the second half of the night watch, still nursing an icy nugget of ill feeling behind his ribs.

When the wind kicked up ferociously three hours later, Kalbi's words seemed viciously premonitory. Behind the wind came slashing rain the likes of which none of them had ever experienced before. The droplets of water were fat, and hit with stinging force. Nobody could hear themselves yelling over both the wind and the crashing sound of the waves on the beach below. The ark itself seemed to take on an acoustic amplification affect, broadcasting the moaning of the wind—through the ribs—and the roar of the ocean too. So that Wyo had to literally scream into the ear of the person standing next to him.

"We can't stay out in this!" he said to Captain Fazal, who'd hurriedly pulled his security teams back from the perimeter.

"But where else is there to go?" the captain shouted back.

They each had waterproof hand lanterns which swayed on waterproof rope handles. The rain pelting down around them came by the bucket. Sleeping bags, open crates, the stoves, everything was getting drenched. Including the people themselves. Wyo shivered, both from cold, and from fear.

Lady Oswight and her majordomo were way ahead of the rest. Two lanterns were already weaving farther into the ark's interior. Wyo shouted after them, waving his hands up and down, but could get no response. He got back in Captain Fazal's ear and roared, "You see to your troops! I'll go after the Lady!"

Wyo thought he saw Zoam Kalbi huddled miserably beneath a waterproof tarp—wrapped like an old woman's shawl.

Wyo went as quickly as he could, in the wake of the Lady Oswight. His steps had become slippery, as water pooling on the surface made footing treacherous. Where exactly those two were going was impossible to say. Wyo guessed that they were simply heading in any direction which seemed to offer temporary respite from the fury of the atmosphere. When he finally caught up with them, he screamed, "We have to stay together as a group!"

"She's panicked!" Axabrast bellowed. "Wouldn't heed me when I called for her to stop!"

Lady Oswight brushed past both of them, and continued to stumble farther into the wreck.

"My Lady!" Axabrast screamed after her—the roaring of the wind, combined with the crashing of the sea, making for a dreadful midnight symphony around them all.

Wyo pursued, and quickly realized Axabrast wasn't directly behind him. He turned to see the old man lying face-first in a puddle of water. He rolled over and tried to get onto his hands and knees. When he held up his lamp, he pointed a finger directly behind Wyo, who turned and saw Lady Oswight's lamp going crazily into the half-deconstructed interior of the ark. She was climbing over, or ducking under, everything in her path. And getting farther and farther away with every second.

For an instant, the two men met each other's gaze. Elvin

was hurt. He couldn't get up, and merely nodded his head at the lieutenant commander. Then Wyo was running after Lady Oswight, trying desperately to avoid slipping. The erratic light from her lantern was all he could see, and his zipsuit squeaked and sloshed with water as he stayed on her trail. Eventually he realized they were getting into parts of the ark which were almost recognizable. Flashes from storm lightning revealed hatchways and corridors.

Suddenly, Lady Oswight's lantern went out. Maybe fifty meters ahead.

Wyo sprinted the distance to try to get to her—or where he thought he'd seen her—then realized his feet were kicking uselessly in midair. The drop-off had been unexpected. He yelped with fright, and felt himself falling, before he thumped into smooth, angled metal, and was suddenly being carried down and away. Water gushed around him, and he sat up, realizing he was being carried through the interior of a huge pipe. His lantern showed very little, except for the walls of the pipe rushing past, and several times he yelped again as further drop-offs left his stomach in his throat.

Until finally, Wyo plunged down at least five meters into a pool which seemed to have no bottom. Swimming lessons—from long ago—kicked in, and Wyo kicked for the surface. He broke through, gasping, and brought his lamp out of the water, while treading with his free arm. A torrent plummeted from overhead into what appeared to be a cavern, though the walls appeared to be almost as smooth as the pipe through which Wyo had just traveled. He spotted the second lantern bobbing at the cavern's far end, though he couldn't see Lady Oswight.

Wyo took the handle of the lantern in his teeth, and swam for all he was worth. In short order, he had the Lady's lantern in hand, and was calling her name with as much breath as he could manage. She was nowhere he could see.

A moment of futile anger swept through him, and he began slamming both lanterns down into the water at his waist—over and over again—while he bellowed Lady Oswight's name into the din of the waterfall.

Her rushing hands almost knocked Wyo over. She came at him through the waist-high water with such force—fingers clawing for balance—he had to wrap his arms around her to contain her terror. She was sobbing, with hair matted across her face and neck, while she shook intensely from both the cold and the adrenaline pumping through her veins.

"I've got you," Wyo said into her ear, though not shouting his words this time. "Hang on tight. We've got to find a way out of here. Just don't let go."

And she didn't. She couldn't say anything, but she allowed herself to be led through the darkness, arms wrapped around his chest, as Wyo held both of their lanterns over his head, trying to find some way out.

Eventually he discovered what appeared to be a metal ladder—the rungs rusty, but solid—and he urged Garsina to climb. She numbly went up, but so slowly that Wyo was afraid she might lose her strength and fall. He came up behind her, pushing her buttocks with a gentle shoulder, until she rolled off the top of the ladder onto what felt like a dry ledge at the ladder's top. Wyo came up alongside her, and took her lantern out of his teeth, setting it down next to her face. Her eyes were wide with fear, and she had bitten her lip. Blood trailed from the wound.

"You and me both," he muttered, and collapsed onto the ledge next to her.

Like the ladder itself, the ledge was metal. And seemed to disappear into dry darkness, away from the echoing drumbeat of the waterfall behind them.

But Wyo didn't have the strength to go farther. He simply cupped Garsina's quivering body to himself, wrapped his arms tightly around her arms—which were already coiled across her chest—and closed his eyes.

The noise of the waterfall got farther and farther away, until it was no noise at all.

# CHAPTER 34

"WE DON'T DARE SEND DOWN AN AEROSPACE PLANE IN THE STORM," General Ekk said, as he pointed to the orbital visuals displayed on Golsubril Vex's wall-sized flatscreen. Once again, she was entertaining an audience in her quarters aboard the *Alliance*. They had arrived in orbit about the target world, with no further surprises from the Constellar ships they were chasing. But unlike the starliners, who had gravity-assisted toward the big jovian at the system's center, *Alliance* and her two sister destroyers were staying put. Vex had no interest in civilian ships, except as ancillary prizes to be taken later. For now, her attention was on the planet itself. Specifically, the images of the pyramid her ship had passed over, just prior to the cloud front occluding *Alliance*'s view.

"How long?" Vex asked.

"Difficult to say," General Ekk said. "The weather could last hours or days. I don't have much experience with such things, to tell you the truth. But analysis estimates that wind speed and shear factor are too dangerous for a landing at this time. Though, we think we may have picked up signs that several Constellar drop modules came down at random points over the land mass."

"Ground operations," Vex said. "Do they pose a threat to our landing as well?"

"Not at that distance. I think our Constellar friends had some problems during deceleration. They were coming in extraordinarily fast when their parent starliners cut them loose. Much faster than any competent Nautilan commander would allow for a similar exercise. They all overshot the target as a result. In some cases, by a hundred kilometers or more."

"All? Are we sure?"

"Analysis indicated that the starliners each carried nine drop modules. In order to execute their deceleration maneuver, some of those drop modules had to have been cannibalized for their retro thruster, which would then augment the pods on the modules which *were* dropped. Tricky business, I say. Too tricky for Constellar, given the results. So, once the weather clears, I think we can proceed to the surface without expecting too much in the way of resistance. Perhaps no resistance at all? Except, there is one odd thing."

"Oh?" Vex said, using her grip slippers to hold herself steady in front of the flatscreen, while her arms were crossed over her chest.

"The repetitive transmission, it's stopped."

"You mean, the transmission in the strange human language?" she asked.

"Yes, Madam Kosmarch. About ten minutes ago. We don't think it's the storm, although the storm was causing a degree of interference—radio being radio."

"We have to assume that something—or someone—is alert to our arrival," Vex said, her fingertips tapping thoughtfully at her biceps. She didn't believe in a coincidence at this juncture.

"That's the most probable answer, yes," Ekk said. His posture in front of the kosmarch remaining ramrod proper, with his palms linked behind the small of his back.

"Prior to the storm, did you see or detect anything which might endanger a landing?"

"We arrived in orbit directly on top of the storm, Madam, so it's difficult to say for sure. We only caught a glimpse of the target—that pyramid—before darkness and clouds blocked the way. Once things are clear, and we get some daylight, I think we can do a proper orbital survey, prior to dispatching our expedition."

"How are preparations?" she asked.

"Going well," Ekk said, and switched the flatscreen's view to his own data table which showed variously colored readiness levels for the different types of stores, people, and equipment which would be going to the surface—along with *Alliance*'s single aerospace plane. The sleek hypersonic ship could hold twenty people, plus the two pilots in the nose. Capable of atmospheric entry, vertical takeoff and landing, as well as a return to space, the aerospace plane was a marvel of modern Nautilan design. Such craft had been in use around the Waywork for a long time, but unlike the bulky clippers—designed to operate with little or no atmosphere—the aerospace plane was built to work in only a few, very specific places in the Waywork. One of them being Nautilan's capital, to which Kosmarch Vex returned from time to time.

This time, though, the craft was being fitted out for rougher operations. The landing gear—built to handle smooth tarmacs—had been replaced with a more robust, bulkier set of splayed-foot touchdown pads, which would not sink into whatever surface the plane found upon landing. Also, the plane's ordinarily vacant missile cradle had been outfitted with a dozen guided rockets of various explosive yields. And the cargo bay had been stuffed with a variety of arms, consumables, and equipment, while the luxurious passenger cabin would be inhabited by Nautilan shock troops wearing full armor, and carrying Nautilan battle rifles.

If there was to be resistance, Vex and her cohort would be ready.

Though Ekk himself would not be joining them.

It had been an argument of some duration. The general being quite adamant that he intended to accompany the kosmarch to the surface. But he was old, not much good in a tactical firefight, and unlike Colonel Jun—the expedition's resident Waymaker expert—possessed no specific knowledge which might prove valuable once the kosmarch had entered the pyramid itself. Because that was her intent. She wasn't much interested in the Constellar forces which had landed ahead of them, nor even in the huge, partially dismantled spacecraft which sat on the beach not far from the pyramid. Those humans who'd come to this place in the past had obviously had a specific interest in the pyramid. Which appeared for all intents and purposes to be alien—not because of the shape, as much as because of the fact that the pyramid had resisted both time and the elements, where the little cluster of dwellings between the wreck and the pyramid had not.

Colonel Jun seemed convinced that the pyramid was a Waymaker artifact, and couldn't help drawing comparisons to the many ancient pyramids known to have existed on Earth prior to Earth's destruction. Was there a connection? Polyhedrons of that style were among the classic shapes of geometry. Any advanced alien civilization would discover and use them early, just as humans had. They were clean, stable, and symmetrical. Aspects which appealed to Vex's own sensibilities. But did this tantalizing congruence of the practical, and the aesthetic, possess real meaning?

Colonel Jun couldn't say, except for emphasizing that they couldn't know more before conducting a thorough boots-on-ground survey. For which the old man would be present, despite his ill health, and despite the fact that Vex didn't like his attitude. Jun had continued to display a flagrant level of nonchalance in Vex's presence. If she'd had another option—a different Waymaker guru—in her employ, she'd have taken that person without a second thought. But Jun was the only man to be had, so to the surface he would go.

Meanwhile, Ekk would remain with *Alliance,* to keep the space around the clement planet secure. With General Ticonner's squadron presumed missing or destroyed—along with the Constellar force he'd been attacking—General Ekk was now all that stood between Vex and additional Constellar ships which might be coming across the Waypoint at any hour. If Vex felt regret at the loss of her number two officer, she didn't show it. Like Ekk, Ticonner had been useful. But she didn't attach emotional significance to any of her men, just as she didn't attach emotional significance to people in general. These could be points of weakness which a military or political rival might exploit. So, Vex had received news of Ticonner's demise with only mild interest—for the sake of the destroyed ships, and their Keys, but not much more. The new system was going to require a thorough salvage sweep once the situation had been stabilized. There were too many Keys now drifting loose in interplanetary space. But the pyramid...that was the clear priority.

Once Vex had what she'd come for, she could leave a small garrison detachment behind, return to orbit with whatever Waymaker knowledge and technology could be taken with her, and return to Jaalit space for the next phase in her plan to conquer this new world.

Colonel Jun had suggested calling it Cheops—the ancient name for a ruler who had existed during the time when Earth men were still actively building pyramids.

"Madam Kosmarch," Ekk said, clicking off the flatscreen, "given the fact that my counterpart's squadron has been destroyed, and the Waypoint now lies unsecured at this system's border, don't you think it would be wise to send at least one destroyer to reconnoiter the Waypoint's perimeter? At this great distance, if any ships do cross—ours, or somebody else's—we won't know about it for precious minutes. And there will be nothing to stop additional Constellar incursion."

"I think at this point, General, we can assume two things. One, if Constellar was capable of moving additional ships across the Waypoint—as a second wave—they'd have done it by now. Just as we'd have done the same. Two, the fact that neither of us have done this, tells me that the odds are still in our favor. It will take more time for Starstate Constellar to reconfigure its defensive posture—in order to move ships into position to cross to Cheops space—than it will for Nautilan reinforcements to arrive in Jaalit space, and make the crossing. Our numerical superiority is our single greatest advantage in this regard. They cannot afford to spare the ships. We *can*. By the time Constellar could send additional ships, it will be far too late. This system will be ours to do with as we please, as will whatever knowledge and technology can be gleaned from the Waymaker pyramid on the surface."

"And if the pyramid itself resists us?" Ekk asked.

Vex considered. The thought of the pyramid posing a threat had not occurred to her. Mostly because the Keys had proven so benign, for so long, what danger could the artifact on Cheops' surface pose? Still, the general had made a valid point. If the pyramid itself was dangerous—boobytrapped, to prevent future meddling by an unnamed enemy?—she would need to designate a course of action.

"Nuclear response, General," Vex said.

"How many?" Ekk said, his face showing a bit of astonishment.

"Assuming I am dead, or incapacitated, use as much of your onboard arsenal—and the arsenal of our two companions in orbit—to level everything. The wreck, the pyramid, all of it."

"Even Keys cannot be destroyed in this way," Ekk said.

"But the site can be irradiated to such a degree that it's practically a no man's land. General, let me be frank. If I cannot possess whatever information and tools are waiting for me down there, *no one can.* You won't be blamed, of course. I'll make the order explicit in your log, prior to my departure. Kosmarchs coming to Cheops after me may be frustrated by the fact that you will have made the artifact untouchable. But then again, if it resists me in any way, why would it not resist them? They can have its secrets when they are smart enough to unlock the puzzle of why it's so dangerous—assuming it even *is* dangerous, which I am not convinced is true."

"Madam Kosmarch, I trust your intuition."

"Thank you, General. And thank you for the latest update. Please alert me when you think the storm has cleared completely enough for us to consider landing. I would like to begin the ground survey as soon as possible."

# CHAPTER 35

ADMIRAL MIKTON WAS ILL. THE *DAFFODIL*'S SURGEON HAD DIAGNOSED Zuri with a serious case of radiation damage. Whether or not it would prove fatal remained unclear. Suffice to say that the medical bay's antirad regimen had been put into full effect, so that instead of conducting operations from the command module, Mikton was doing business from her hammock in the medical bay itself—with tubes running in and out of her arms, while liters of medicated fluid mingled with her blood and tissues. The cells lining her stomach and intestines, had begun to die first. The medicine being streamed into her body was designed to mitigate this problem, as well as combat chromosome damage. But even the best treatments Constellar medical science could come up with weren't proof against truly severe radiation exposure.

Admiral Mikton thought she had maybe a fifty-fifty chance. Which really didn't bother Zuri that much, given what had happened to her Task Group. Losing a beloved officer like Urrl was merely the insult to injury. It was the loss of ships which hurt Constellar the most. Now, more than ever, Zuri's plan *had* to work. And in order for that plan to go the way Zuri wanted, she had to convince the captain and crew of the *Daffodil* to attempt suicide.

"No," said the *Daffodil*'s skipper, who was floating upright next to Zuri's hammock in the medical bay.

"I'll make it an order if I have to," Zuri said. "But I'd rather not."

"Ma'am, we should be collecting Keys, and getting them

273

back to Oswight Space," the *Daffodil*'s captain said firmly. "With those keys in our possession, we can quickly turn around some of Commodore Iakar's security flotilla, and be back across the Slipway in short order. If protecting Uxmal system is the priority, I see no reasonable alternative."

"And then Nautilan simply blows away whatever ships we've moved, and we're back to square one," Zuri said. "No. Trust me. I've seen this show before. I know how it ends, Captain. The only chance we've got is to throw out the script, and do something they'll never expect us to do. Even if it means *Daffodil*'s destruction. It will buy Starstate Constellar the time necessary to move heavy assets. Destroyers and cruisers. The big stuff. While Nautilan is girding its loins for another strike on their side of the Waypoint, Constellar can reallocate enough capital ships to Oswight and Uxmal space alike, to make a second Nautilan attempt on Uxmal incredibly difficult. But we have to strike *now*."

"The Keys are too important—" the captain began, and was cut off.

"Even if we collect whatever Keys can be easily found, and try to shuttle more of Iakar's ships over, they don't have enough Waypoint pilots for the work. And not every ship in Iakar's force can be quickly converted to Key use, regardless. So, we wait, and lose. Or we do something crazy, and maybe win."

"Admiral, it's not that I can't see the potential benefit of your plan. I can. It's just that we don't even know if we can successfully wire the Nautilan code box into our communications array without damaging the code box beyond repair. That's sensitive Nautilan technology being joined to sensitive Constellar technology, and our systems aren't able to talk to each other very well at all. We'll be lucky if the two engineering specialists I have aboard are up to the task. We're not exactly fitted out for this kind of work, you know."

"I know," Zuri said. "And I am sorry things can't be done in a more regimented fashion. In a sane universe, we'd collect the Keys, take the code box back to Oswight space, and turn it over to DSOD forensic intelligence for a careful dissection. But Uxmal has changed things, and we're not necessarily allowed to take the safe road anymore. In fact, I strongly suspect it's been us taking the safe road—all this time—which has gotten us into our hole against Nautilan in the first place. They know our doctrine like we know their doctrine. And their doctrine is specifically designed to wait out our doctrine. Decade, after decade, after decade. The numbers are firmly on their side. And have been all of our lives. Constellar is not going to win against that. Not unless we do something unexpected. And there is no better time than the present."

*Daffodil*'s commander still seemed hesitant.

"Please, Captain Garmot, don't waste this chance. Commodore Urrl paid for it with his life. So did the crew of the *Hallibrand*. We can't go back to Oswight space reporting that we lost the First Family yacht without significant payoff. There has to be a *reason* for it all."

"You mean, *you* need a reason, Admiral," the captain said.

Zuri closed her eyes, and swallowed. Then opened her eyes again.

"That too," she said. "I've led a lot of people to Uxmal space to die, apparently. And I might be one of them. Clearly, I've not asked anyone to do anything which I am not willing to do myself. But we've got to think about long-term ramifications. If Starstate Nautilan claims Uxmal, it might snuff out the only candle flame of hope Constellar's seen in the Waywork for a long, long time. We have to keep Uxmal under our flag. There has been nowhere else for Constellar to go, while Nautilan slowly eats us alive. And when they're done with Constellar, it'll be Starstate Yamato next—whom they hate almost as much as they hate us—then they'll go for their sometimes allies, Starstates Amethyne and Sultari. And when the whole Waywork is under Nautilan control, what future will there be for the human race? From which world will a successful rebellion spring?"

Captain Garmot stared at his grip shoes, which rested lightly on the deck.

"You know I'm right," she said.

"Doesn't make it any easier," he replied. "What am I supposed to tell this crew?"

"Tell them they're doing it for their brothers' children. And their sisters' children. Hell, tell them it's for the sake of all children across the Waywork. A moment in human history when, if we're successful, everything pivots. Look, Captain, for all I know, even if I order you to do this, once you walk out of the medical bay you could tell your crew whatever you want. Declare me medically unfit. In your position, I'd be tempted. But I am begging you. Please don't sell out the future."

Captain Garmot slowly looked up at his boss, and pushed a hand out toward her.

"May God favor the bold and the free," he said with resignation in his tone.

"Victory with honor," Zuri said, and shook his hand.

# CHAPTER 36

WYODRETH ANTAGEAN STIRRED AWAKE. HIS MUSCLES WERE COLD, and cramped. It was agony uncurling himself from around Garsina Oswight's damp, warm body. But he thought he'd heard something other than the sound of water splashing in the distance.

Gently rolling over—body silently complaining—Wyo looked up into a human face. The woman was old. With skin the color of light chocolate, and wavy white hair, bordering on curls. She held one of their two lamps in one of her hands, revealing a flowing smock which appeared to have been handmade, and a similarly handmade tunic over the top of the smock. She'd certainly dressed appropriately for the weather, though Wyo couldn't begin to guess who she actually was. A lovely flame motif had been woven into each of her sleeves, at the cuff. And the smock sprouted a healthy bundle of turtlenecked fabric under her chin.

The woman's brown eyes watched Wyo, without blinking.

"Who are you?" Wyo asked, realizing his voice was almost gone. He'd shouted so loudly, so many times, his vocal chords were battered to a rasp.

When the woman didn't say anything, Wyo asked again. Then, something in his brain kicked him for not thinking more clearly, and he switched to using Mariclesh.

Now, the old woman reacted. She smiled slightly, and stood up.

"A friend," she said, her Mariclesh fluent, but the accent strange—like nothing Wyo had ever heard in the Waywork before. Was she possibly from Starstate Amethyne? Of the international traveling Wyo had done—for the company—Amethyne was the one Starstate he knew least well.

"The trip through my water catchment system could have killed you."

"I'm surprised it didn't," Wyo admitted, looking down at his soaked zipsuit and armor, neither of which had prevented about a gallon of water from pouring down his neck, filling the cavities between the suit and his skin with an uncomfortable *squishiness*.

"Is she alive?" the woman asked, motioning to Lady Oswight with the lamp.

Wyo checked Lady Oswight's neck.

"Yes," he said. "But I don't know what kind of mental shape she'll be in when she wakes up. The storm scared her senseless."

"Storms are why I live down here," the old woman said. "Been a while since I had visitors."

Wyo stared at her.

"How...how *long*?" he asked.

"That's part of my problem," the old woman said. "It's been so long, I honestly have no idea. You got a name, son?"

"Wyodreth Antagean," he said.

The woman's mouth silently made the odd—for her—vowel and syllable motions.

"Wyo for short," he said.

"*Why*-ohh," she said carefully. "Not the usual sort of man's name, like John or Patrick."

Now it was Wyo's turn to silently sound out the unusual vowels and syllables.

"You don't know those names?" she asked.

"No," Wyo admitted.

The woman grunted at him, then turned on a heel, and began walking away from the edge of the ledge, with their lantern still in her hand.

"Wait, where are you going?" Wyo asked, his voice still raw from shouting.

"The hell away from here," she said. "You better follow. And bring her too."

The lieutenant commander stood up—very shakily, and feeling extremely sore—then stooped to pick up the Lady Oswight. She was heavy in his arms, and limp, but not so bad that he couldn't cradle her to his chest. After a few steps, she murmured and stirred, then instantly wrapped both arms around his neck, and let out a squeaking shriek into the plates of armor on his chest.

"It's okay," Wyo said. "I've got us. Or, well, *somebody* has got us."

The Lady Oswight gradually turned her head to look over her shoulder, at the old woman's back as she walked purposefully through the metal-walled corridor. It led away from the ledge where Wyo and the Lady Oswight had taken refuge.

"Who...?" the Lady Oswight whispered.

"No idea, yet," he whispered back to her.

The corridor twisted and turned, appearing to make several switchbacks, until it ultimately terminated in an oval-shaped, high-ceilinged room decorated with what appeared to be chandeliers. The light hurt Wyo's eyes, and he stopped momentarily, blinking away spots, before taking a few more steps—and stopping again.

The old woman was standing in the middle of a painstakingly tiled global map, though of what globe Wyo could not be sure. It could have passed for one of the Waywork capitals, or even Uxmal itself, save for the fact that the shapes of the land masses and the seas were totally foreign to Wyo's eyes. Lady Oswight looked down, and then patted Wyo quickly on the shoulder. He gradually set her on her feet, allowing her to brace herself on one of his arms as she stared at the design, then she looked up at the old woman—who simply watched them with a kind of dispassionate curiosity.

"Do you recognize it?" the Lady Oswight asked him.

"No," Wyo said. "But I get the feeling she could tell us more."

The Lady Oswight took a few hesitant steps, futilely attempting to straighten her half-dried, frizzy hair, then brought herself up to a proper First Family posture and said, "I am Garsina Oswight, of the First Family Oswight. I am visiting your planet on a mission of exploration. How may I address you?"

The old woman merely continued to watch, and said nothing.

"Mariclesh," Wyo hinted. "It's the only thing she's understood."

The Lady Oswight repeated herself, this time in the ancient international tongue.

"You sound like royalty," the old woman said, and took a few steps closer. She slowly circled the Lady Oswight, looking the younger woman up and down, then stepped away and pronounced, "Brazilian."

"What?" Garsina said, startled.

The old woman went to one of the land masses on the floor map, and tapped a toe in its upper corner.

"Right here," the old woman said. "If I didn't know better."

Garsina stared at Wyo, her mouth half open, then looked back at the old woman.

"We don't understand what that means," Wyo said. "We're from Starstate Constellar."

The old woman stepped over to Wyo now, and gradually circled him, looking from head to toe. Then she stepped back and pronounced, "Euro, but with some other blood mixed in, so make it American."

This time she went to a different land mass on the map, and tapped her foot.

"Again, if I didn't know better."

"Is that . . . is that supposed to be *Earth*?" Garsina asked, trying to be gentle—her voice every bit as hoarse as Wyo's.

"Yes it is. I was born there."

Wyo and Garsina exchanged glances, then he asked, "What's your name?"

"I'm called Lethiah," the old woman said.

"Are there other people here like you?"

"None like me," she said firmly. "Haven't been any like me in a long, long time."

"*How* long?" Garsina asked.

The old woman considered, her mouth making a sour frown, then she shrugged. "Like I told him, that's part of the problem. Too much time goes by, the human brain . . . gets fuzzy on certain details. The men of Earth used to chase immortality. I am here to assure you it's *not* all it's cracked up to be."

Wyo and Garsina exchanged still more startled glances, then Wyo stepped forward a few paces and stood on the continent where the old woman had most recently stood.

"What is this 'American'? Is it a place?"

"*Was* a place, and a people," Lethiah replied. "Hasn't been an American in the universe for a long, long time."

"But you said your memory is . . . fuzzy. How can we trust anything you're telling us?"

"How can you *not* trust what I am telling you?" the old woman said, the corner of her mouth curling up slightly. "You're here, on this planet, because I *wanted* you to be here."

"Is this because of the Waymakers?" Garsina asked.

"Do you mean the *Others* who made the starlanes over which you travel?"

"Yes! They lived a long time ago. They weren't human."

"Lord, don't I know it," Lethiah said, her face taking on a bitter expression. Then she turned and started walking to a different corridor which branched away from the oval room with the floor map.

"Wait—we just want to ask questions!" Garsina said.

When Lethiah did not stop, Garsina walked after her, and Wyo walked after Garsina. The water in his zipsuit still made things uncomfortable, but he ignored the feeling, and stayed on Garsina's trail. The new corridor twisted up and around on itself, in spiral-ramp fashion, until the old woman stopped at what appeared to be a glass doorway into a mammoth hydroponics facility. Inside, more lights—this time, glaring as brightly as the sun itself—hung down from the ceiling. The floor was all rich brown, moist soil, with row upon row of familiar-looking plant life. Corn. Tomatoes. Peas. Lettuce. Potatoes. And around the perimeter of the bay, large fruit-bearing trees, out of which strolled a host of floppy-eared versions of the very same animals Waywork people routinely slaughtered for beef. The beasts stopped short of the vegetables, barred by what appeared to be thin wire running around the tilled rows. An electric fence?

"There's enough vegetables and meat here to feed tens of people," Garsina said, looking through the transparent wall in front of her.

"Like I said, gone," Lethiah murmured. "Just like you all, if you don't do something about it soon."

Wyo froze in place.

"What?"

"I told you, son, I brought you here for a reason. The Others didn't give us much of a clue when we landed. We tried the best we could to figure out how their shit works. Crazy-making stuff, really. But then, you all know that, if you've been using those starlanes. What is it you call... the Waywork? The Others built it. But the Others didn't stick around. Wish they had. Or maybe we can be glad that they didn't? I've gradually started to think the Others don't have minds like people have minds. Their thoughts go in... very strange directions."

"If what you say is true," Wyo said, "and you had something to do with the new Slipways opening to this system—why did you do it? What are we supposed to be afraid of?"

"I can't be too sure," Lethiah admitted, then turned away from them, and walked back down the spiral corridor, returning to the floor map room. Wyo and Garsina quickly followed.

"This isn't making sense," Garsina said, becoming frustrated. "Are you aware that there's a war going on right now? Men and women are being killed."

"War," Lethiah said, grunting, with a knowing frown on her face. "It's probably the one common denominator that makes us all human. Been going on since Cain slew Abel, if you believe in that kind of thing, like my daddy did. You think you're in a war now? I'm here to tell you, you don't *know* war yet. Because something's happening out there. I've been watching the rest of the galaxy for a long, long time. You all think it's all about the Others and their Waywork. But there are bigger, stranger things in the universe than the Others. And pretty soon, you're going to be meeting them. Or they're going to be meeting you, whichever."

"How?" Garsina asked. "Can they use the Waywork like we do, with Keys?"

"Keys?" Lethiah asked.

Garsina crouched, and mimicked a Waypoint pilot putting her hands on the spherical surface of a Key.

"Ohhhh," Lethiah said, nodding her head in understanding. "You mean the Anchors."

"Is that what you call them?"

"Yup. Some of them are big, some of them are small. Not all of them are for the same function. A few of them have many functions. They're the physical manifestation of Otherspace as it touches *our* universe. We can use them to do certain things."

"We only ever use them for starships," Wyo said. "My...*daddy*, he built a whole company around this kind of activity. We use the Keys to transport people and goods across the Slipways—your starlanes—all over the Waywork. We used Keys to come here, to this system, using three of our starliners, in fact. If a Key can be used for anything else, we've never discovered what it might be."

"That's because the Others didn't want you taking apart their playground equipment," Lethiah said. "Or at least that's what we assumed, once we came here. It took me *forever* to learn how to use the Anchors well enough to get a pair of starlanes opened up when the need was urgent. Been watching your Waywork for a long time too. Couldn't do anything about it until now."

"Are you saying you can *make* Slipways?" Garsina asked incredulously.

"Not me," Lethiah said. "I had to go up to the Temple and convince the machines. They're the ones who did the work."

Wyo listened, and looked around him. Wherever they'd ended up during the storm, it was clearly hidden from the surface. Were they still inside the ark? It seemed as if this strange person had been expecting them, and she talked as if she knew a great deal about things which had been mysterious until now. But was anything she saying credible? Wyo's misgivings—about Lethiah's mental state—continued to grow.

"Ma'am," he finally said, "we've got people who are still out in that storm. I don't know where we are right now, but we need to get back to them."

"Yes, we do," Garsina agreed.

"Storms don't last more than a few hours this time of the year," Lethiah said. "It's the Temple you need to worry about."

"Are you talking about the pyramid?" Garsina asked.

"Yes. That's where the machines live."

"We haven't gone there yet. We wanted to find the source of the human-made beacon first."

"And so you have," Lethiah said, bowing with her arms open wide, then stood up straight. "I turned the beacon on so that anyone who used the starlane would know where to come. Once I found the two of you, I turned it off."

"Others will come," Wyo said. "Starstate Nautilan is sure to land an expedition of their own."

"Is that bad?" Lethiah asked.

"Of course it's bad!" Garsina replied loudly. Then seemed to think better of herself, and said, "Starstate Nautilan will kill or imprison all of us. Especially you, Lethiah. They'll think you have the answers they want."

"Answers to what, exactly?"

Wyo and Garsina exchanged glances.

"The same questions we have," she admitted.

"And you won't kill or imprison me?" Lethiah asked. She said it without blinking.

"Absolutely not," Wyo said. "We have rules about that."

"And how do I know I can trust your 'rules,' young man?"

"Well, the fact is . . . uhhh . . . look, we're strangers to you, and you're a stranger to us. I'd like to find out how Captain Fazal and his TGO troops are doing, in addition to Mister Axabrast and Mister Kalbi."

"Your friends on the surface?" Lethiah asked.

"Yes. But our wireless communications have been terrible since coming here."

"That's the machines at the Temple again. They do that sometimes."

"Why?" Garsina asked. "And what are they?"

"Who knows why. I said it before: The minds of the Others went in strange directions. The machines they left behind think in strange directions too."

"*Thinking* machines?" Garsina blurted.

"I have a feeling you two might feel better if you freshen up. You look and smell like a couple of drowned rats. I have a place—not used in a long time—where you can do that. And there's food if you want it."

Wyo's stomach rumbled.

"We'll accept whatever hospitality you care to offer," Wyo said.

Lethiah bowed again, then straightened, and led them to another corridor which seemed to run roughly on the same level as the map room. Eventually they came into another high-ceilinged chamber which had a number of plush, overstuffed couches and chairs arrayed around low tables on which sat various pieces of nonrepresentational sculpture. There were closed doors at regular intervals around the exterior of the room. Lethiah opened one of them, and waved her hand over a small panel in the wall just inside the door. Lights quickly brightened to reveal a large bed, another overstuffed couch and chair, as well as what appeared to be an anteroom that could have been a lavatory. When Wyo walked in, he stared at the space. It didn't look too different from the executive suites aboard his starliners, save for the fact that there were no gee hammocks. The linens on the bed looked use worn, but serviceable, as did the furniture. Everything appeared to have been kept immaculately clean.

"Meet me back in the big room in thirty minutes," Lethiah said. "I'll bring something hot, and something cold."

Without waiting for a reply, Lethiah turned to walk away.

"Just one room for both of us?" Wyo asked.

"Is that a problem?" Lethiah said.

"Well, it's just...We're not..."

"We're not *together* like that," Garsina finished for him.

Lethiah's eyes widened, then she slapped a hand over her face—the tendons and knuckles looking particularly pronounced with age.

"My fault for assuming," she said. "When I found you both balled up together on the ledge like that...well, my mistake. Of course. This way, girl."

Garsina was shown to a doorway on the opposite side of the room from where Wyo stood, and entered.

Wyo went to the lavatory first, and evacuated not just his bowels, but the hygiene system of the zipsuit too. Swift-running water washed everything away, as Wyo had seen when using similar facilities on the Constellar capital. Facilities on a starliner were quite different, by necessity, as were lavatories on many terrestrials where water was at a premium. Uxmal had no lack of water, thus Lethiah could afford to use it any way she wished. Or so it seemed.

Wyo hung the various pieces of his armor and zipsuit on a row of hooks in the lavatory wall. Overhead, he could see a bank of lights that was not on, as well as what looked like a grate for a fan. Moving his hand over the control plate near the lavatory entrance both activated and deactivated the lights, and the fan. Then he discovered the heat lamp, and was grateful for both the warmth, and the dry air moving across his skin. He decided to leave them on—to dry his zipsuit and equipment—while he experimented with the huge wash basin. When the water coming out of that spigot proved scalding hot, he pushed his fingers on the control plate—everything controlled by proximity or contact, not switches per se—until the temperature eased off. And before long he had a robustly hot pool.

Cabinets revealed towels, robes, and large chunks of what appeared to be soap.

"The boys on the surface will want some of this," Wyo muttered to himself as he climbed in. The water felt glorious. After so much time using gee showers—water also being at a premium on a starliner—it was an almost obscene luxury to be able to sit in a tub for a quick, hot soak.

Wyo gave himself five minutes to just savor the sensation, then used one of the chunks of soap to lather up, followed by a vigorous brushing with the palm scrubber sitting at the basin's lip. When he was done, he put one of the towels on the tile floor, and stepped onto it, while using one of the towels to wipe himself off. The moving air, combined with the heat lamp, dried him very quickly. And there were even brushes and combs on shelves near the wash for washing hands. All as one might expect for civilization across the Waywork.

Checking his zipsuit, Wyo decided to give it more time, and instead opted for one of the robes he'd found. It was all-natural fiber, and felt both delightfully smooth and crisply dry to the touch. Like the linens on the bed. There were also some sandals for his feet.

Padding out of the lavatory, and then out of his assigned room, Wyo couldn't help but wonder who had lived there before him.

He found Garsina already seated on a stool at a bar along one side of the room. Lethiah had put out bowls filled with steaming, cubed potatoes, several kinds of hot vegetables, three or four different sauces, and a large roast from which healthy slices had been taken, and laid on three plates. Lethiah was already eating—her portion seeming dainty compared to Garsina's, which was huge—and Wyo's stomach again rumbled at him as he took his seat.

"You grow, harvest, butcher, and cook all of this by yourself?" he asked the old woman.

"Only way it can be done," she said, chuckling.

Wyo looked at his plate, and at the utensils and cloth napkin to either side.

"If you're worried about being poisoned, Lady Oswight seems to think it's just fine."

"It's not that," Wyo said. "It's just…this is all very strange, and very unexpected."

"To me as well," Lethiah said between small bites. "When I convinced the machines in the Temple to build starlanes to the rest of your Waywork, I had no idea what I might be getting myself into."

"How did you even know we were there?" Wyo asked. "And if you did, why didn't you let us know *you* were here? I mean, sooner than now?"

Lethiah carefully set her fork and knife down, and laced her fingers together under her chin.

"It's like this. When we set down on this world, we didn't even know your Waywork existed. All we knew was that this place was the first hospitable world we'd seen since we left Earth."

"You *cannot* be that old," Wyo said. "Nobody lives that long."

"Nor should they," Lethiah said, the tone in her voice—still using fluent Mariclesh—sounding regretful. "But I'll get to that in a minute, son. My point now is, we had no idea who the Others were, nor that they had created the starlanes adjacent to this star system. All we saw was a world where we might be able to grow things. Start over again. It had been such a long time since we left Earth, and a lot of people had already died. By the time we set down here, I was one of the few originals left. I was surrounded by the grandchildren and great grandchildren of men and women who'd been my own age at departure."

"So if *you* survived this long, how come nobody else did?" Wyo demanded, putting his own utensils down, and glaring at the old woman.

"Back on Earth—a long, long time ago—people became obsessed with longevity medicine. That was one of the things which started the fighting. Only the very wealthy had access to longevity treatments, and everybody else did not. Also, the treatments worked differently for each individual. Some people benefitted enormously. Others, almost not at all. Only a few of us seemed to get the maximum benefit."

"Which was?" Garsina asked.

"I'm still here, aren't I?" Lethiah said. "I am the outermost outlier at the very edge of the bell curve. The freak. Like Methuselah. Do you even know who that is?"

Wyo and Garsina shook their heads.

"In very ancient Earth times, he was the man who lived longer than them all. The Great Flood got him, finally. And sometimes I think he must have been grateful for it too."

"He died?"

"Killed by the wrath of God, but yes."

"Why would anyone be grateful for death?"

Lethiah stared down at her plate—at the meager meal, still only half eaten.

"It *is* possible to grow weary of life, son. You're too young to understand. But when you've been alive as long as I have, you realize that life is a kind of prison. There is only so much you can see, and so much you can do. I've taught myself dozens of vocations and professions. Become adept at any number of crafts and hobbies. Including musical instruments. But eventually you get bored with it all. And you can forget. I always thought it would be like learning to ride a bicycle."

"What's that?" Wyo asked.

"Two wheels, with pedals, and you push them to make yourself go," Lethiah said, mimicking her hands on handlebars. "What I mean to say is, once you learn to ride a bicycle, you never forget. But I've lived long enough to realize you can't know everything, and make it stick. You have to pick and choose which things to keep up on, and which things to let go of."

"Everybody does that," Wyo said, still not sure he believed what he was hearing.

"But, boy," Lethiah said, slapping her hand on the bar, "I've forgotten more in my time than you could *ever* hope to know in yours. And that's *depressing,* you understand? Why go to the trouble to teach yourself something, when you'll have to decide to eventually let it all fall away again later? Took me at least a couple centuries to figure that one out."

"But even if you're as old as you say you are," Wyo said, "where are the other humans who should be here? Where are their descendants?"

"That's the Temple again," Lethiah said.

"I don't understand," Garsina said. "Is the pyramid bad?"

"It's not good, nor is it bad," Lethiah said. "The Temple just is. It's the workshop where the Others built the starlanes. Or at least where they created the machines who built and still maintain the starlanes. The Others aren't around anymore. I don't think they've been around for a very long time."

"We know this already," Garsina said. "There are artifacts left. I've studied some of them. Just scraps, really. But we know that the Waymakers haven't existed in this region of the galaxy for hundreds of thousands of years."

"That's about right," Lethiah said. "Though we didn't know the truth at first. We thought the machines in the Temple *were* the Others. We learned better. And the people who came with me to this planet? We found out very quickly that living in the

Temple's shadow has a price. We obviously landed where we landed because we wanted to find out who the Temple builders were. We'd never seen actual aliens before. We'd speculated that they must exist, but never before had any living human discovered proof. And the Temple was proof! But it cost us."

"How?"

"After we landed, we immediately got to work trying to explore not just the Temple, but establishing a city as well. We partially dismantled our ship—you've seen that already—and used what we could of the local materials to create new buildings. Everything went wonderfully. We were thriving. Or so we thought. Then, some of the women began to complain. They weren't having children. Also, the crops and animals we introduced to the surface eventually died without reproducing. The only place we *could* grow food successfully was here. In the farm spaces, like the one I showed you earlier. As long as we didn't grow those animals or those plants on the surface, they did okay. But the people? All of us had been on the surface, and especially inside the accessible places in the Temple. When it became apparent that we were sterile—even the children—it was too late to do anything about it."

"That's horrible!" Garsina said, her eyes wide with shock.

"Yes it was," Lethiah said. "You have no idea how badly that single piece of news hurt us. Even those of us who'd had the longevity treatments. Or maybe I should say, *especially* those of us who'd had the longevity treatments? We got to watch everything slowly fall apart. The suicides. People simply giving up. Eventually it was down to just a few dozen of us. Like I said, the freaks. We knew we were doomed, but we made it our mission to try to understand as much about the Temple and the machines as we could. Especially the Anchors. Though we couldn't use those too much without losing our minds."

"The same is still true for us," Garsina said. "Prolonged Key use is guaranteed to induce insanity, as well as death."

"Eventually we became aware of the fact that other ships—survivors from Earth—had found other hospitable worlds in the relative vicinity of ours. Though we didn't dare announce ourselves. Why invite more people here, to share our fate? It would have been cruel, especially knowing that our warnings for them to stay away would not have been heeded. So we stayed quiet.

And watched the skies. And listened with our radio telescopes. And also with some of the devices in the Temple, which we gradually came to understand on a limited level. We only learned after the fact that the starlanes were possible. But by then most of us were gone, and there was no hope of resurrecting industry sufficient to build new spacecraft. Our original plan had been for future generations to do that. And of course, there *were* no future generations."

Wyo stared at his plate. He'd not made much time for relationships, to say nothing of a family. He'd followed in his father's footsteps, and allowed Antagean Starlines to become his focus. But now that he was listening to this strange old woman talk, he realized how devastatingly lonely she must have been.

Tears were dropping down Garsina Oswight's face, and one of her hands had moved over to grasp Lethiah's forearm.

"I'm so sorry," she said. "It must have been agony."

"It was," Lethiah agreed.

"But we've seen life on the surface," Wyo said. "Down at the beach."

"Primitive life that's *native* to this planet," Lethiah said. "Life that got used to the Temple during its construction and the early days of full operation. We did seismographic studies. There's a shaft of some sort, directly under the Temple. It goes all the way down through the planet's mantle. To the core, we figured. And it's *using* the core for power. So much so, this entire planet's geological cycle abruptly ground to a halt about the same time as the Temple's appearance. Do you understand? All the energy from the radioisotope decay of an entire *world* is being funneled up into the Temple. Where the machines subsist on it, and use it."

"To form new Slipways," Garsina guessed.

"Yes, and to keep the extant starlanes maintained."

"And this is connected to the sterilization of Earth life?"

"You asked me about why your communications aren't working. The sterilization is connected. Something about the functioning of the Temple throws out particles, or waves, or something else entirely. It's the strange, non-Einsteinian nature of the Others' technology, and their ability to access a universe beyond our own."

"We call it Overspace," Garsina said. "It's where starships exist for an infinitesimally short span of linear time when they are in transit between Waypoints—which are the specific regions of space

at the edge of every star system in the Waywork, where the Keys—
your Anchors—can be used. But if the pyramid is causing some
kind of Overspace disruption that is harmful to Earth life, how
come nobody who's used the Waywork ever experienced a problem?"

"The starlanes are not the source of their own power," Lethiah
said. "And neither are the Anchors."

"Assuming everything you've said is true," Wyo said, choosing his words, "I still don't understand how you can be the only
survivor left alive from Earth. We know there were many arks
launched before Earth was destroyed. Some of them found the
Waywork. Others—like yours—went elsewhere. There must have
been other people who received the longevity treatment, and
survived?"

"Maybe there are," Lethiah said. "And if so, I pity them. I
pity us all. God did not intend for people to live forever. Not
since He threw us all out of the Garden."

"What does that mean?" Wyo asked.

"I think I know what it means," Garsina said. "We have a
belief in the Waywork, called the Word. Some people take it seriously. Most do not. Part of the Word says that when the universe
was created, people—our essence—was one with God. But when
we chose to live corporeal lives, we descended to a lower plane
of existence. Became mortal. And could never go back again.
Except only at death."

"That's about what Daddy said, when I was a little girl,"
Lethiah said. "Even the First Man had to die some time, and he
lived much longer than most. I lost track of my years, but I have
a hunch I've beaten them all by now. And if there are more like
me—out there, somewhere—it's a hell of an existence. Listen to
me, you two. You have to get *off* this world, and soon. Before
whatever sterilized me, sterilizes you too. Don't let the Others'
infernal technology take away your babies. Find somebody. Hell,
you'd make a fine couple yourselves. Give yourselves to the new
generation. Make them smart, but more importantly, teach them
how to be wise."

"What's the difference?" Wyo asked.

"Knowledge is what you *think* you know, boy. But then you
take what you think you know, and you hurl it against the wall
of reality so that it smashes into little pieces. What you pick up
off the floor? *That* is wisdom."

"Was it wisdom that spurred you to convince these Waymaker devices—these machines—to build the new Slipways?" Garsina asked.

"I hope so," Lethiah said. "Because something is coming. None of you know it yet. But I know it. The machines know it too. They don't care. But *I* care. Because if your civilization in the Waywork is obliterated, humanity might be extinguished from the galaxy."

"What could possibly destroy every system in the Waywork?" Wyo said, letting his fork clatter on his plate in exasperation. "For all we know you've been telling us lies. How are we supposed to trust any of this?"

"I can take you into the Temple," Lethiah said. "I can show you some of what I've seen. Including how I talk to the machines. Maybe then you'll believe me? Because it's important that you do. Too many lives are depending on it."

"Starstate Nautilan might get there first," Wyo said. "They've got to be in orbit already. And if the storm has broken, they might even be coming to the surface."

# PART FOUR

# CHAPTER 37

GOLSUBRIL VEX'S AEROSPACE PLANE DESCENDED INTO CHEOPS'
atmosphere with ease. She rode in a gee chair directly behind the
pilot, with Colonel Jun sitting in a gee chair in the aisle across from
her, and their detachment of troops behind them. Vex's only change
to her plan prior to departure had been to add the young Waypoint
pilot whom Vex had observed earlier in the expedition. She was a
nervous little thing, unused to the physical sensation of atmospheric
flight. While Jun craned his neck and looked out his window,
the Waypoint pilot kept her face buried in a crash pillow braced
on her knees. Jun had promised to tell her when it was all over.

The surface of Cheops was mostly barren. Though water
stretched across vast distances, it was the same uniform green-
blue throughout, and there was no foliage on the land. Some of
the escarpments and fields of boulders appeared to harbor primitive plant life, clinging to the surface of the rocks. But there were
no forests, nor large animal life from what anyone could see. Just
kilometer after kilometer of blank, promising desolation. Aching for
someone with a vision to take hold of it, and remake it to her liking.

Vex closed her eyes, and imagined—at some future point—the
surface studded with cities, and vast tracts of farmland spread
throughout. It would take centuries. Vex herself would not live
to see the project through to its completion. But her fingerprints
would be deeply embedded in this world, which would serve as
her stepping stone—Nautilan's gateway—into the wider galaxy.

Vex eagerly looked out her window as they approached the

pyramid. It was even larger, when viewed up close, than it had appeared from orbit. At least two kilometers tall. Or more? A tiny tuft of cloud hung around the pyramid's peak, while the sides gleamed perfectly in the post-storm sunlight of the new morning. An etched pattern of geometric lines covered the pyramid's surface, repeating itself on each of the four faces. What those lines meant was just one of many puzzles to be solved. Vex was eager for a personal inspection. Especially since Constellar posed little threat to her now.

"Anything on wireless?" she asked the pilot.

"No, Madam Kosmarch," the man said. "And our connection to *Alliance* has broken up. That's normal during atmospheric entry, but we shouldn't still be having problems. I'll keep trying."

"But the beacon—coming from the beached vessel—hasn't repeated?"

"No, Madam."

"What about Constellar signals on the surface?"

"Their wireless is encrypted, just like ours. We wouldn't be able to decrypt it."

"But it would be detectable."

"Yes, Madam. Nothing yet."

Colonel Jun looked over at her.

"It's entirely possible the storm got them," he said.

"It is," she agreed. "But I somehow suspect our Constellar friends can't be gotten rid of so easily. Their drop modules were scattered, not destroyed. And if the occupants of the module which landed near the beached wreck were able to seek shelter within? They could be alive and well."

"We should send the spaceplane up immediately, to bring down more men," Jun said.

"I agree, Colonel. I've already given instructions to that effect. But first things first. We need to find a way into that pyramid. Everything we came all this way for—what our men and women have died to obtain—is in there."

"Assuming we can even *get* inside," Jun said.

"Do you really think the Waymakers would build it without an entrance?"

"They built the Keys with no obvious way to access their interior. We've been trying to figure that mystery out for as long as we've known about the Keys. If this pyramid is the same, you may have come all this way for nothing."

Vex eyed the old man. He should have added *Madam Kosmarch* on the end of his sentence.

"No," Vex said. "The humans who originally came to Cheops found something there. I see every sign of it."

"Maybe what they found was too much for them to handle?" Jun opined. "We've been using the Keys for so long, to such good effect, we forget that we don't understand anything about the Waymakers or their motives. If this is a Waymaker artifact—and I think we're absolutely correct to assume it is—what we discover about it may not be to our liking. What if the pyramid is a weapon of some sort?"

"A weapon to do what, Colonel? Against whom?"

"Again, we can't read the minds of the Waymakers, who aren't here to tell us what they intended. But whoever these first people were, something went very wrong for them after they landed their ark. These were men and women from Earth, or at least their descendants. They would have been very eager to remake this world in Earth's image, just as the founders of all the Starstates were. Yet, for whatever reason, the humans who came to this world went extinct. They landed, took half their ship apart for technology and raw materials, began the construction of the first city, and... stopped. Just seemingly quit the project. Or died off before it could be completed?"

"You mean, killed," Vex corrected the colonel.

"I'd say that's a distinct possibility," he said.

Vex didn't say anything more, as the pilot continued to circle the pyramid, then slowly dropped down toward a flat stretch of ground not far from the pyramid's northwest corner. The vertical takeoff and landing system was a series of nozzled thrusters lining the belly of the aerospace plane. During level flight, they remained shut behind louvered hatches. But when it came time to use them, the hatches louvered open, and the thrusters engaged. Reaction-control exhaust gusted out from around the aerospace plane on all sides, until the craft's landing pads engaged. Vex held her breath for a few seconds until she felt the vehicle settle securely, then the pilots spent several minutes performing a routine touchdown check, as well as an external atmospheric analysis—to determine if the air outside was dangerous.

"It's breathable," the pilot finally announced. "Though, Madam Kosmarch, I cannot guarantee against biological hazard."

"I know that," Vex said. "As long as there are no toxins present, we can proceed—and accept the danger of a germ threat."

"As you wish, Madam Kosmarch," the pilot said. "Nitrogen and oxygen content is consistent with clement atmospheres. There isn't as much carbon dioxide as there should be, but this won't be a problem for humans."

"No large fauna," Colonel Jun said, still looking out his window.

Now that they were on the ground, Vex could see the bleakness of the land in fine detail. Little patches of green and brown lichen covered most of the exposed stone, with larger clumps of moss forming near the depressions which collected water during storms. Not so much as a single flower showed its lovely face to the sun. The life on this world had not evolved enough.

Vex imagined surrounding the Waymaker pyramid with a square-shaped garden, kilometers in circumference. Such an artifact—in pristine condition—deserved to be beautified. She would make it one of her priorities, once she had enough manpower moved from Jaalit system to justify the effort. For now, it was enough to dream.

The security detail accompanying the detachment were already out of their gee chairs and adjusting their armor and equipment. Every man carried a battle rifle with full kit, to include hundreds of rounds of ammunition, several antipersonnel grenades, some demolitions explosive, and a pack containing both water and rations for three days. They were big—per Nautilan guidelines regarding infantry—and they followed their battle sergeant's commands without asking questions.

"Madam Kosmarch," the battle sergeant said, "once my team has secured a perimeter around the plane, you and the colonel may descend safely to the surface."

"Understood," she said.

The loading ramp popped out of its stowed position in the side of the plane, then the hatch at the top of the ramp unsealed with a hiss. Vex felt the change in pressure in her ears, and had her breath taken away by the sudden gust of moist, thick air that came up into the aerospace plane's cabin. The security team trooped down the ramp on the double, and quickly fanned out around the plane at regular intervals, where they each took a knee and brought binoculars up to their faces. As each trooper finished a one-hundred-and-eighty-degree visual sweep, he reported over the security net to the battle sergeant, who finally said, "Madam Kosmarch, there are no threats detectable within our vicinity. You may come down. Once you are down, half of my men will return to the plane to retrieve our equipment, and begin setting up a camp of operations."

"Just find us a way into the pyramid," Vex said, walking purposefully down the ramp, and out onto the soil of Cheops. It was mostly sand, albeit mixed with decayed plant matter. The grayish uniformity of the sand matched that of the rocks, and also the battered heap of a mountain range which Vex could see very far off in the distance. It had been a long time since that range had been thrust up, and worn down. With no new geologic activity to break up the monotony of the geography in this region of the planet.

The side of the pyramid itself was perhaps a hundred meters from the battle captain's perimeter. The slope of the two sides—meeting at what appeared to be a perfect forty-five degree angle—was distinct. And the pattern of etched lines, now seen up close, was huge on the pyramid's immense, smooth surface. Which appeared to have been untouched by time, or the elements. Sunlight glinted on the semireflective surface like off the surface of a still pond. Depending on which way Vex faced, she had to shield her eyes from the glare.

Beginning at roughly the middle of the side which faced the far off wreck, a jumbled heap of disused brick buildings rose out of the sand. This collection of dilapidated structures ran all the way from the pyramid to the wreck itself, and appeared to be composed of mostly one-story and two-story structures, the majority of which had slumped in on themselves. Without forests, there had been no trees from which to harvest wood—which would have been the most natural choice for early construction materials. The brick itself did not appear to have been fired, but rather dried and cured in the light of Cheops home star. Which explained why it had so poorly survived the time since their original occupants disappeared.

"Now that we're here," Colonel Jun said, "it's all somewhat depressing, don't you think? No people. Not even bodies or skeletons. Though I am sure if we did a detailed archeological examination, we'd find those eventually. Whatever happened here, it wasn't sudden. The settlers had time to evacuate. Or clean up after themselves. Before the weather began its ceaseless work, season after season."

"You sympathize with the men and women of the ark?" Vex asked.

"Of course I do," Jun said. "You'd have to be a machine not to! Think about it. They had abandoned the only home in the galaxy humanity ever knew. Spent hundreds of years crossing interstellar space at slower-than-light conventional velocity. Finally arrived here, at this planet, which seems to offer so much potential, and then...the whole thing went to hell. Something very, *very* wrong happened. We don't know what. Yet. But we may find out soon."

"Could the Waymakers have returned to this place, and extinguished the human settlers the way we might fumigate a housing block for roaches?"

"It's possible," Jun said. "Human life might not have even registered as intelligent on their scale. Though it's difficult to know for sure. We've never found anything that could be described as a Waymaker fossil. Nothing to suggest the shape or size of their craniums—assuming they had those. Which they may not have. We know intelligent Earth life comes in a variety of shapes and sizes. How does an octopus perceive the sea through which it swims? Is everything else that swims around it just food, or a threat? Or are their more subtle thoughts lurking in that complex—for an animal—mind?"

"Madam Kosmarch," the battle sergeant said, approaching respectfully. "I believe we've identified a potential entry point."

He handed her his binoculars, then pointed to a spot at the pyramid's base, not far from where the brick human buildings began.

Vex looked. There seemed to be something akin to a portico, made from the same material as the pyramid, but partially obstructed by crumbling brick from the human settlement.

"Very good," she said. "Instruct the pilot to take off as soon as we clear the perimeter. Battle Sergeant, bring half your men with us, and leave the other half to handle the camp. I don't want to waste any more time speculating."

The battle sergeant saluted, then relayed her instructions to his team, and to the pilot. When they were three hundred meters along the base of the pyramid—sweating, now that the sun was high in the sky, and the wet sand beneath their feet proved particularly arduous to traverse—the roar of the aerospace plane's engines pounded off the pyramid's surface. Vex did not turn to watch the craft take off, but it thundered over their heads and out across the face of the sea, before climbing sharply for orbit. Vex knew it was a risk to use the plane as a cargo taxi, but it was the only means they had for putting men and equipment on the ground in a reasonable amount of time. Destroyers—as a matter of Nautilan military doctrine—did not have the capability for drop modules as the Constellar expedition had used.

Which reminded Vex. Once a sufficient amount of Nautilan materials and equipment were on the surface, to sustain life for several days, she wanted the general to send one of his destroyers to reconnoiter the big jovian planet at the center of the Cheops system. Those civilian starliners were still out there, and theoretically, still armed with some form of Constellar military weaponry. She didn't want to directly engage. Rather, she wanted at least one of her ships to do a flyby. To confirm that the starliners were in fact still there. Versus trying to execute a maneuver which might put them on course back to the Waypoint, to rendezvous with the picket ship still waiting out there. If that happened, Ekk would have to intervene. But as long as the starliners stayed put, Vex could afford to be hands off about it. Nautilan reinforcements would arrive soon enough. And when they did, Vex intended to have seized the power of the pyramid for herself.

The portico—once they arrived—wasn't much to look at. People had built an additional hall around the alien entrance, which had since disintegrated. But there seemed to be a fresh path cleared through the rubble, so that Vex, Colonel Jun, their Waypoint pilot, and the battle sergeant with ten of his men, were able to walk single file into the base of the pyramid.

The interior wasn't what Vex had expected. A long, hexagonally cut corridor stretched off into the distance, illuminated from both the floor and the ceiling by a repeating hexagonal pattern of what appeared to be glowing cracks in the surface of the pyramid material. The light cast was blue hued, but not bright. Giving everything a kind of indirect illumination which was not unpleasant on the eye. The air inside was also fresh, and seemed to be circulated according to principles of positive interior pressure—since a slight breeze flowed perpetually out of the hexagonal corridor into the air beyond.

Walking on the pyramid material felt like walking on solid metal or stone. The hexagonal pattern in the floor did not change when you stepped on any of the lines. The light coming up from below was cold. Without any specific source point. Which seemed to be true of the ceiling—as if the pattern had been scratched into the pyramid material's surface, allowing it to glow through the scratches from within.

There was a bass droning in their ears. Not loud. In fact, after a few moments, they had to stop and specifically pay attention to hear it. But it was there.

"Amazing," Colonel Jun said as they slowly walked inside. The old man's sickness fatigue seemed to desert him as he ran his hands appreciatively along one of the sloping corridor walls—like touching a lover.

"What's your first impression?" Vex asked, the heels of her expedition boots making a regular, sharp noise on the corridor's floor.

"The Waymakers clearly had a fondness for geometry," he said. "Pyramids. Hexagons. Notice also that this corridor is much taller than would be necessary for an ordinary human. We can guess somewhat about their size, as creatures. I'd estimate they were at least half again as tall as an average man. Perhaps as much as double? They must have had eyes which perceived the world in the visual spectrum, as ours do, too."

"Why would it be otherwise?" Vex asked.

"There are species of bats which perceive their surroundings almost entirely by reflected sound waves."

"But wouldn't that make it difficult for a technological civilization to evolve?" Vex asked.

"I'd say yes, but who knows what's really possible? Part of my problem—as a man who's studied the Waymakers for so long—is that we only have our one civilization to compare, against so little evidence left over from theirs. It's been almost impossible to come to any definitive conclusions about who they were, what their lifestyle may have been like, what their physiology was, and so forth. Now, perhaps finally, we can get some solid answers."

They walked down the long corridor, carefully searching for anything that might look like a hatchway, a portal, a door, or a tool. But the smooth surface of the pyramid was unbroken by anything other than the hexagonal illumination both above and below.

Reaching the corridor's end, they stopped, and Vex ordered the Waypoint pilot to put her hands on the corridor's slope-walled surface.

"Can you detect anything?" Vex asked.

"Madam Kosmarch, what is it I am attempting to do?" the young woman asked.

"I think she's wanting you to try to see if the interior surface of the pyramid responds to you the way a Key would," Colonel Jun said gently.

"Yessir," the young woman said, and placed her hands on the surface. Her eyes closed, and she breathed deeply for several seconds, then pulled her hands away.

"Nothing," the Waypoint pilot said.

"Farther in, perhaps?" Colonel Jun suggested, pointing to the right angle the corridor took.

Vex estimated they'd penetrated about half a kilometer into the interior.

"Battle Sergeant," she said. "Are you able to communicate with your troops back at camp?"

"Negative, Madam Kosmarch," he said. "There seems to be something interfering with our wireless."

"It's this place," Colonel Jun grunted. "I'd have been shocked if it *didn't* interfere. In fact, I'd wager all our communications problems, since arriving in the atmosphere, can be traced to this structure."

Around the right angle of the corridor they discovered two sets of ramps which proceeded gradually through a series of switchbacks, one going up and one going down. When the battle sergeant and the colonel eyed each other, then their boss, Golsubril Vex, chose up. Down is where she reasoned the "plumbing" of the pyramid might be. Control centers or other places of power would surely be up. When she explained her thought process to the colonel, he *tsked* and shook his head.

"We can't be sure they think as we do," he said.

"But you've already deduced some aspects of their physical character," she said. "What sane species puts their control rooms in the basement?"

"A species seeking to protect their leadership from orbital bombardment? Or perhaps they have a hierarchical instinct we can't begin to guess at. For us, notions of *up* have always held significance. A man *climbs* to power. He sits *on top of* his chain-of-command. We *rise* through the ranks. The Waymakers may have looked at the universe through very different eyes."

"Nevertheless, we have to choose one direction or the other, and I choose to ascend," Vex said smartly.

Jun merely shrugged, and followed her. As did the rest.

The ramps had a hexagonal cross section and hexagonal

floor-and-ceiling lighting pattern, just as the entry corridor did. After having risen perhaps fifty meters, Vex and her entire group were huffing and puffing.

"Surely the Waymakers thought of a lift!" Colonel Jun lamented, while sponging at his brow with a sleeve. Like all of them, the old man had adopted a field uniform made from tough fabrics, with minimal insignia or rank. Dark spots were forming at his armpits and around his neck.

"You were the one lecturing *me* about how we shouldn't judge their mentality based purely on our own human perspective," Vex scolded, enjoying the old man's annoyance.

After over a hundred meters of switchbacks, the ramp emptied out into a large hall which stretched over one hundred meters in either direction. Like the corridor and the ramp, the cross section of the hall was hexagonal. Unlike the corridor and the ramp, which had been featureless saving for the lighting pattern, which also repeated in the hall, there were numerous floor-to-ceiling hexagonal columns, and artifacts at some of the bases.

Colonel Jun forgot all about his physical fatigue, coughing spastically into a handkerchief while he ran to the base of what appeared to be a statue.

"Look at it!" the old man exclaimed, then took a knee and choked out several long, wretched, lung-wringing gagging fits. When one of the battle sergeant's troops took a knee alongside the colonel, to see if she could assist, the colonel gently waved her off, took many deep breaths, then slowly got back to his feet.

The artifact was roughly three meters high, and columnar in build. But with something like a ribbed beetle's carapace, from which sprouted various insect-segmented limbs which dangled from irregularly placed shoulder joints. There was nothing like a face any human would have recognized. Rather, the head seemed to be nothing but a curved shield with a grill in the center. The very top of the shield was open, with a span of metal rounding up and over the grill, almost like an arch. And there were several more artifacts just like it spaced at regular intervals around the hall.

Jun reached out to gently touch one of the limbs on the artifact before which he stood.

"It's made of the same thing as the pyramid," he said. "And seems about as lifeless too."

"Could this be what the Waymakers looked like?" asked the battle sergeant, who surprised Vex with his curiosity.

"Maybe," Colonel Jun said, stepping back a few paces, and looking back and forth between two of the artifacts. "Each one is similar, but still a bit different. Not all of them have the same number of limbs. And not all of the limbs are segmented in the same way. Also, some of them have differently sized thoraxes, though I am sure 'thorax' is a bad way to look at it. Notice also that the sound we've been hearing, ever since we entered? It's gotten louder."

Vex inclined her head, and closed her eyes. He was right, the drone in the background *had* gotten louder.

"Obviously, the pyramid has power," she said. "But drawn from what source? A reactor, like we would use?"

"It would need to be refueled with hydrogen extracted from the sea," Colonel Jun said. "I somehow think the Waymakers wouldn't resort to using a power source as pedestrian as ours."

"But nuclear fusion is a supremely reliable source of energy," Vex said.

"Our ancestors on Earth once thought wood was an extremely reliable source of energy," Jun said, making a scoffing sound. "No. The Waymakers would have used something different. Something which could survive half a million years, or more, of isolation. Without need of refueling or repair. Something that couldn't wear down, or wear out."

"Madam Kosmarch, what if these are robots?" the Waypoint pilot—a lieutenant whose name Vex hadn't bothered to learn—asked. She stepped gingerly to one of the statues, and ran a hand over one of its dangling, spindly limbs.

"What do you mean?" the colonel asked.

"Somebody has to be keeping up the place, sir," the Waypoint pilot said. "Haven't you both noticed that there is no dust nor dirt anywhere in here? The minute we crossed the threshold back at the entrance, the interior of the pyramid became immaculately clean. There are not fractures in any of the surfaces. None of the lights are out, nor blinking irregularly, like you find in a standard housing block back home. If the Waymakers themselves are no longer here, maybe they created these mechanical servants to maintain the building?"

Colonel Jun laughed, and patted the young woman's shoulder, tapping a finger to the side of his nose.

"When you retire from Waypoint duty," he said with a smile, "you're being assigned directly to the Nautilan bureau for Waymaker study and expertise."

The Waypoint pilot blushed.

"Thank you, sir," she said. "I never thought of myself as a xeno scholar."

"The best xeno scholars seldom do," he said. "Where do you think I got *my* start? I was a ship's surgeon before I became interested in Waymaker artifacts. Sometimes it takes a fresh set of eyes—seeing the same thing as yourself—to give you a new perspective. So, let's go with your idea. The Waymakers are gone, but these are something they created and left behind. For tending the pyramid. Obviously they're not active now. I wonder when—or if—they do become active? From what source are they controlled? Or are they independently minded?"

"How can a machine have an independent mind?" Vex asked.

"It's not hard to imagine," Jun replied.

"Just impossible to program," Vex said. "Humans have been trying to build an artificial person since before the Exodus. We've gotten good at making computers which can *fake* being human, but only to a point. Because sooner or later, computers lack the ability to adapt quickly enough to changing situations, changing data, and so forth. If you were a surgeon in your youth, I cut my teeth on coding problems. The entire Waywork relies on automation for a multitude of routine, monotonous, and dangerous jobs. But those machines rely on an army of programmers, technicians, engineers, and manufacturers to keep the automation working. Are you suggesting the Waymakers developed an automation system capable of doing all of that, for itself?"

"I am," Jun said. "So, the system is self-repairing as well as self-sustaining. But when nothing is out of sorts—parameters of one type or another have not been exceeded—the automation remains dormant. These artifacts could slumber for years before getting called to perform a task."

The lieutenant had wandered while Vex and Jun speculated. Then the young woman shouted for their attention, practically jumping up and down while she pointed to something much farther down the hall.

Vex rushed to where the Waypoint pilot stood.

"It's a Key," Vex said.

"It's *many* Keys," Colonel Jun corrected her. "Of many sizes."

A gallery of spheres lay before them, each one half-submerged into a small platform. The biggest was taller than a man in diameter, while the smallest was approximately the size of a grapefruit. Having seen and used Keys all her professional life, the Waypoint pilot had no doubt what she was looking at.

"Can you use them?" Vex demanded.

"Madam Kosmarch, I am not sure what I'd use them for, this far from a Waypoint."

"Within the confines of this pyramid, the Keys may do much more than simply allow travel across Slipways," Colonel Jun said. "I too would like to know if they can be used. But you are the only one with the gift. It's why I suggested we bring you with us."

Again, the Waypoint pilot blushed.

"Which one should I try first?" she asked.

"This one," Vex said. She'd stepped a few paces through the gallery, until she stood before a particularly large sphere, perhaps twice the size of an ordinary Key. It also had a slightly different metallic hue compared to the rest. Even in the strange, blue-white light given off by the floor and ceiling.

The young Waypoint pilot approached the Key with mixed eagerness and trepidation. When she applied both her hands to the sphere's surface, nothing happened. Several seconds passed, with the lieutenant slowly moving her hands over the Key's surface, and still nothing happened.

She opened her eyes and said, "I can't sense anything. It's almost as if . . . well, the Keys we use for the Waypoints are never *off* the way we turn off a human device. But this one seems off to me."

"What about the others?" Vex asked. "Begin trying them one at a time."

The young officer complied, while Vex watched impatiently, her arms folded over her chest. All around her, the potential power of the Waymakers seemed ready for grasping. Yet, she was forced to work through interlocutors. Because Golsubril Vex did not have the gift, as Colonel Jun had called it. She had no aptitude with Keys, and never would. Which was immensely frustrating. Especially while they were on the brink of discovering how to unlock the pyramid's potential.

The Waypoint pilot's back suddenly arched, and she stared vacantly into the air over her head—mouth moving silently to form half-thought words.

The Key she touched was about two-thirds the size of a Waywork Key. As Vex had seen before, when the Key became active, its surface took on a translucent quality, revealing a sphere inside the sphere, but covered with a network of geometric patterns which lit up from within themselves. The lieutenant's body quivered, and her hands shook.

"Tell us!" Vex demanded. "What can you see?"

"T-h-h-the Waymakers—!" she stuttered.

"Please, Vex," Colonel Jun hissed, putting a restraining hand on Vex's bicep, "our Waypoint pilot is clearly overwhelmed by what she's experiencing!"

"Touch me again," Vex said, violently shrugging the man off, "and I will ensure you painfully regret it, *Colonel.* The lieutenant's state of mind is obvious. But she needs to talk, and talk *now.* Lieutenant, this is Kosmarch Vex. You will control yourself, and explain to me what is happening."

"T-h-h-hey...their programming...machines...*in my mind!*"

At once, the lieutenant cut loose with a blood-curdling shriek that filled the hall. Almost simultaneously, all of the statues—which Vex and her group had been examining early—suddenly came to life.

"Security!" the battle sergeant shouted, and ten men instantly deployed around Vex and the colonel, their battle rifles pointed at whichever artifact was closest.

When the machines began to raise their insect-like appendages, with grasping claw-like digits extended from the tips, one of the troops flinched, and cut loose with a shot, which sent a bullet whirring off the carapace of the machine not twenty meters distant. And then the entire squad was firing, the din from their weapons drowning out the Waypoint pilot's horrific wail. Vex ignored her men, and focused on the lieutenant, who still clutched the glowing Key with both hands.

"Control! Control!" Vex shouted, physically grabbing the young woman's bicep in both of her hands. "You must control it! *You must!*"

But the Waypoint pilot didn't seem to be aware of Golsubril Vex at all. Her mouth was stretched open, teeth bared crazily, while a wavering scream poured from her throat.

"Stop shooting, you idiots! Stop!" Colonel Jun was shouting.

Men began to be flung bodily, as the machines ignored the bullets caroming harmlessly off their metal armor, and attacked in a blur of swinging insect arms.

# CHAPTER 38

*DAFFODIL* PULLED TWO GEES TOWARD THE WAYPOINT. THERE WAS another ship significantly ahead of them, but of undetermined national origin. She'd switched off her identification code computer, or the code computer had been damaged. Whichever. It didn't matter. The other ship was going to hit the Waypoint first. If the other ship was friendly, she'd be back in Oswight space, and find herself in the care of Commodore Iakar. If she was not friendly, she'd be heading back home to tell the rest of Starstate Nautilan how things were going in the Uxmal system.

"It's the *Hallibrand*," Zuri said from her gee chair, having relocated to the ship's command module against surgeon's orders. As long as she kept her vomit bags handy, Admiral Mikton didn't make too much of a mess. But trying to keep her mind on the tactical situation—versus the intense sensation of nausea which dominated her stomach—was a devilish chore.

"Are you sure?" asked Captain Garmot.

"Pretty sure," Zuri replied.

"I think Commodore Urrl missed a destroyer," the captain said. "That was a hairball of a fight, back at Objective Epsilon. Anything could have happened."

"*Hallibrand*'s fallback orders were to return to Oswight space, if all else failed," Zuri said.

"Then why won't she respond with identification?" the captain asked.

Zuri didn't have a good answer for that one.

"Assuming it *is* one of the destroyers," Zuri said, "I don't think we change our plan. Assuming the destroyer lingers near the Waypoint in Jaalit space, it's just one more target for us to acquire when we emerge. How have your engineers been doing modifying the launches to carry nukes?"

"That's been the easy part," the captain replied. "We simply open the nose, remove the broadcast package that's inside, and insert one of our nukes with its proximity computer wired to the launch's proximity sensors. Granted, those launches aren't the smartest machines in the Constellar fleet, but they are pro-grammed to operate in a ship-like fashion. Once we drop out of the Waypoint, we'll have to deploy them fast, to make ourselves look like the Nautilan fleet that came across originally. Nine ships. So, eight launches, and us. That gives us eight potential targets to identify—the second we're over—then the launches go. If the codes we scraped off the memory of that Nautilan box still work, the security flotilla won't be aware that there is a problem. Unless the codes are individually identifiable for individual Nautilan ships."

"Our codes do that," Zuri said. "Every Constellar vessel in the registry is in the memory of every Constellar warship, large or small."

"So, if you're the watch commander on the other side of that Waypoint, Admiral, and you suddenly see nine versions of the same ship popping up on your tactical display, what do you do?"

"It's what I am hoping they *don't* do that counts," Zuri said, then turned her head to the side and wretched into one of the vomit bags. An intravenous feed unit had been belted to her stomach, pushing medication directly into the areas which had been most sensitive to the radiation. The lining of her intestines, and the cells of her stomach wall, were deciding minute by minute whether to disintegrate totally, or rally for one more go at healing. If Zuri somehow made it back home alive, she was quite sure she wouldn't be eating solid food for several months.

"They shouldn't," Zuri said, wiping her mouth with a nap-kin, "open fire on a friendly signature. The fact that there are duplicates won't initially indicate hostiles, just as multiples of the same signature on *our* side would not immediately indicate hostiles. We'd order the ships to keep a safe distance, and invoke two-step authentication using the backup audio-video process. That takes minutes. During which we can have those launches deployed, and moving toward their targets. Which shouldn't immediately set off any bells, because the launches are physically too big and bulky to be missiles. A lot depends on how much distance their security flotilla keeps between themselves and the Waypoint. Too much distance, and the launches will never make it in time, before somebody gets wise and takes the launches out with point-defense or antimissiles."

"Stupidly bad odds," Captain Garmot said. "Last time you took on odds that poor, it cost you all of the Task Group."

Zuri thought about it—as her insides continued to debate dying.

"Okay, what if we modify the plan?" she said.

"This late in the game?"

"Sure. It'll be a while until we get to the Waypoint anyway. So, we don't deploy launches immediately. We keep them. One ship, one signature. It's a signature their security flotilla will recognize. We tell them we've had battle damage, and are heading for drydock in the inner system. Tell them to remain vigilant at the Waypoint. Bypass the flotilla altogether. At that range, and with a code their systems recognize, it shouldn't be too hard to slip by them. They won't be able to tell what class *Daffodil* is until or unless they're on top of us. But we won't give them enough time to do that."

"Running immediately would look suspicious," Garmot said.

"Maybe we tell them we have a VIP aboard who's hurt, and needs treatment at a groundside facility? Hell, I can produce the barfing sounds to make it convincing."

Zuri wretched again into her vomit bag, sealed the zipper, and let herself be miserable. The gee chair had been fitted with an extra layer of padding, but that didn't change the fact that Zuri was suffering worse than she could ever remember having suffered. Every part of her felt awful. The surgeon speculated that even if Zuri survived, she'd cut untold years off her life on account of the induced malignancies which were going to be in her future. The human body just wasn't built to withstand that much radiation exposure in such a short span of time. Not without dreadful consequences.

Part of her didn't care. Making it or not making it was not the point anymore. Zuri had sacrificed everything for the sake of an idea. An idea she still thought was worth trying.

Or was it simply that Admiral Mikton wanted to make Nautilan hurt?

Chaplain Ortteo and his focus on the Word had gotten Zuri to thinking. If worthiness really was the deciding factor in this supposedly larger-than-life drama in which they were all participating, which objective was better? Attacking a Nautilan system for the desired strategic delay it would cause, or attacking a Nautilan system because Zuri wanted to make sure the Nauties *felt* her? At long last. Right between their eyes.

She knew the answer. But Ortteo wasn't here to lecture her anymore. He'd died with *Catapult,* and was finding out firsthand whether the Prophecies were true or not.

Admiral Mikton wanted to believe that it could be a bit of both, and God—or whoever was paying attention—would be satisfied with a mixed motive. Versus no motive at all.

# CHAPTER 39

ELVIN AXABRAST WAS FRANTIC, NOT TO MENTION FURIOUS. NOT once in all the time he'd served Family Oswight had he ever failed to keep the Oswight children safe. Oh, there'd been a bump here and a bruise there. The usual kids' stuff. But when it came to standing between real danger and those two boys and their sister, Elvin had stood like a cement wall.

Until last night.

He winced every time he took a step, feeling the sprain in his ankle. It wasn't broken. But Elvin's tendons and ligaments weren't as elastic as they used to be. He would be feeling it for weeks. Assuming they managed to make it that far.

"Keep after it, lads," he urged the men and women around him. Captain Fazal's platoon of DSOD TGO troops had been gainfully employed looking for Lady Oswight since the sun had come up. It had been a hell of a night before that, with all of them huddled in whatever makeshift shelter they could find. Most of them came out of it drenched, hungry, and tired to death. But that didn't stop Elvin from rousting everyone the moment light crept its way over the horizon. And it *wouldn't* stop him until Lady Oswight had been found. Or he was dead first. Whichever.

Since none of their wireless was working, they had to tackle the project compartment by compartment. A chore which might have been interesting, if Elvin had been spared the time to do it in the name of archeology. The insides of the ark weren't all that different from the insides of any other large spacecraft.

Staterooms, lavatories, refectories, they tended to have the same general configuration as those in the modern era, except many of them—the ones which could be easily accessed, at least—had become choked with sand, or filled with water, or clogged by a mixture of the two. There were even hydroponics facilities, like those found across the Waywork. One such bay held the desiccated, lifeless remains of livestock. Pigs, from the mummified look of them. Another had been used for rice farming, but had all of its topsoil washed out, so that the nested moisture tubes ordinarily covered by dirt were exposed.

Not once did any of the searchers find a human body. Not the remains of an original ark inhabitant, and—thankfully—not the corpse of someone who'd come down with them in the drop module.

If Lady Oswight were still in the ark, and Elvin felt she had to be, they would discover her sooner or later. Even if it took him uttering all the oaths and curses in the Constellar dictionary, and Dissenter folklore, to do it.

The sky suddenly made a noise. Everyone stopped the search, and looked up. Elvin shielded his eyes with a palm at his brow, while the sleek, predatory shape of an aerospace plane flew overhead. The craft looked nothing like any of the drop modules which had been hastily mated to Antagean's starliners. And unlike the drop modules, the aerospace plane could return to orbit again. Which meant Starstate Nautilan had a way to get back to space, where Elvin and his cohorts did not. They watched as the aerospace plane descended to the northwest corner of the pyramid, using its vertical takeoff and landing thrusters to set down on a flat piece of ground not far from the pyramid itself. Elvin's binoculars whined as he dialed the magnification up as far as it would go. He couldn't make out individual people, but he could see vapor blowing off the aerospace plane's ducted engine nacelles, where the fusion-driven turbofans converted atmosphere to thrust. Later, in the boost-to-orbit phase, the nacelles would close off, and the aerospace plane would climb into low planetary orbit using direct fusion-rocket power.

If the ship had not belonged to Nautilan, Elvin might have admired it.

As it was, he muttered curses aplenty on the plane, then put his binoculars away, and went to find Captain Fazal.

The TGO officer looked dead on his feet.

"What d'yah think, lad?" Elvin asked, his own voice sounding hollow and exhausted in his ears.

"We knew they were coming. Now we know they're here. And they certainly know *we* are here, if they saw the drop module on the beach. Which I doubt they would have missed during that flyover. Our one piece of luck is that they're more interested in the pyramid than us. So, we can keep looking for Lady Oswight. Though I can't say what our plan should be once we find her. If the Nauties are taking control of the pyramid, we've got nothing left to gain on this world."

"Gunfight them," Elvin urged. "A plane that size c'ldna take more than a score o' men. Maybe a few more? We've got the troops and the weapons."

"We have to assume they will return to orbit, and bring down more people," Fazal said, crouched down on his haunches, and drinking heavily from one of his canteens. That had been the single benefit of the storm. Plenty of fresh water to top off their bottles.

"Then we bloody hit the plane before she's back in the air," Elvin said.

"You really were a colour sergeant of the old school, weren't you?" Fazal said, smiling slightly.

"Damned right," Elvin said.

"But then we're well and truly stuck here, Mister Axabrast. Antagean's starliners have no way of bringing us back up off the surface, even if they could get through the destroyers in orbit. We *need* that plane, as much as they need it too."

Elvin ran a hand over his face and beard, feeling the fresh dots of stubble that poked out of his cheeks. As a man who prided himself on his groomed appearance, he realized he was going to wind up looking mighty shaggy after a few days. Shaggier than Garsina Oswight had ever seen him, that was for sure.

"Sir!" one of the TGO troops shouted.

Elvin and the captain shot to their feet, making their way over to where several TGO people were clustered around what appeared to be a large funnel.

"Is this where you last saw her?" Captain Fazal asked.

"'Twas damned bloody dark and I couldn't see a damned bloody thing except her lantern," Elvin growled, staring down into the hole at the funnel's bottom. Unlike the rest of the ark which they'd been searching through so far, this particular portion appeared to have been recently modified. Little streams of water were still runneling out of different places in the ark, and into the funnel basin. Almost as if the funnel had been specifically built here, to take advantage of a natural depression in the ark's hollowed-down internal landscape.

"Big enough for a man," Captain Fazal said, pointing down at the hole, which was a good ten meters below them. The sides of the funnel were not steep, but their smoothness made it apparent that nobody who fell down it could hope to climb back up. Especially during a storm.

"Aye," Elvin said, getting a prickly feeling on the back of his neck. "And it could be a bottomless pit to nowhere."

For a moment, the majordomo imagined Garsina Oswight trapped in the dark, down at the bottom of wherever that hole ultimately led to. Maybe half shivering to death? Maybe drowned already?

The old man shuddered, and shook such thoughts out of his head.

"It's worth a try," he said. "But only if we don't lose more men, Cap'n."

One of the troops knelt by the opening, and began shouting into it, "*Heeeeeeeeellllloooooooooo! Caaaaaan annnnyonnnne heeear meeeee?*"

Her voice echoed down the funnel, but there was no response. They all looked to Captain Fazal for guidance.

"We've got assault rope. We could lower somebody down."

"And how much will it take to get to the bottom?" Elvin asked.

"Who knows?" the captain said. "But do you have any better ideas? We've been searching all through this wreck for hours. Even frantic like she was, I don't think Lady Oswight could have gotten much farther on foot than this. You said Antagean went with her, and now both the lieutenant commander and Lady Oswight are proving extremely difficult to find. If they had holed up in a compartment somewhere, I think they'd have heard us calling for them, or knocking on hatchways. And now that Starstate Nautilan is here, our time is running out. Sooner or later, they're going to put enough troops on the ground to send a security force our way."

"Aye," Elvin said, staring at the funnel.

He nodded his head in agreement.

Five minutes later, they had one of the smallest, lightest females in Fazal's TGO group tied off securely, with an impromptu climber's seat arrangement. Lowering her down into the funnel—with three different lanterns attached to her body—they played out the rope slowly, with half a dozen men on the line, working in concert. Elvin had insisted on being at the front. His ankle may have hurt, but he knew ropes too. A pair of heavy gloves from his pack kept his hands from getting burned as he gradually let the line go down, and down, and down some more. As the end of the rope hit the back man, they paused, he tied off another length obtained from another TGO trooper's pack, and then they would start again.

It was supremely frustrating not having wireless for the job. The corporal on the business end of the detail couldn't give them an immediate report on what she was seeing. Occasionally, the line would slack a bit, as she hit a flat part in the tunnel below, but then the line would go taught again as she approached a vertical space.

Captain Fazal was directly behind Elvin, both of them breathing deeply, and sweating, as they worked.

"You might be right," Fazal wheezed, "about there being no bottom."

"Just don't let the line get too loose," Elvin grunted.

At almost five hundred meters, the rope—or series of ropes, knotted together—went very tight, and then became very slack. For a few moments, Elvin wondered if one of the knots farther down had come undone. Then he felt the rope jerk three times in succession, a solid *yank-yank-yank,* which was the signal for them to all begin pulling.

"Here comes the sweaty part," Elvin said, and shouted for the team to reverse what they'd been doing. Instead of gradually paying out line, they began to gradually reel it back in. Which was a much more muscle-intensive chore. Several other TGO troops rallied to the job, and soon a dozen of them were hauling rhythmically, for many minutes. At the end of which the corporal emerged from the bottom of the funnel—soaking wet—but with a grin on her face.

"There's a big compartment down there," she reported. "It's got thousands upon thousands of gallons of fresh water in it.

But what's more, I saw a ladder leading up to the top of a ledge. Guess what I found when I checked up there?"

The corporal produced a tiny blue elastic hair tie. The kind Lady Oswight often used to put her hair into a bun.

"Merciful God," Elvin breathed, reverently taking the hair tie, and turning it over and over again in his large, gloved hands. "But you didn't see the Lady herself? What about the lieutenant commander?"

"Both gone," the corporal reported. "When you get up on the ledge you can see a long tunnel that goes back into the wreck. Wherever the lieutenant commander and Lady Oswight went, it's back there somewhere."

Elvin and Captain Fazal looked at each other, then Elvin snatched one of the corporal's lanterns away from her, went to the lip of the funnel, and unceremoniously shoved himself off. He could hear the captain shouting his name as he dropped, but he didn't care. The water still flowing into the funnel smoothed his way. When he passed through the hole, he worried that his bulk might get stuck, but the hole was more than large enough to accommodate him. Suddenly, he was being whisked along through a series of watery twists and turns. He kept his feet facing downward and kept the lantern raised to his chest. The way ahead was a blur of smooth-sided metal pipe, which didn't give him any clues about which way it might twist, turn, or drop. Several times, Elvin almost bit through his tongue, the drops were so sudden. But then he hit the final drop, and was in over his head, feeling the cold, fresh water up his nose and into his ears.

Pushing back to the surface, Elvin burst through the top, choking and coughing, but with his lantern still firmly in hand. He scanned around the space until he saw the ladder the corporal had been referring to, and swam vigorously toward it. Climbing up to the top, he saw the tunnel too, and limp-marched his way forward, favoring his sprained ankle as little as possible.

The tunnel's end was a shock. Elvin emerged dripping and sputtering into a huge chandeliered space, almost like a ballroom, except for the fact that there was a mosaic covering the floor, composed of countless little pieces of tile, portraying a map. He reached a shaking hand down to his sidearm, unclipped it from his gunbelt, and drew it slowly. With his thumb, he clicked off the weapon's safety, and kept his index finger outside the trigger guard while he slowly advanced. Where there were lights, there was power. And where there was power, that meant people. Which meant Lady Oswight and the lieutenant commander may have run into someone who couldn't be counted as friendly—even if they weren't necessarily from Starstate Nautilan.

Elvin paused in the middle of the map to marvel at the intricacy of the thing. Huge blue oceans and green-brown land masses were arranged in a configuration the majordomo had never seen before. It certainly wasn't the Constellar capital. And it looked nothing like Uxmal either. This planet—if it was an accurate depiction—looked nothing like any world Elvin had ever seen.

Several branching corridors presented themselves. Elvin paused, and listened intently, trying to see if he could hear anything. When he finally discerned what sounded like very distant voices, he picked his path, and proceeded with caution. After several more minutes of painful—because of the ankle—feather-stepping, Elvin discovered a huge room with numerous doors ringing the exterior, and couches and chairs filling the space in the middle. He thought he smelled delicious beef in the air, but was all eyes for Lady Oswight, who stood next to the lieutenant commander. She was in her zipsuit, and Antagean was in his zipsuit plus armor. They were having an animated conversation with a third person Elvin couldn't see, with the Lady and the lieutenant commander's backs to him.

"Oy!" Elvin cried loudly.

Lady Oswight spun on a heel, her mouth hanging open. Then she rushed up to Elvin and threw her arms around his neck.

"Good timing, Mister Axabrast," Antagean said, walking up to him.

Elvin safed his sidearm, deposited it back into its holster, then detached from Garsina and took Antagean's extended hand. The two men shook strongly, their gaze meeting for a moment— just as it had the night prior, when Elvin had fallen and hurt himself—then Elvin dropped the handshake, and peered past the lieutenant commander to the old woman standing behind him.

"A new friend?" Elvin asked, looking from Antagean's face, to Garsina's face, then back to Antagean's.

"You might say that," Garsina said enthusiastically. "She knows a lot about the Waymakers, Elvin! She's going to take us to the pyramid!"

"I'm afraid that's a dicey proposition, lass," Elvin said, wiping water and perspiration from his brown.

"Nautilan?" the lieutenant commander asked.

"Affirmative," Elvin replied. "Nauties landed in a wee sexy aerospace plane, not too long before we discovered where you'd both gotten off to. I would have liked the ride better, Lady, if I'd not been half afraid to find you drowned at the bottom of it."

"We almost did," Antagean said. "We owe Lethiah here for providing us with a place to dry off, and a hot meal. Not to mention one hell of a story."

The old woman walked up to Elvin, and circled him slowly, looking him up and down. The lieutenant commander and the Lady shared knowing glances, while Elvin suddenly felt highly uncomfortable.

"Ahem," he said. "Even when I was a young, braw lad, I never had a lass be as forward as you."

"British Isles," the old woman said, using Mariclesh. Then she peered a bit more closely at Axabrast's face and added, "Or maybe Australia?"

Elvin couldn't make sense of those words, and looked at Lady Oswight with pleading eyes.

"Did you see the big map on the floor?" Lady Oswight asked.

"Aye," Elvin said.

"Island nations, both," Lethiah said. "One of them, in the northern hemisphere, the other in the southern. But what's this about the Temple? People are already there?"

"She means the pyramid," Lady Oswight said.

"Aye," Elvin said regretfully. "I'm afraid the Nauties beat us to it. If they haven't taken off again to go get more troops, they will soon."

Lethiah shook her head, and *tsked* loudly.

"We've got a problem," Lieutenant Commander Antagean said.

"The problem is *theirs*," Lethiah said. "The machines in the temple react differently, to different stimuli. Most of the time they remain dormant. But if someone who can use Anchors went to the Hall of Anchors, there could be trouble. That person won't know how to talk to the machines the way *I* know how to talk to the machines."

"I'm afraid you have me at a disadvantage," Elvin said. "What are 'anchors'?"

"She means Keys," Garsina said.

Elvin raised an eyebrow.

"If we're going to go, we'd better go now," Lethiah said.

"Madam," Elvin said, doing his best to remain polite, "as I've tried to say to you, there won't *be* any goin', so long as Starstate Nautilan controls the pyramid. To get inside we'll have to get through their security detail first. Which may or may not be possible with the few Constellar troops we have."

As if on cue, Captain Fazal staggered up. Like Axabrast, he was soaking wet.

Lethiah promptly performed her walkaround.

"Jordanian, or maybe Syrian," she said. "Somewhere in the Levant."

"What?" Fazal said, looking at Elvin.

"Long story for later," Lieutenant Commander Antagean said. "Where are the rest of the men?"

"Still up top," he said. "I told them to wait until I come back and tug on the rope."

"If ye haven't noticed," Elvin said, "we've been using the *service* entrance."

Puddles of water were forming under Elvin's and Captain Fazal's boots.

"Ye wouldn't happen to know a faster, *dryer* way to get back to the lobby?"

"Of course I do," the old woman said. "But before we do anything, I have to warn you all. The Temple isn't built for men. I go in there only when I absolutely have to. A lot of the ones who tried to study it extensively, way back when we first got here? They went crazy after a couple of years. And that was with us being as gingerly and unprovoking as we knew how to be, when we were doing our initial survey. Is Starstate Nautilan violent?"

"They can be when they feel like it," Elvin said gruffly.

"Which is often," Lieutenant Commander Antagean added.

Elvin nodded at the man in agreement.

"Then I can't guarantee how the machines will greet us when we get there."

"*If* we get there," Elvin reminded. "I don't see us just walking past the Nauties who are setting up to keep the place permanently."

"Just how *many* people are we talking about?" Lethiah asked.

"Three destroyers," Lieutenant Commander Antagean said.

Lethiah shrugged, and shook her head—the words had meant nothing to her.

"If they can bring down every last jack with a gun in his hand?" Elvin said, "It'll be a couple hundred at the very least. Starstate Nautilan wants this planet, just as they want every other world in the Waywork."

"But this world isn't part of your Waywork," Lethiah said.

"Which just makes Uxmal a juicier target!" Elvin said, exasperated.

"Uxmal?" Lethiah said, testing her pronunciation.

"It's what we named this place," Garsina said. "Before we knew somebody still lived on it."

"That's fine," Lethiah said. "After a few hundred years, I stopped caring that it even *had* a name."

Elvin looked at Garsina and mouthed, *A few hundred??*

She waved him off with the flick of a hand.

"The fact remains," Elvin said, "that Uxmal is now Starstate Nautilan's number-one objective for domination. Even if we can get through their security line, and enter the pyramid, that doesn't get rid of the destroyers in orbit. And as long as those destroyers are in orbit, Uxmal belongs to them—no matter what we might say about it."

"Uxmal belongs to the *Others*," Lethiah said bitterly, "and always has. You children just haven't figured it out yet. The machines will make sure it stays that way too."

# CHAPTER 40

GOLSUBRIL VEX AWOKE TO FIND HERSELF SURROUNDED BY A small heap of bodies. The attack by the machines had occurred so quickly that there'd been little time to react. Vex had been focused almost entirely on her Waypoint pilot, who appeared to be nowhere that Vex could now see. She reached a hand out to feel the neck of one of the soldiers who was sprawled nearby, and discovered warmth, as well as a pulse.

Colonel Jun was slumped against her, snoring lightly.

They weren't in the hall anymore. The room they occupied was much, much smaller, with no Keys of varying sizes, nor any of the menacing machines who'd come to life earlier.

All of the troops' weapons were gone.

"They didn't kill us, but they won't let us fight them, either," Vex said quietly, trying to will herself to stop having a headache. The very last thing she remembered was being tossed like a rag doll, then the record in her head went blurry.

When she tried to dislodge the colonel, he groaned, and sat up slowly.

"You'd think I tied one on," he moaned, rubbing at his fore-head. "Where are we?"

"Somewhere in the pyramid still," Vex said. "Though I can't say how we got here. Our Waypoint pilot is gone, which cannot be a mistake."

"Poor girl," Colonel Jun said. "Activating that Key must have flooded her perception. It's a tough enough profession, being a

Waypoint pilot who merely has to use the Keys to take a ship from one star to the next. If these Keys in the pyramid are more powerful, or come equipped with a two-way interface, our Waypoint pilot may have been exposed *directly* to the Waymaker network which clearly runs this facility."

"What do you mean?" Vex asked.

The colonel struggled into a sitting position, eyeing the troops around him.

"Alive," Vex said. "For now. Just like us."

Jun frowned, then said, "A thought occurred to me, once the shooting started. We've been assuming that the technology in this pyramid is passive. It doesn't do anything until we do something to activate it. But *once* it's activated, we have no idea what it's all programmed to do. Or to what lengths any of it will go to protect itself from a perceived threat. I am thinking now that those machines are all part of one big artificial intelligence. It doesn't notice humans at the singular level, but it *does* notice us if we try to interact with it through its Keys. Now that it's aware we're here—and may have rather intimate knowledge of us, depending on how well it's managed to interrogate the mind of our Waypoint pilot—we have to be very, very careful. We came here, after all, assuming that this would be *our* world to do with as we please. What if the pyramid doesn't agree?"

Vex made a scoffing sound, as others in their group began to stir.

"Report," groaned the battle sergeant, who rolled over on his hands and knees, and began slapping the legs and arms of some of his compatriots.

"Detained, and unarmed," Vex said matter-of-factly.

The battle sergeant quickly did a self–pat down, and cursed, realizing that all of his grenades were gone, along with his weapon, and the magazines for same.

"You act like this place has a will of its own," Vex said to the colonel.

"Doesn't it? Even if there are no true Waymakers here with us, this pyramid and all of the machines within it bear the Waymaker legacy. Those machines which attacked us—acting as sentinels—might simply be the pyramid's way of dealing with infestations. It would explain why the people from the ark are all gone. Something they did must have triggered the pyramid. So it took care of them."

"An entire population?" Vex said. "Using what?"

"We don't know. But we might—unfortunately—have a chance to find out."

"It may not matter," Vex said. "I left explicit instructions with General Ekk that if I do not return, he is to bombard this site from orbit."

"Now *that's* an encouraging thought," Jun said, laughing sarcastically.

The rest of the men were staring at Vex with no small degree of horror.

"Madam Kosmarch—" the battle sergeant started to say, but she cut him off.

"Every line soldier must understand his ultimate duty," she said sternly. "I will *not* allow this facility to fall into enemy hands, be it a known or unknown enemy. General Ekk won't act until he is certain the expedition is a failure. At this time, we don't know if the rest of your men are even aware of what's happened in here."

"I left instructions that if we did not return before the sun sets, as soon as a full platoon's worth of troops had been brought to the surface, a follow-up squad was to be sent into the pyramid."

Vex checked her chronometer. "I'm going to guess that the sun set a long time ago, battle sergeant."

"Yes, Madam Kosmarch."

Vex stood up slowly, and stretched out. Her head still hurt, but she felt unharmed otherwise.

"If only we could figure out some way to talk to them," she said.

There was a whispering sound, followed by the distinct smell of electrical ozone, and a space suddenly appeared in the wall, where none had been before. Through it staggered the Waypoint pilot—or what had formerly served as the Waypoint pilot. The lieutenant moved like a badly puppeted marionette, with halting steps, and her head cocked at a poor angle. A line of saliva leaked from the corner of her half-open mouth, and she held one of the Keys—much smaller this time—in both of her hands. The Key glowed softly, its interior matrix shining brightly through the translucent surface.

"Talk," the lieutenant said, though the word was slurred, with neither inflection nor emotion. "You ... talk ... through this one."

Colonel Jun's face had gone deathly pale.

"That's obscene," he said. Coming to his feet, he walked carefully over to the young woman, and reached out a hand to stroke her hair. She neither blinked nor flinched. Using one of his handkerchiefs, he wiped the spittle from her mouth.

"Can you hear me, Lieutenant?" Vex asked.

"Lieutenant . . . not hear . . . you . . . we hear you . . . instead."

"And who is 'we' that we might know you?" Colonel Jun asked.

"We . . . are the ones who remain . . . we . . . keep the place of . . . power."

"This pyramid?" Jun asked.

"Yes . . . place of . . . power."

"Is that what you've been programmed to do?" he asked.

"Programmed . . . we are . . . what we are . . . you are . . . very different."

"Yes," Jun admitted. "But I think we might be able to understand each other eventually. We didn't know how to contact you. Did you build this place?

"We . . . did not build . . . we . . . are the ones who remain."

"So you are not the Waymakers?"

"Waymakers . . . are the creator . . . we . . . are that which was created."

"And does that which was created serve the creator?"

"We . . . serve the creator . . . we keep the place of . . . power."

"What happened to the humans who came to this planet long ago? Their ship is on the beach not far from this pyramid."

"Those . . . were not the creator . . . they . . . did not suffice . . . all except . . . one."

Jun looked at Vex, who had been carefully watching the whole conversation. She motioned for him to continue, as the lieutenant's eyes did not seem to see any of them, and only blinked in a very slow, mechanical fashion, every thirty seconds.

"Who is the 'one' that sufficed?" Jun asked.

"She . . . came from your old world . . . she . . . is of the planet called . . . Earth."

"Earth!" Vex blurted.

"Yes . . . she . . . is the one . . . we know best . . . she . . . convinced us to open the . . . connections to your Waywork."

"Why?" Jun asked.

"We . . . do not know . . . only she . . . knows."

"The woman from Earth?"

"Yes."

"She still lives?"

"Yes."

Vex stopped Jun before he could ask another question.

"Will you free us?" Vex asked.

"Free . . . you."

"You're detaining us against our will," Vex said impatiently.

"Will . . . there is only one . . . will . . . and that is the will of . . . the creator."

"Is it the will of your 'creator' that we be kept here?"

"We . . . are not sure . . . we . . . will ask the one from . . . Earth."

"And what about the lieutenant?" Jun asked. "Will you release her to us, at the very least?"

"What are you doing?" Vex hissed.

"Like I said," Jun hissed back, "this is obscene. Look at the poor girl!"

"This 'poor girl' knew her duty, Colonel. And now she's our translator for these *sentinels* as you called them. We need her to be their mouth and ears."

"But at what cost?" Jun said. "Slavery to these revenants of Waymakers who've long since departed? To them, she's just a sack filled with meat! She's not a living mind as they would recognize. They've *repurposed* her!"

"Maybe. But they apparently hold this 'one' in high regard," Vex said. Then turned her attention back to the lieutenant—or at least, the lieutenant's body.

"Can you summon this woman from Earth?"

"No . . . she will come . . . when she is . . . ready."

"Does she live in the wreck on the beach?"

"Yes . . . where the others of her kind . . . once lived."

"Will you let us go if we promise to bring this 'one' back for discussion?"

"Cannot trust . . . your motives . . . you are . . . not known to us."

"If we bring the 'one' back, as promised, this might help you learn to trust us?" Vex suggested.

"Your kind is . . . so confusing . . . we understand our . . . creator . . . but your minds go in . . . so many directions."

"They got that right," Jun muttered, as he began to pace nervously.

Suddenly the Waypoint pilot's head jerked up, and her eyes fluttered with consciousness. The Key in her hand dropped to the floor, going dark. She looked around the room, then stared at Colonel Jun, and collapsed toward the old man, who caught her and gently settled her onto the floor.

"Make them stop," the young woman sobbed, clutching at her head, "make them stop, make them stop, make them stop... they're in my brain!"

Jun made comforting noises, while Vex stepped over and picked up the Key in one hand. If it was aware of Vex's presence, the Key didn't show it. She eyed the opening through which the Waypoint pilot had come a few minutes earlier; it remained open.

"Come on," Vex said. "Battle sergeant, you're in the lead. We're getting out of here."

"Something happened," Jun said, holding the young woman in his lap. "What caused them to release her?"

There was an echoing sound, very, very far away. Like an explosion, but so distant as to be little more than a muted clap of thunder.

"My God," Jun said, "has Ekk begun the orbital strike already?"

"No," the battle sergeant said, "that was conventional. Something's happening outside!"

He motioned for his men to follow, with Vex in the middle.

"Come on, Colonel," Vex urged. "If you have to, leave her."

"Go to hell, Kosmarch," the old man said.

"I could have you executed for saying that," Vex said plainly. "I could have your *family* executed too."

Colonel Jun's harsh laughter filled the room, making the soldiers on the end of the escape detail look back and forth between Vex and the colonel with nervous faces.

"You cannot touch me," he said, "and you never could. I came here to learn the truth about the Waywork, but *you* came here for the sake of your personal ambition. Neither of which is worth the price being paid by this young lieutenant. *You and I both owe her more than to just leave her here.*"

"Then pick her up and bring her," Vex said. "Or stay, and be at the mercy of the sentinels."

Jun struggled to get the lieutenant to her feet. She sagged on him uncontrollably, while her arms flopped limply. Two soldiers stepped back in and put the lieutenant's arms around their shoulders, and together they began dragging the Waypoint pilot out of the room. Jun slowly stood up, and walked to the exit, pausing where Vex stood. Her eyes burrowed into his, but his burrowed right back. No, this one could not be intimidated. It was rare to find anyone so reckless or so fearless, that he would challenge Golsubril Vex's authority. She had half a mind to order the old man shot once they returned to camp. But she still hoped to get some use out of him.

"We'll finish this later," she said, and allowed Colonel Jun to pass.

The troops—weaponless—double-timed their way through several hexagonal corridors, until they reentered the hall which featured the gallery of Keys. The sentinels had resumed their motionless resting state, though at different places around the hall. Vex eyed them carefully as she jogged past, then the whole team was trotting down the switchbacked ramp to the ground-floor corridor, which elbowed back to the main entrance corridor. As they neared the portico, they could smell the explosives from rifle rounds, and hear the irregular chatter of weapons being fired. Another horrendous boom made the bricks directly outside the portico shift unsteadily, raining sand onto the portico floor.

The battle sergeant and his men had grouped up at the portico, but didn't dare go beyond it.

"Madam Kosmarch," the battle sergeant said, "I cannot guarantee your safety beyond this point. Someone has engaged our forces from the camp."

"You mean, Starstate Constellar has engaged our forces?" Vex asked.

"I think that's the logical assumption, Madam," the sergeant said. "Without our wireless we can't ask for assistance. I've sent two of my men to quickly reconnoiter the ruins beyond the portico. We might be able to take shelter, and determine if there is a safer route back to camp."

# CHAPTER 41

IT HAD TAKEN THEM MOST OF THE DAY TO CREEP TOWARD THE pyramid, using the brick ruins for cover. In that time the aerospace plane had gone to orbit twice more, and returned with additional Nautilan soldiers, munitions, and equipment. By the time they were within striking distance, Captain Fazal estimated that at least sixty Nautilan troops were on the ground, compared to his thirty—which included the lieutenant commander, Mister Axabrast, Garsina herself, and Zoam Kalbi, who had only allowed himself to be brought along for fear of being left behind. He was most unhappy about being forced to participate in an offensive ground-combat operation. Even if he wasn't be expected to do any of the shooting.

Lethiah herself had come of her own free will, and didn't seem particularly bothered by the potential danger. Garsina kept watching the old woman out of the corner of her eye. Lethiah had the same kind of calm poise Garsina had witnessed among some of the matriarchs of the First Families—like Garsina's mother. Unafraid. But not foolishly so. Eyes wide open. Spine kept straight. Steps confident. She walked while others scuttled and crouched. Only allowed herself to duck when either Elvin or Captain Fazal demanded that she do so.

Garsina herself was scared almost to the point of being giddy. There was nothing in her experience which could have prepared her for what was about to happen. Unlike Kalbi, Garsina *was* armed—clutching the small carbine which Elvin had brought for her from the starliner, and which Elvin had retrieved again during the storm—though she felt horrendously awkward trying to mimic the movements of the TGO soldiers who surrounded her. They darted and zigzagged their way through the ruins. Using a movement pattern of cover-overlap which allowed the men and women behind the bounding formation to ensure that those going forward were not moving unsecurely. Like a slithering snake, the loose battle formation made its way to the edge of the ruins just as the sun dropped below the horizon. From there, Garsina and the others in the leadership council—as Garsina had come to think of it—made their plans.

"The aerospace plane hasn't returned," Lieutenant Commander Antagean said, using his binoculars to survey the camp on the pyramid's northwest corner.

Garsina's own binoculars showed several bivouacs erected within a perimeter that encircled the aerospace plane's landing site, which had been jet-blasted down to the stone. On that perimeter, Nautilan troops using big squad weapons—large-caliber, rapid-fire, high-capacity guns—had sandbagged in several defensive fighting positions. Including pieces of thick steel being used as overhead cover. The barrels of the squad weapons swiveled back and forth continuously, as the men in those fighting positions surveyed their respective quadrants.

"Gotta hand it to them," Captain Fazal said, "they're a pro bunch. I don't think I could have set it up any better myself."

"So what do we do?" Garsina asked.

"Our two advantages are darkness, and the fact that they don't have any air cover," Elvin said.

"Our single greatest disadvantage is that there are two or three of them to every one of us," Wyodreth Antagean said, putting his binoculars back into their case attached to his battle pack. "Which means any way you slice it, we can't take them on directly. We have to get their attention somehow, if we want a clean corridor to the pyramid entrance. And *then* we have to hope that they're not already inside."

"Unlikely," Captain Fazal said. "Posting troops inside would be the first thing I'd do, once the aerospace plane landing zone was secured."

"Which means they'd be shooting at us in a thoroughly unfamiliar environment with indeterminate possibility of cover or concealment," Elvin said.

When Garsina simply stared at the old man, he cleared his throat and said, "There would be no guarantee we'd find anything to hide behind."

She nodded.

"Which begs the question," Lieutenant Commander Antagean said, this time in Mariclesh, "what exactly is it that we're trying to *do* inside, that necessitates all of this risk?"

All eyes turned to Lethiah, who'd been watching the conversation, but not understanding any of it, until Wyodreth's last sentence.

"Out here," the old woman replied, "we are powerless. But in there? I can talk to the machines. It's not easy. I was never the kind of Anchor adept, as you've described to me—the people who have a natural talent for using the devices. It's taken me a lot of mental self-training and discipline, and then I've not exposed myself to the Anchors any more than I've felt is necessary. I saw what happened to those who did. I didn't want to lose my mind that way. But if we can get to the hall where the different Anchors are kept, I can convince the machines inside to intervene on our behalf. The power of the Temple will be—not exactly ours to command—but more likely to swing in our favor."

"What exactly *are* these machines, anyway?" Zoam Kalbi asked.

"I can tell you what they think they are," Lethiah replied. "The Others are who they think of as their creator. Singular. They don't really make a distinction, regarding individual Others. It's possible there may not have *been* an individual distinction? Some of my peers—before they died—speculated that the Others may have been a single intelligence shared across multiple sapient organisms. But the machines regard the creator as the source of definitive knowledge and guidance. The machines don't necessarily have a will of their own, as you and I understand it. There is what the creators want, and there is...everything else. Which is either interesting to the machines, or not. The only reason I was able to convince them to *finally* open starlanes to your Waywork was the fact that I got the machines interested in the potential destruction of the Waywork by an outside power. Not human. Not creator. Something new."

"Which is what *I* personally want to know about," Lieutenant Commander Antagean said. "And I think Admiral Mikton would too. DSOD will want explicit details on this outside threat. Assuming you can provide us with details."

"That's just it," Lethiah said, the whites of her eyes showing brightly as the moons of Uxmal began their slow journey across the clear night sky. "I can't be sure about details. I wish I could. I only know what the pyramid's own long-range sensors can tell me. They're tuned into the Overspace somehow."

"I thought the Waywork was the Overspace," Captain Fazal said.

"We think the Overspace is everywhere, all at once," Garsina responded. "The Waywork is merely a map of explicit travel paths opened on the 'surface' of the Overspace. Using these paths is an instantaneous process in our linear universe. But the Overspace itself goes far beyond the Waywork. We've been wondering if our Waywork is just one of many which might exist in the galaxy. Perhaps there are tens, or even hundreds, or maybe thousands of other Wayworks? Each one distinct from the others, built by either the Waymakers themselves, or other advanced species which have discovered how to manipulate the Overspace as the Waymakers have—using the Overspace as a kind of road bed."

Lethiah tapped the shadow of a finger to the side of her nose.

"My people and I reached the same conclusions, and the devices in the Temple support these deductions. It was while trying to monitor the extent of the Overspace—well outside of your Waywork, and far from anywhere men have ever traveled—that I noticed a problem. A *shadow* is occurring in the Overspace."

"What does that mean?" Garsina asked.

"Exactly what it sounds like," Lethiah said. "It wasn't there a few hundred years ago. But it's there now. And it's growing. Your Waywork hasn't noticed it yet, because your Keys are only useful for traveling the starlanes. But the shadow is growing near to you. If it overtakes you, it may destroy your Waywork, and the ability to rapidly travel from star to star with it. When I focused the Pyramid's conventional telescopes on this same region of the galaxy, I see hints that there may be a force at work in our linear universe causing the Overspace to unravel."

"Unravel..." Antagean said, with the same disbelieving tone he'd often used with Lethiah. "Why? For what purpose?"

"That I can't say," Lethiah said. "Only that proving the existence of the shadow to the machines in the Temple was a very long, very arduous project. Once I had their attention, they agreed with me that something ought to be done. But because they didn't have contact with their creator anymore, they didn't have any active guidance on how to respond to the shadow threat. So I suggested the starlanes—the Waywork—as a potential ally."

"If you'd have known about Starstate Nautilan beforehand," Elvin said, "you might have changed your mind."

"Even Nautilan may eventually prove a vital ally against the enemy I believe is coming," Lethiah said. "If what you've told me is true, Nautilan believes that only a united Waywork—beneath Nautilan's flag—can decipher the secret of the Keys, and open the Waywork to a wider galaxy. They're many days late, and numerous dollars short."

"Begging your pardon?" Antagean said, unfamiliar with the phrase. Which Garsina had never heard before, either.

"Right, sorry," Lethiah apologized. "I mean that Nautilan won't have *time* to unite the Waywork, before it's over. Severed from each other—unable to quickly jump the distance, star to star—humanity will be utterly vulnerable before the shadow. So it's important that you not only have advanced warning, but I also wanted you to come here. To this planet, in person. I can't use the Temple or its tools the way they might be used, to prepare for what's ahead."

"If everything you've told us is accurate," Garsina said, "*nobody* can use the pyramid—or what's inside—for very long, without it proving harmful. To our bodies, and our minds."

"This is true," Lethiah said. "But it's the only thing I have to give you all. I'm the last of my people. Perhaps, even, the last woman from Earth. I can't fight wars for you, nor can I defeat your enemies. But I can point you to the tools you might need, to do the fighting for yourselves. And *that* is why we have to go in there."

Garsina felt the force of Lethiah's words, and could sense their effect on the others. Antagean was still skeptical, but sobered enough by the possibility of a threat outside of the Waywork to take the matter seriously. Captain Fazal was an infantryman who understood clear objectives, and the will to take them. Elvin was a fighter at heart, who'd served Starstate Constellar and Family Oswight with equal fidelity. Garsina herself was not a fighter, but realized nothing in the universe remained stable forever. If this shadow had not come to disrupt the Waywork, something else would have done it. The time for humanity to be unleashed had arrived. That opportunity was worth more to her than her own life. Especially if it meant potentially keeping the power of the Waymakers out of Nautilan hands. Where it would surely be abused, to the detriment of all.

They talked more, about tactics this time. Captain Fazal used a dim, red light from his combat pack to illuminate the dust at their feet. He drew lines and symbols in the dust, explaining himself to his men, as well as to the leadership council. He would make a feinting attack on the bivouacked landing site, drawing off the attention of the Nautilan troops, while Antagean—with Axabrast acting in the role he knew best—made for the pyramid's portico. Any enemies discovered inside would be Antagean's and Axabrast's to handle. To make the feint truly effective, Fazal couldn't spare any of his men.

Zoam Kalbi was left to choose which team he wanted to be with.

The little infotainer—glasses forgotten for the moment—had sulked all evening. If he'd found the expedition fascinating or fun to that point, now that it came down to actual shooting, the man's mood had soured considerably.

"I've said it before," he groused, "we're working against Starstate Nautilan when we ought to be working *with* them."

"Enough of that nonsense," Elvin snarled. "If you won't actively help us, then you can stay here. On your own. Whatever happens to you is not our problem."

Kalbi took several deep breaths, then mumbled about going with Antagean's group.

"Fine," Elvin said, "but you stay the hell out of our way. There will only be five of us, with just two armed."

"Three armed," Garsina said, holding up her carbine.

"Lady," Elvin said, "we never did get around to showing you how to use that properly."

"I'll have to learn on the job," she said.

"By my side, Lady, please," Elvin implored her.

"Of course, Elvin. Of course."

"I think it's settled, then," Lieutenant Commander Antagean said, and put out his hand—a mere shadow in the light of the moons—to Captain Fazal. Who shook it.

"No wireless is going to play hell with our ability to talk to each other," he said.

"That's a disadvantage both sides will have to deal with,"

Wyodreth said. "I think once you hit that camp, there'll be no question on our part—as to when we should run for the pyramid entrance. After that, we'll have to depend on Lethiah. Captain, don't feel inclined to stay and spectate. Once we're inside, and you and your men have had enough fun for one night, make a hasty retreat for the wreck. They won't be able to successfully track you through the ruins until morning, at which point you and your men ought to have gone to ground. We'll either have been able to do something with the machines inside, or not. If the answer is 'not' then... well, dammit, Captain, I can't say much more than good luck."

"May God favor the bold and the free," Fazal said.

"Victory with honor, hurrah, hurrah," the entire group said quietly amongst themselves—save for Kalbi, who merely prepared himself to follow wherever Antagean and Axabrast led.

Hours crept by, as Captain Fazal carefully moved his troops to where he wanted them. Despite the moonlight, the ruins made for excellent cover. The security on the wire at the aerospace landing site never seemed to notice, if ever they detected any movement. Eventually, all of the TGO personnel were gone, and their weapons and equipment with them. Leaving Garsina to stare at the portico with the others. She saw no movement of any kind from within, though the light coming from the interior was quite noticeable. In fact, with the ruins being a warren of shadows, the portico was now the brightest thing in any direction.

"Uh-oh," Wyodreth said.

"What's wrong?" Garsina asked.

"I'm looking over at the camp. There's a squad moving out toward the pyramid. Maybe ten people. I hope Captain Fazal sees that. If they get to the entrance before we do..."

The answer to the lieutenant commander's question came a few moments later, in the form of antipersonnel rockets which lanced from the ruins—at least a kilometer away from Garsina's position—and struck the bivouacked landing site along the length of its perimeter. A loud, automated warning horn began to blow, down on the landing field itself, and dozens of troops began to spill from the bivouacs out toward the sandbagged defensive positions, which opened up with their heavy weaponry. The cracking stutter of the big guns could almost be felt, even this far from the landing site. Little arcs of tracer fire—bullets made luminescent in the darkness—speared at the ruins, from which the rocket attacks had come.

Suddenly, a second set of rocket attacks blasted from the ruins, even father away from Garsina's position than the first. The unguided missiles hit one of the sandbagged security positions, several shots at once. The sandbagged hole went up in a fireball which illuminated the night sky for several seconds.

"That detail headed toward the pyramid is double-timing back to help their comrades," Wyodreth said, with no small degree of satisfaction. "Remind me to put Captain Fazal in for a commendation. Meanwhile, Mister Axabrast. Shall we?"

"Aye, lad," the older man said, drawing his sidearm. "Lady? Mister Kalbi? Madam Lethiah?"

Antagean went first, with Lethiah on his heels, Kalbi in the middle, Garsina behind him, and Elvin bringing up the rear. Garsina crouched and ran at the same time, remembering having watched the TGO troops do it earlier in the day. Then realized nobody else was crouching, and simply stood up, putting one foot in front of the other as fast as her legs would carry her. The moonlight shining down on the ruins in front of the portico made it plain that there would be nowhere to hide. They'd be fully exposed for at least the last fifty meters. And they still didn't know what waited for them inside.

"Go, go, go," Elvin said to Garsina's rear as she pumped her legs, the bandolier of ammunition slapping uncomfortably across her chest, and the carbine feeling heavy in her hands. She was careful to keep her fingers away from both the trigger and the safety while she moved. The last thing she wanted was to accidentally shoot herself, or anyone else in the remaining leadership group.

Wyodreth went into the portico first. Almost immediately, there were shouts, screams, and the sound of the lieutenant commander discharging his battle rifle. The shots were like physical impacts on Garsina's ear drums, and she cringed, resisting the urge to slap her hands over her head. With Elvin close behind her, she crowded into the portico behind Kalbi and Lethiah, who were crowded behind Antagean, who was angling his weapon down the length of the corridor at the backs of several fleeing people. Three bodies lay on the illuminated floor—their blood staining the hexagonal pattern of glowing lines which spread a diffuse light throughout the hexagonally cross-sectioned space. They'd each been struck at neck level, where their armor didn't cover.

Elvin aimed his sidearm over Garsina's shoulder and discharged several shots at the fleeing enemy, which *did* make Garsina drop her weapon—to dangle by its sling—so that she could slap her hands over her ears.

Elvin then quickly swiveled his head to look to their rear, and reversed himself—aiming back the way they had come. Garsina thought she saw a flicker of movement in the ruins. Several more shots erupted from Axabrast's sidearm, and two human-shaped shadows toppled out of the darkness. They awkwardly pawed forward half a meter, then collapsed completely. Not to move again. Elvin grunted with satisfaction, and ejected the magazine from its housing within the weapon's single, use-worn handle. Without looking, he removed a fresh magazine from its perch on his gunbelt, slapped the magazine into the sidearm, worked the sidearm's action, then turned his attention to the men Wyo had killed.

Antagean stared at the people lying on the floor of the entrance. They didn't look any different from Constellar troops, save for the fact that their uniforms were a different style and a different color. They were also young, and male, their eyes staring in empty surprise at the alien ceiling. Almost as if the last thing they had expected, at the pyramid's main entrance, had been an enemy officer using a rifle.

"How many?" Elvin demanded.

"Didn't ... didn't count them," the lieutenant commander said, still staring down at the bodies. His eyes were large, and he looked sick.

Elvin—for once—took pity on the man.

"It's a terrible thing, lad," he said. "And you won't be able to make it okay with yourself for a while. Just keep moving, see? We've come this far. Don't let the gears seize up in the engine now. Keep moving, keep moving, keep moving."

Antagean literally shook his head, swallowed several times, seemed to hear the ongoing battle at the Nautilan aerospace site not far from the portico, and said, "Right. Sorry. Uhhh, okay. Sorry. Let's go."

Elvin slapped the lieutenant commander on the shoulder, and the businessman's son, who'd turned soldier, stepped over the dead, and trooped off down the corridor. Lethiah—who didn't seem bothered by the bodies at all—followed, then Kalbi after her. The infotainer seemed even more horrified by the sight of the dead Nautilan troops than Wyodreth had been, and he had to be prodded to continue.

"Follow Antagean!" Elvin roared, pushing the small man in front of Garsina, "or we leave you behind!"

Kalbi moved, but his actions were robotic. Forced.

Garsina moved too. Seeing the blood was something she knew she was never going to forget. It had been fresh, and dark, filling the air with a slight coppery sent. Who those young men had been, and where they had come from, Garsina would never know. As Elvin had patiently explained to her, back aboard the starliner, good people did bad things to each other in war. It was just the way of things. You couldn't stop and judge it in the moment. Forces were at work, well above the consciences of single men. Though single men—and women—would bear the burden for those deaths well beyond the battlefield.

They reached a right angle in the corridor. Beyond appeared to be two ramps, one of them switchbacking down, and the other switchbacking up.

Everyone was panting.

"Did ye notice?" Elvin said.

"What?" Garsina asked.

"No weapons on those unlucky fellas."

She hadn't thought about it before, but what Elvin said was true. The bodies at the portico had been unarmed. Antagean must have fired in pure reflex. Would Garsina have done the same?

"Up or down?" Wyo demanded of Lethiah.

"Up," the old woman said. For someone claiming to be her age, she was remarkably quick on her feet when she wanted to be.

"Those switchbacks could be deadly," Wyo said.

"We'll cover you," Elvin said, nudging Garsina, who brought her carbine up in both hands—still being careful to keep her fingers away from the safety, and the trigger.

"Okay," Wyo said, looking at her, then her weapon, then back at her. He nodded once, which got a similar nod from Elvin, and then the lieutenant commander was spinning around the first switchback, with Elvin and Garsina directly behind. They pointed their weapons straight over him, as he went up the ramp, and then crouched at the landing for the next level. Garsina and Elvin followed Antagean up, then all three of them peered around to the next ramp, which Antagean sprinted up again, waiting at the next landing, and so on, and so forth. If the Nautilan troops were going to make a stand of some sort, they certainly weren't going to do it here. Garsina was thankful, simply because for every level in the ramp they cleared without resistance, she didn't have to do anything more deadly than sprint.

At the ramp's top, a huge hall revealed itself. Like the rest of the internal parts of the pyramid, light shone from a hexagonal pattern in both the floor and the ceiling. This light reflected off the metallic casings of what Garsina could only describe as machinery built in the vague mold of insects.

"The machines," Lethiah said.

Only, they didn't seem to move, nor react to anything else going on around them. As for the Nautilan troops who'd been encountered earlier, they scattered. All save for an old man who'd crumpled ten meters away. He was on all fours, coughing and gagging horribly, with a handkerchief clutched over his mouth. He paid no attention to Antagean as the lieutenant commander approached, his battle rifle raised to the shoulder. The DSOD Reservist stopped one meter away, and said in Mariclesh, "If you don't surrender, I will shoot you."

"Shoot him anyway," Elvin growled.

Now the man on the floor looked up. His face was wrinkled, pale, and sweaty. A trail of blood led from the corner of his mouth, down his chin, and leaked across the front of his uniform.

"Starstate Constellar, in the flesh," the old man wheezed in Mariclesh, with a surprisingly clean accent.

"According to Constellar Law of War, I am taking you into custody, Colonel," Wyodreth said. Garsina didn't know how Antagean knew the Nautilan man's rank, but guessed it had something to do with the little pins and insignia on the man's uniform. Which wasn't fantastically different from the uniforms DSOD troops wore, except for the fact that the old man did not use armor.

"Doesn't matter whose custody I am in now, I am as good as dead," he replied.

"Lad, we don't have time for this," Elvin said.

"No, wait," Lethiah said, leaving the top of the ramp to

walk over to where the Nautilan officer still kneeled. She knelt at his side, and used one of the handkerchiefs he'd dropped on the illuminated floor to wipe the blood from his face. Then she helped him to stand.

"Much obliged, madam," he said, still using Mariclesh. Then he put both hands on her shoulders and squared her to him. His eyes got large.

"You must be the 'one' they talked about," he said, almost reverently.

"Who is they?" Lethiah asked.

The Nautilan officer motioned an arm weakly about them, aiming a finger first at one of the machines, then at another, and then another still.

"You talked to them?" Lethiah said, her own eyes getting big.

"More like, they talked to us," he said. "Through a poor young Waypoint pilot who's mind is now jelly because I was foolish enough to bring her here, hoping she could help me divine the secret of the Waymakers."

"Where are the others? Where are their weapons?" Wyodreth demanded.

"Too swift for me, as you can see, Lieutenant Commander. Regarding our weapons, the sentinels took care of that. Though I don't know why they bothered. Armor-piercing bullets never even scratched them."

"You *shot* at the machines?" Lethiah said, her mouth hanging half-open.

"Not me personally, woman, my men! Well, the Kosmarch's men, anyway. I was never anyone's idea of a foot trooper. Which is now more obvious than ever. So if it's a prisoner you want, it's a prisoner you have, Lieutenant Commander. For as long as the cancer lets me live. Which might not be long."

The old man started coughing again, making wretched noises as he doubled over, spitting blood onto the floor.

Garsina looked around her, at the spectacular machines which dominated the hall. They were huge, intricate in design, yet imposing, and oh so alien.

"Will they hurt us?" Garsina asked Lethiah.

"Difficult to say," the old woman replied. "We never shot at them before."

"If you *are* the 'one' they talked about," the Nautilan colonel said, "you have a place of special status in their strange hierarchy. It's one thing to guess about the motivations and intentions of the Waymakers—I've been doing that most of my adult life. It's another thing entirely to parley with one. Or at least, parley with a Waymaker representative."

"What did they say?" Lethiah asked.

"We confuse them, as much or even more so than they confuse us. But they seem to think you're special."

"Can you do what you need to do?" Wyo asked the old woman. "In this room?"

"I should be able to," she said, and walked quickly to where a collection of different Keys were all recessed into compact platforms which appeared to sprout from the floor itself. She walked up and down the rows, looking for something, then shouted an obscenity that Garsina did not understand, save for the specifically profane way in which it was shouted.

"It's gone," she said.

"What's gone?" Elvin asked.

"The Anchor I use to talk to them. It's a specific one. It's the only one I've ever had any luck with."

"Was it smaller than most?" the Nautilan officer asked.

"Yes."

"I am afraid my kosmarch scooped that up. That's the one our Waypoint pilot had in her hands, when she was being pulled by the sentinels' strings."

"I don't understand," Garsina said. "Why can't you just use another?"

"I've never had any of the Anchors go missing," Lethiah said. "If I knew how to use any of the others, I would. But I've never had any success. There's just the one, and now it's gone."

Antagean's hands gripped the handle on his battle rifle so hard, Garsina could hear the polymer squeaking in complaint. His jaw was particularly prominent—even more than normal—with muscles flexing up and down both sides of his face.

"What do we do now?" he asked.

Which was when the bullet hit him squarely in the back.

# CHAPTER 42

*DAFFODIL* HUNG JUST OUTSIDE THE EFFECTIVE RADIUS OF THE Waypoint, awaiting its commander's final go-ahead for crossing. There was no visible sign that this region of Uxmal interplanetary space was any different from the rest of the system. In fact, none of *Daffodil*'s conventional sensors could detect that the Waypoint was even there. Only the Waypoint pilot could tell, and relay his instructions to the ship's conventional pilot, who gently pushed the picket ship with occasional bursts from the reaction control thrusters.

Admiral Mikton's stomach was beginning to recover, despite the lack of gees. She watched the tactical hologram over her head—reclined as she was, sitting forty-five degrees to the angle of the deck—and pondered what she was about to order *Daffodil*'s commander to do. Once they executed the Slipway crossing, there would be no going back. In an instant, they'd be over the light-years of distance separating Uxmal system from Jaalit system. Sitting squarely in Nautilan space. A Constellar ship pretending to be a Nautilan ship, which she clearly wasn't to anyone who could make a visual inspection. She'd be depending on her dummied-up identification system telling the Jaalit security flotilla that *Daffodil* was another vessel entirely. That, and having enough distance between herself and the flotilla proper that visual identification would be impossible before *Daffodil* was on her way.

The new plan had seemed even more straightforward, in Admiral Mikton's mind, than the old plan. Instead of trying to fake out the security flotilla with nine bogus signatures, *Daffodil* would try to do it with just one. And—assuming they passed out of range of the flotilla unscathed—get a chance to penetrate deep into Jaalit system. Which Constellar intelligence actually knew very little about, beyond the usual planet-finder charts which every Starstate military kept on every other nation's planetary systems. You could tell a lot about a place, even at light-years of distance, as long as you had the correct satellite telescopes for the job.

Once they'd penetrated to the inner planets, there would be targets of opportunity. Including Jaalit itself, which was not—so far as any Constellar chart showed—clement. It was a small, rocky planet perhaps two-thirds the size of Planet Oswight, and possessing negligible atmosphere. Which meant most of Jaalit's vulnerable infrastructure would be subterranean. Beneath hundreds or even thousands of meters of rock.

So, skip Jaalit. Focus on hitting something else. Where would the shipyards be? All systems had them, either for routine docking and repair or for large-scale construction, as was the case with Planet Oswight and its moons.

Anything big and soft—meaning, it had a high potential price tag attached to it, and it wouldn't fight back—would be begging for *Daffodil* to shoot one of her nuclear-tipped launches. But of course, once that happened, the ruse would be over. *Daffodil* would be exposed. And while her ability to wreak havoc might go unchecked for minutes, or even hours, eventually Jaalit's comprehensive defense network would catch up with Admiral Mikton, and that would be the end of the mission.

*Mission,* she thought, almost laughing at the word. It wasn't any kind of mission. It was a stunt, designed to spook Starstate Nautilan so badly they would delay sending more ships to Uxmal space before Starstate Constellar had sent additional reinforcements to Oswight and Uxmal space alike. Zuri had no official approval for her plan. No one outside of *Daffodil*'s captain and crew knew about it. If the captain and crew were nervous, they kept their anxiety to themselves. She would not—could not—blame them. After all, she would be taking them on a one-way trip. *Daffodil* was too small and fragile to survive the pounding of an extended interplanetary fight. It would take just one nuke, with not even a particularly high yield, to blast the picket ship to bits.

So, Zuri hesitated. At the final moment of maneuver execution. With *Daffodil*'s captain peering at her from his own gee chair, where he floated gently against his restraining straps.

"Problem, ma'am?" he asked.

"We never did identify the ship ahead of us," she said.

"No, ma'am," Captain Garmot said. "Does it really matter at this point?"

"Probably not," Zuri replied. And kept staring up at the tactical display.

Ordering the ship home would be easy. Simply instruct the Waypoint pilot to choose Oswight space, versus Jaalit space. Let the *Daffodil* link up with Iakar's force once again—for the first time in weeks—and allow herself to be transferred to one of Iakar's corvettes, which would speed her back to Planet Oswight for treatment at a DSOD groundside facility with all the drugs Constellar's DSOD medical procurement officers could buy. To sit comfortably in a gurney, day after day, waiting for her body to recover from the brutalization it had received. As damaged nucleotides potentially spawned little cancers, over and over again, until one day, her immune system would no longer recognize friend from foe, and the cancer would be allowed to grow. Spread. Make her sick. Put her back in the hospital again, until they could dump even *more* drugs into Admiral Mikton's body, trying to fight a disease of its own making.

Or...

*Daffodil* would go out with glory. She'd talked Garmot over to her way of thinking, and Garmot's word was law on the picket ship. Once Zuri told the Waypoint pilot to execute, it would happen.

But there had already been so much death. Multiple ships and crews lost. Men and women who would never go home to see their families again. *Daffodil*'s modest compliment was all that remained of Zuri's force—save for the Antagean liners, which were still taking their chances in the inner system, with Nautilan's destroyers. Was it worth it to take these men and women to their graves? Such a tiny crew. Not like *Catapult*'s, which had been far bigger. What did the lives of individuals matter, weighed one for one? And would Zuri be judged rightly or wrongly for her decisions, when it came time for her to answer? Whether it was an actual God with a beard and robe—as imagined by some of Chaplain Ortteo's contemporaries—or the consciousness of the universe itself, as Zuri sometimes imagined it. The ebbing and flowing of so much life energy. Countless organisms being born, living, and dying. Short lives. Long lives. Each and every bit of it cosmically connected to all the rest somehow. The universalists insisted that it was possible. The Waywork itself was possible only because a kind of space literally above and beyond ordinary space existed. Was that where souls came from, and to which souls eventually returned? Zuri couldn't make herself believe it all ended with nothing. She refused to accept the model of a pointless universe, where entropy and randomness ruled. But she wasn't convinced it was a designed thing, either, with some supernatural version of a human being perched on a throne, overseeing the entire thing. Picking and choosing sides. That didn't seem enlightened at all.

So, if God did exist, what was a third option? Could God at once be a real manifestation of the sum total of the universe's living essence, but also a unique, individual mind capable of seeing, hearing, and feeling what was going on in the cosmos? Even down at the granular level, where ordinary men and women dwelt? Little people with little lives, who were just trying to get through their days?

Would God notice, or appreciate, what it was Zuri was about to do?

Or were the radiation meds simply playing with her emotions, making her giddy at the moment of truth?

"Admiral," Captain Garmot said sternly.

"My mother always said the universe hates a coward," Zuri whispered to herself, then she sat up straighter in the gee chair, cleared her throat, and ordered, "Captain, begin broadcasting identification codes on Nautilan bandwidth. Waypoint pilot, execute Slipway crossing to Jaalit space."

As had happened during the crossing from Oswight space, the moment of travel—one place in the galaxy to another—was accomplished in less than the blink of an eye. Which left a kind of false afterimage in the mind, like a funny taste that's barely eluded the tongue.

"Did we come out where we think we should?" Zuri asked.

"Checking the stars now," Captain Garmot said. His command module crew was silent, their faces stoic. A few of them were sweating, even though the command module wasn't warm.

"Yes, ma'am," the conventional pilot reported. "Charts indicate we are in fact in Nautilan territory, vicinity of the Waypoint in Jaalit space.

"Passive scan," Captain Garmot ordered. "Tell us what the situation is."

The tactical hologram over their heads remained blank for a few moments, then began to slowly populate with signatures. Many more than Zuri would have expected for a security flotilla guarding a system like Jaalit. Unless—

"Damn," Zuri said, instantly intuiting what had happened.

"Four cruisers, four destroyers, at least a dozen support craft." Captain Garmot read off the bad news as their tactical computer figured out the configuration for the new ships.

"How close?" Zuri asked, and used her gee chair keyboard to zoom the tactical display view in until it focused exclusively on their immediate vicinity.

"Good God," Garmot said, "they're almost collocated with us."

"We're getting screamed at to vacate the Waypoint," the communications officer reported. "And on open channels too."

"If we can make them out, they can make us out," Zuri said. "But they haven't fired yet. The code box is confusing them. They're seeing one thing, but their computers are seeing something else. Captain, deploy the launches. I don't care what you shoot them at, just shoot them!"

"Copy that, Admiral!" the *Daffodil*'s skipper said.

In the void of space, weaponized, automated, miniature interplanetary spacecraft—originally intended to be messenger ships—split away from the *Daffodil*. At a distance measured merely in thousands of miles, the launches ignited their fusion motors, and flashed toward their targets. Which did not, at first, recognize the launches as hostile. *Daffodil* had literally popped out of the Waypoint into the middle of the Nautilan follow-up force, which was getting ready to make the crossing to Uxmal space—having aggregated over the past few weeks at Jaalit's Waypoint. It had taken major logistical muscle movements to shuffle so many big ships in such a short span of time. And it was, Zuri suspected, merely the first of many such relief efforts, designed to solidify Nautilan's hold on the Uxmal system.

Antagean's starliners would never have a chance.

Suddenly *Daffodil*'s threat alert began to blare across the command module.

"We've got weapons in space, hot," said the tactical officer—the only one aboard the ship, who often did double duty as a reactor specialist.

"Targeting us, or the launches?" Captain Garmot asked.

"Impossible to say at this distance, sir."

Zuri watched the tactical hologram. The launches raced to meet their targets, like spears thrown with the fury of tiny suns. Their signatures mingled among the many red icons which identified the various pieces of the Nautilan fleet.

Suddenly, a cloud of antimissiles cluttered the tactical view.

"We're too close," Captain Garmot said. "All of us packed in too tight."

"Which hurts them, and helps us," Zuri said.

"Antimissiles!" Garmot commanded. "Deploy at will!"

*Daffodil*'s supply was relatively miniscule. Nowhere close to the number necessary to eliminate all the warheads which appeared to be incoming. But with so little space between all the individual ships, the chance that one or more of the Nautilan warheads would proximity-detonate next to a Nautilan ship was tremendously increased.

"Give them something to *really* panic about," Zuri said. "Dump the rest of your nuke magazine!"

Garmot opened his mouth to give the order, but the single man at the weapons station had already done the deed. *Daffodil*'s remaining warheads—just ten total—were hurled into space, seeking randomly assigned large targets. With this many Nautilan ships so close, it was going to be almost impossible to miss. The point-defense systems would be firing like crazy.

Balls of light bloomed in the tactical display.

"Hit, and hit, and hit," said the tactical officer.

"Which ships?" Zuri asked.

"Uhhhh," the officer said, and couldn't answer.

Individual, much smaller spheres of light appeared, and were gone, as Nautilan antimissiles and Constellar antimissiles sought out and destroyed their targets.

"Hit again," the tactical officer said.

"That's four," Garmot said. "Any kills?"

"Impossible to say, sir. We're continuing to score hits. Five. Six. Seven..."

The number of inbound warheads looked like a wall of wasps

constricting on the *Daffodil*. Garmot's antimissile barrage would thin them out somewhat, as would the railguns. But there were simply too many. Meanwhile, Zuri could see two of the Nautilan cruisers, three of the destroyers, and at least two of the other ships blinking in the tactical hologram—as the computer tried to figure out their status. The launches had worked. As in Uxmal space, Nautilan's antimissile and point-defense computers weren't programmed to recognize anything as large as a launch as a weapon.

If any of the follow-on nuke launches had done the Nauties damage, that was to be determined. *Daffodil*'s ten-warhead volley was still tied up with the cloud of antimissiles. With so many large and small contacts so close together, it was a wonder the antimissiles could function at all. Zuri had never engaged so many ships, so abruptly, in such a small area.

In the relative darkness of deep space, at the edge of Jaalit's domain, the Jaalit Waypoint had become a tiny pocket of hell. Debris from destroyed and damaged ships, missiles, antimissiles, the repeated firing of railguns, all expanded outward from the sphere of battle, like a smoke ring. The Nautilan fleet, which had been tidily formed and queued for Waypoint crossing, was now in disarray. Surviving ships had fired their main reactors and were attempting to clear the area. Especially the support ships, which were more ill-prepared than any for the unexpected fight.

*Daffodil* was only moments from certain obliteration.

Zuri hoped desperately that it would be worth it. She used her gee chair keyboard to activate the shipwide speaker network.

"This is Admiral Mikton." Her voice reverberated throughout *Daffodil*'s interior. "Thank you for your service, ladies and gentlemen. On behalf of my command. And also on behalf of the DSOD. Starstate Constellar survives, because people like you are willing to hold the line. Be proud of yourselves, in this moment. Be proud of who and what you are."

"Victory with honor!" Captain Garmot shouted.

"Hurrah, hurrah!" the command module crew responded back.

Five different Nautilan nukes simultaneously made it through *Daffodil*'s point-defense, and detonated within a hundred meters of the hull. There was no moment of terrible realization for the crew. One instant, the ship was there. The next? She became a white-hot point of fusion fire in the vacuum of space. The shockwave traveled outward, taking the molecules of vaporized steel, titanium, aluminum, polymer, flesh, and bone with it. Other nukes in the relative vicinity, sympathetically detonated. Competing shockwaves roiled the mix. Which didn't touch the Waypoint at all. But simply added to the existing mess of debris which would make the space in the immediate vicinity of the Waypoint a dangerous mess for weeks. Possibly months? Eventually the Waypoint would shift beyond the battle site, since it did not orbit Jaalit's home star the way everything else did. But until that happened, any ship attempting to cross was going to wind up with a severely compromised shield dome. Not to mention secondary damage from anything that hit below.

# CHAPTER 43

WYO HAD NEVER BEEN SHOT BEFORE. THE SENSATION, THROUGH his armor, felt like being clubbed in the spine. He went down hard, gasping. Other shots filled the hall with loud echoes, and the little group of Constellar people scattered. Wyo himself barely had the sense to drag himself behind one of the motionless machines—the sentinels, as the Nautilan colonel had called them. Peering past, it was difficult to tell from where in the hall the shots were coming from. It was a big space, and the acoustics didn't lend themselves to identifying a specific direction in which to look. His ears rang badly. The shots had seemed impossibly close!

There, he could see a small group of Nautilan troops hiding behind one of the machines, just as Wyo was. He thought he saw a single woman with them. Though he couldn't be sure. If they'd been unarmed at the pyramid entrance, they were apparently armed now.

Looking in a different direction, Wyo could see Lady Oswight and Elvin Axabrast crouching at the top of the ramp, using the ramp's wall for cover. Lady Oswight was hurt. How badly, Wyo couldn't tell. She clutched at her side, and there appeared to be blood on her fingers.

The Nautilan colonel was dead. A bullet had burrowed into his skull. He lay motionless on the floor, the light from the hexagonal pattern illuminating vacant eyes.

Lethiah and Zoam Kalbi were gone.

A bullet suddenly *panged* off the metal of the machine behind

353

which Wyo lay. The alien device didn't move, but Wyo did. He got on all fours and bolted across the hall—over the dead colonel's body—and rolled to the top of the ramp, where he joined Axabrast.

"Where's Lethiah?" Wyo asked.

"Bloody hell, lad, Kalbi's got her! He's the one who shot you and the Lady, here. As well as killed our former prisoner."

"Kalbi?" Wyo said incredulously. "He wasn't even armed!"

"Son of a bitch pulled out a small pistol and started pulling the trigger. If I'd not grabbed Lady Oswight and thrown us both back toward the ramp, she'd be dead now."

"Lady, how badly are you hurt?" Wyo asked.

"I'm in a lot of pain. I think a couple of ribs might be broken. But the zipsuit kept the bullet from fully penetrating."

"Good thing it wasn't a rifle bullet," Wyo said, then asked, "Is there any other way out of here?"

"I think the ramp is it," Axabrast said. "And we're guarding it."

"I don't understand," Wyo admitted, still feeling like he'd had the wind knocked out of him. After a few moments, he got enough breath in his lungs to shout, "Zoam Kalbi! You bastard! You won't get out of here alive!"

"Wrong, Lieutenant Commander," the small man's voice said—though the echoes made it impossible to tell from which direction. If he had Lethiah, he was hiding her.

"You murdered a prisoner of war," Wyo shouted, "plus attempted murder on a First Family heir, and a DSOD officer! That's a guaranteed death sentence from any court in Starstate Constellar, military or civilian!"

"It's simple, Antagean," Kalbi said. "We're surrounded by Starstate Nautilan's forces. Both inside the pyramid, and also in orbit. You bet our lives on the idea that Lethiah could use one of the Keys in this hall to change the equation. She can't do that because Nautilan has the only Key Lethiah knows how to use. Now *I* have Lethiah, and I am wagering I can use her to bargain with Nautilan for a settlement."

"A *settlement*?" Wyo said incredulously.

"I've said it several times, Lieutenant Commander. We should have tried to work with Starstate Nautilan, not against them."

"But you're a Constellar citizen!" Wyo yelled.

"Allegiances to Starstates are meaningless, Antagean. You'd

know that if you were in my line of work. One way or another, Starstate Nautilan is going to own it all—the entire Waywork. It's just a matter of time. They already control this planet. You're just too stubborn to admit it. I am taking my fate out of your hands, and getting myself a better deal."

"Nautilan won't deal," Wyo said. "No matter what leverage you think you've got."

"Lethiah is all the leverage I'll need," Kalbi said. "She's able to communicate with these things. And this place. That makes her valuable. You need her, and Nautilan needs her. I gain nothing by working with you. I gain a great deal by working with Nautilan. You'll be fortunate if they take you prisoner, Lieutenant Commander. I on the other hand, am now in a position to broker for myself a superior option."

"Lunatic," Axabrast muttered.

"Or too smart by half," Wyo said coldly. "Where in the hell did he get a weapon? I never once saw him carrying."

"I only got a glimpse of it," Axabrast replied. "Looked like a sleek semiauto, specifically designed for concealment."

Very far away, back down the ramp, the noise from the battle outside could still be heard.

"Nautilan officer or sergeant!" Kalbi's voice shouted in Mariclesh. "Can you hear me?"

"Yes, I can hear you," replied a woman's voice, also in Mariclesh.

"Your colonel said you were looking for the 'one' who could communicate with the Waymaker machines in this structure."

"We are," replied the woman.

"My name is Zoam Kalbi. You may or may not know who I am, depending on how much Starstate Nautilan monitors Constellar's public media. I have what you want. I have the 'one' as the colonel called her. Are you in a position of authority to treat with me?"

"I am Kosmarch Golsubril Vex of Starstate Nautilan. On this world, and also the planet Jaalit, my word is absolute."

"A kosmarch!" Kalbi said. "It surprises me that someone of your stature would risk coming to this place. But it doesn't matter. Can you guarantee my safety?"

"That greatly depends on whether or not I am able to communicate with my general officer in orbit. If he begins to suspect that the situation here on the ground has gotten out of control, he may follow my final directive, and take drastic action."

"Have you had any more luck with your wireless than Constellar?"

There was a pause, then the kosmarch admitted, "No."

"Then I offer you the 'one' in exchange for full political immunity—for myself. I have no quarrel with Starstate Nautilan, and never did. As an informationalist, I have traveled all over Starstate Constellar, and many places beyond. I know what the future of the Waywork looks like. I intend to be on the right side of history."

"Kalbi, you idiot!" Wyo shouted in Mariclesh. "When you think you've got what you want, they will just shoot you and take Lethiah anyway!"

"Not true," Vex said. "I will honor our agreement. The woman, for full immunity. It is a reasonable arrangement."

"What about your general, Kosmarch?" Wyo said to Vex. "What does 'drastic' look like?"

"Nuclear bombardment of the entire site," she said.

"What about the ark?" Wyo asked.

"Human artifacts are not as valuable to me as this Waymaker facility."

"Even if the pyramid survives, there's no guarantee that you will."

"This is true," she said. "But your future is even less certain."

"We control the only way in or out of this hall," Wyo said. "You can't get outside."

"Soon, my men from the aerospace landing zone will gain the upper hand. Once their perimeter is resecured, they will enter the pyramid searching for me. You won't have a chance against so many soldiers. Neither will your surviving Constellar troops outside. Not unless you surrender."

"Like I told the traitor Kalbi, I don't believe you'll keep any agreements which might be made. When you have the opportunity, you will simply kill us all, and take what you want. As Starstate Nautilan always does."

"Who are you?" Vex asked.

"Lieutenant Commander Wyodreth Antagean, Constellar Deep Space Operations and Defense. Kosmarch, I know you don't have any weapons. These machines—the Waymaker sentinels—took them from you. Kalbi has Lethiah, who can talk to the machines. But you have the Key that Lethiah needs. I can't allow Lethiah, or this Waymaker installation, to fall into Starstate Nautilan's hands. If I have to, I will kill every single person in this hall to prevent that from happening."

*What are you doing?* Garsina mouthed at Wyo, her teeth clenched in pain.

Wyo held up a hand, begging off. Then looked at Axabrast, who seemed to get the hint.

"Aye," Elvin said loudly. "'Tis a good night for sheddin' Nautie blood. And it would be a fine trophy, adding a kosmarch to my score."

"Nobody seems to be interested in what *I* have to say on the matter," said a different female voice. Lethiah's, using Mariclesh.

"You are the person who can talk to the Waymaker machines?" Vex asked, from the other side of the hall.

"I am," Lethiah said.

"Let me see you."

Kalbi slowly shuffled out from behind a column, with Lethiah by the arm. He appeared to have his pistol pointed into her ribs.

The kosmarch also stepped out from behind the motionless sentinel she and her people had been clustered behind. She produced a small Key, which lay dormant in her hands.

"There are a great many opportunities I could offer you," the kosmarch said. "Service to Starstate Nautilan can come with many rewards."

Lethiah's laughter was scornful.

"Your enticements amuse me," she said, "but as I've already explained to the lieutenant commander and Lady Oswight both, there is far more at stake now than the petty battles between your rival nations. The entire human race—what you know of it—is now in jeopardy. I don't care about what you can offer me, Kosmarch. I've lived long enough to learn that material things and physical ease are empty things, when you've got nothing left to hope for. *Ouch*, quit that!"

Kalbi had jabbed the barrel of his small pistol into Lethiah's side.

"Do we have a deal, Madam Kosmarch?" Kalbi said. "Immunity, for the woman?"

"Consider it done," Vex said.

Wyo reflexively raised his weapon to his shoulder, and sighted on the kosmarch. Who seemed to be ignoring him, except for the small flicking of her eyeballs as she switched her gaze from

Lethiah, to Wyo—who still remained partially hidden by the wall of the ramp—then back to Lethiah.

"Don't," Kalbi warned. "If the kosmarch gets shot, Lethiah dies too. I think I know enough about you, Lieutenant Commander, to be sure that you won't risk this old woman's life. Nor will you kill her outright, not even to keep Waymaker technology out of Nautilan hands. That's just not the kind of man you are."

"Do you really want to test that?" Wyo said, rapidly switching his aim from the kosmarch to Kalbi instead. "How about I shoot you, before you can shoot her?"

Kalbi tugged Lethiah in front of him, so that only his eyes and the top of his head were visible to one side, and the brandished pistol to the other. Wyo no longer had a clean shot.

What could he do? More importantly, what *should* he do? He momentarily moved his head to look over his shoulder—at the Lady, and her majordomo. They both looked anxious.

"It's a sour pickle, lad," Axabrast admitted with a whispering voice. "There may not be a right answer here."

Wyo snapped his head back to position on the rifle, his cheek pressed tightly to the stock, while his shooting eye peered through the small scope mounted to the rifle's receiver. An illuminated target reticle surrounded Lethiah's chest. When he switched his aim back to the kosmarch, the image through the scope blurred, then came back into focus with the reticle over the kosmarch.

Back and forth. Back and forth.

How ruthless did Wyo want to be? He could easily shoot the kosmarch, then shoot Kalbi after Kalbi had shot Lethiah. Or try to shoot at Kalbi, and probably hit Lethiah instead. Then shoot him after Lethiah had hit the ground. As long as Lethiah wasn't able to use the Key in the kosmarch's hands, the pyramid might remain an enigma for Starstate Nautilan. The colonel had said that a Nautilan Waypoint pilot was driven mad attempting to use the pyramid's Keys. If even a Key-trained, Key-adept person couldn't handle this technology, it might frustrate Nautilan to no end.

But then, what about Lethiah's warning? What if the pyramid—and everything in it—was the best chance the Waywork had for devising a defense against whatever it was Lethiah suspected might be destroying Waymaker Overspace? Possibly taking the worlds of the Waywork as well?

"Outside," Wyo finally commanded.

"What?" Kalbi said.

"Everyone is going outside, *right now*."

Wyo shifted his aim slightly, and pulled his trigger once. The bullet cracked out—incredibly loud—and caromed off the pillar Kalbi had been previously standing behind.

Kalbi and Lethiah both flinched. As did the kosmarch. But Kalbi didn't pull his trigger.

"Do that again, Lieutenant Commander," Kalbi warned, baring his teeth for the first time, and shoving his pistol against his hostage.

"Do as he commands," Vex said. "Our agreement is valid, Zoam Kalbi. But only as long as the woman remains alive."

"What's the plan?" Axabrast hissed.

"There is no plan," Wyo hissed back. "I'll think of one on the way down. Unless you think of one first, okay?"

Wyo shifted his feet, and began to carefully walk—rifle aimed the entire time—around the hall, until Kalbi was between himself and the top of the ramp.

"Mister Axabrast, Lady, would you both be so kind as to escort the kosmarch and her entourage?"

The majordomo complied, keeping his sidearm aimed at the Nautilan group until they were between Elvin and the top of the ramp. Garsina carried her carbine one-handed, with the other hand still held over her wound. She was even less sure of herself—with the weapon—using one arm than she had been with two. But it did make for a sufficient incentive to get the Nautilan troops moving, with their kosmarch in the lead.

Sudden movement among the Waymaker machines made Wyo stop cold. Garsina gasped, pointing back to the hall. Without taking his finger off the trigger, Wyo waited and listened as he heard the sounds of mechanisms *whirring* behind him.

"What are they doing?" Kalbi asked Lethiah, still using her for a shield.

"It's difficult to say," Lethiah said. "But if I had to guess, I'd say they intend to follow us."

"Why?" Kalbi asked.

"I don't know. Something has attracted their interest. It could be my presence. Or it could be the Key in Golsubril Vex's hands. Or both? It's not like you can stop them. Vex's soldiers discovered that fact, firsthand."

"Will they attack?" Vex asked.

"Why would they?" Lethiah replied. "For them, this is all just observation."

"Ignore it," Wyo said. "Keep going."

The entire group—Vex and her men, followed by Kalbi with Lethiah, then followed by Axabrast, Lady Oswight, and Wyo—went down the ramp. As did the sentinels, who trailed quietly. Wyo chanced a look over his shoulder, and was shocked to see that the machines did not walk or roll. They floated. About half a meter off the floor. That *whir* he'd been hearing was apparently some form of repeller or gravity nullifier, which allowed the robots to move without touching the ground. Human engineers had been trying to invent something similar for the entirety of the Waywork's existence. With no success.

Near the bottom of the switchbacks, the sounds of combat outside grew louder.

"I told Captain Fazal to retreat into the ruins," Wyo said softly.

"Something might have gone wrong," Axabrast replied, also softly.

"I told you," Vex said loudly enough so that everyone could hear, "once my men on the outside have resecured the perimeter, they will be coming for you."

So, Vex understood native Constellar dialects, in addition to Mariclesh. Wyo made himself a mental note to *not* make any more sidebar comments.

They walked, down, and around, then down, and around, until the ramp ended, and they were making the elbow to the main corridor once more. If Lethiah seemed frightened, she didn't show it. The old woman had an uncanny ability to appear unfazed, even when the situation was dire. Or perhaps she really was unfazed? Wyo got a sense from her that everything which transpired—all the drama—wasn't worth getting upset about. Either this was a kind of uniquely heightened perspective, afforded by extreme old age, or Lethiah had simply stopped giving a damn. He remembered her unhappy expression, when she'd talked about how the men of Earth—seeking immortality—should have been careful what they wished for.

It suddenly occurred to Wyo that Lethiah had absolutely no fear of death. None whatsoever.

When they got to the portico, Wyo ordered them out—the new morning sun having barely risen over the horizon.

A quick glance told him that several of the sandbagged fighting positions on the aerospace landing zone's perimeter had been destroyed, but there were still Nautilan troops roaming about, so Captain Fazal hadn't been successful dislodging them; if that had even been Captain Fazal's intent. Since the man had clearly not fallen back to the ruins, per earlier agreement with the lieutenant commander, he was either taking a new course of action based on his own initiative, or the Nauties had flanked Fazal's men, and the captain was trying to avoid being exterminated down to the last man.

Without wireless, there was simply no way to tell.

Columns of black smoke were drifting up into the sky, both from the landing zone and from two places along the edge of the ruins—where Fazal's men had hidden the night before, and from which they'd launched the first rocket attacks.

There was no one—not Constellar, nor Nautilan—guarding the pyramid's entrance.

"Forward," Wyo ordered. "Into the ruins."

"What exactly are we doing out here?" Vex asked.

Wyo put a round into the dirt by her feet.

"Don't stop moving," he commanded.

Garsina's face looked at him, confused. He shook his head once, and waved her off. He couldn't tell her what he had in mind, because the truth was, he honestly didn't know. And when the Waymaker machines followed him out into the sunlight, he realized they were going to keep following him wherever Lethiah—or the Key, or both?—were taken. He just had to try to keep Kalbi from pulling that trigger, while also having Kosmarch Vex under his control. If Lethiah had been Kalbi's bargaining chip, Vex was going to be Wyo's. If it came down to having a discussion with Nautilan military leadership.

A roar in the sky announced the arrival of the aerospace plane. It circled the pyramid once, then activated its vertical takeoff and landing nozzles, for a final approach to the Nautilan camp. Two streaks of white smoke speared out of the ruins— much farther away from Wyo's position than Wyo was from the pyramid's portico—and soared straight for the aerospace plane, which hovered perhaps fifty meters off the surface as the pilot attempted to gently set the craft down.

Then, the pilot saw the threat. Or his systems did. The aerospace plane's turbofans suddenly kicked in, and the craft started to move forward again. But the maneuver came several seconds too late. One of the guided rockets hit the left wing, while the other guided rocket hit the cockpit. Two explosions happened at once, and the aerospace plane tilted over, doing a crazy spiral on one set of nozzles only, until it had done four whole revolutions around the landing zone—jet wash throwing men around like rag dolls.

Then, what was left of the damaged wing touched the ground. The aerospace plane rolled onto its back and smashed across the tops of several bivouacs.

The explosion was tremendous. Hydrogen fuel tanks—meant for return to orbit—ruptured. The slush hydrogen, now exposed to sources of heat and oxygen, turned the entire camp into a gargantuan fireball that ballooned up into the sky. When the fireball had cleared, the entire camp was ablaze. Men. Bivouacs. Equipment. Weapons. Ammunition. Everything.

Elvin Axabrast cut loose with a throaty cheer.

"Your TGO has sealed our fate," Vex said coolly.

"What does that mean?" Kalbi demanded.

"It means her people in orbit are probably watching, and they're going to see that explosion, and assume the worst," Wyo said. "Do I have it right, Kosmarch?"

"Yes," Vex said. "My destroyer group carried just one aerospace plane. Its destruction will be interpreted as catastrophic by the commanding general of the squadron. There is now no way for him to retrieve anyone from the surface, nor send down additional reinforcements to replace our losses. His only choice will be to ready and launch the missiles, per his orders."

"How long?" Kalbi asked, the pistol now dangling limply in his hand at his side. His eyes had turned entirely to the sky.

"Minutes," Vex said. "Depending on how long it takes for General Ekk's tactical officers to correctly analyze what has happened, and report."

"Isn't there anything you can do?" Kalbi demanded, walking over to the kosmarch.

"Without wireless to orbit? This place—those Waymaker devices—seals our fate, as much as General Ekk's orders from me. It would take me thirty seconds to confirm that I am alive and well on the surface. Ekk will only see the imagery of the destroyed camp."

"Is there anything *you* can do?" Kalbi said, turning his attention back to Lethiah.

"What do you suggest?" she asked.

"Make those...things, stop blocking the wireless!"

"The problem is not the machines, but the Temple itself," Lethiah said.

"We have to signal them! Tell them to stop the attack!"

"If there had been more time," Vex said, "we were planning to set up a message laser at the landing site. But that's not going to be a problem now."

Kalbi's frantic anxiety was almost comical, except for the pistol he still held in his hand. He waved it about erratically, not caring who he swept with the barrel. Elvin and Wyo both kept wincing every time the little weapon went anywhere near Lady Oswight, or themselves.

"So that's it," Wyo said, looking up into the blue sky. "As soon as your destroyers are in position, they launch. And this entire place—the wreck, the ruins, and pyramid—gets glassed."

"Essentially," Vex said.

"It's such a waste!" Garsina said, sitting on a small pile of baked mud bricks, still holding her wound with one hand. "We came here to learn about the Waymakers, and we found so much more. To just throw it all away seems maliciously stupid."

"Especially if what Lethiah told us is true," Wyo said. "We need this place—need her knowledge—to get ready for the big war."

"What are you talking about?" Vex asked.

"If you'd talked to Lethiah at all, you might know. She's found evidence that something is coming into this part of the galaxy. Something that might tear the Waywork apart. It's enough to make even these machines sit up and pay attention. But that doesn't matter anymore, because the pyramid is soon going to be a radioactive hot potato. And the one person who seems to know more about all of it, than any of us, will be dead. Lethiah, you said you worked very, very hard to convince the machines that they should create new Slipways to the Waywork. I am afraid we—the Starstates—have done you wrong."

"You've done yourselves wrong," Lethiah said flatly. "In many ways, my life ended a long, long time ago. When I first came to this place, and we learned there would be no future for humanity here. I'm not worried about me. I *am* worried about what will happen if the Starstates refuse to unite against a common enemy."

Wyo and Elvin maintained their guard. But the looks on the

faces of the Nautilan soldiers said it all. They knew what was going to happen. No ability to fight. No time to run. Kalbi may have devolved into a nervous wreck, but those troops...not so different from DSOD personnel, Wyo thought. There would be no histrionics. The men of Starstate Nautilan would die with dignity.

Vex herself seemed like an ice cube. Her eyes saw everything through a lens of dispassion. There was a calculating mind behind those eyes. Wyo had sat across from people like her during contract negotiations. She would seek the path of maximum corporate benefit, but if she felt there was nothing to be gained from concessions, she would happily sink the entire deal.

"Let me see the Anchor," Lethiah said to the kosmarch.

"The what?"

"She means the Key," Garsina said.

"Why?" Vex asked, holding the object tightly between two palms.

"In your hands, it's useless. In my hands? perhaps there is still a chance."

"Like what?" Kalbi demanded, waving the barrel of his gun in her face.

"Give it to her," Wyo ordered, motioning to Vex with the barrel of his rifle.

"No!" Kalbi said, turning his pistol on the lieutenant commander, and pulling his trigger. This time, the hammer felt like it hit Wyo in the sternum. He stumbled backward, trying to keep his rifle up, but all the wind had been knocked out of him for the second time in the same hour. He thudded to the ground, his face to the sky, and thought he heard Axabrast shout, "Enough of this!" and then there were other gunshots—and not just Kalbi's.

There was an intense pain in Wyo's chest. He reflexively took one hand off the rifle, and reached it up to his chest, seeking the blood. But there was nothing to feel. His armor had absorbed the small pistol's energy, though there would be a wicked bruise on Wyo's chest, to match the one he already had on his back.

"Dammit," Wyo croaked, and rolled onto all fours. He raised his head to see scuffling. Axabrast, with Lethiah, and the kosmarch, rolling on the ground. Kalbi simply lay nearby, trying to take breaths through a mouth filled with blood. There was a hole in his stomach that pumped blood into the dust around him, and his pistol lay safely out of reach.

Garsina had her carbine up—safety distinctly off this time—aimed at the Nautilan troops, who kept their hands up, and backed away from the three people rolling around on each other in the dirt. Wyo tried to make himself bring his own rifle up, but the pain in his chest was too intense, and without being able to breathe, his only thought was on trying to draw air into lungs which had decided to momentarily not work.

Suddenly, Lethiah rolled out of Golsubril Vex's grasp, and leapt to her feet. The Key was in her hands. She raised it over her head with one hand, and the Key immediately illuminated from within.

The Waymaker machines clustered around Lethiah, attentive.

Like all Keys, this smaller one became translucent when activated, with a still smaller sphere of glowing geometric patterns within. Lethiah barely blinked as she focused all of her attention on the Key, and the sentinels seemed to focus all of their attention on Lethiah. When the kosmarch got to her feet and tried to intervene, one of the Waymaker machines blocked her, so that the sentinels closed in around Lethiah, until only Wyo, Garsina, and Lethiah were within the sentinels' circle.

"What's she doing?" Garsina said, lowering her carbine, and going back to one knee. If her ribs hurt half as much as Wyo's sternum, it was a wonder she could even stand at all.

Wyo struggled to his feet, feeling air return to his lungs, and watched. Lethiah didn't move. The Key merely took on an added intensity, as the light coming from inside it brightened perceptibly. The Waymaker machines were silent. If they thought or planned anything, it was impossible for Wyo to tell. They had been faceless and implacable since he'd first seen them, and as long as they did not try to directly harm anyone, he wouldn't worry about them.

But something was clearly happening for Lethiah. Her eyes had gone wide now. So wide that the whites were fully exposed all the way around her pupils. But she wasn't looking at Wyo, or Garsina. She wasn't even looking at the sentinels. She was somewhere else. Her mind bent on other matters.

"Can she hear us?" Garsina asked.

"I don't think so," Wyo said.

"Keep your distance, lads," Wyo heard Axabrast say, outside the circle.

The muscles along Lethiah's neck strained to the point Wyo thought they might snap.

Then, Lethiah exhaled slowly, and said, "I think it's worked."

"What worked?" Wyo asked her, staring at the illuminated Key still in Lethiah's hand, raised high over her head.

"The Anchors aboard their ships in orbit...I was able to use my connection to the machines to convince them that the Anchors posed a threat. The machines still don't have any regard for themselves, as individual entities. But I convinced them that the Anchors currently orbiting this planet were threatening the larger picture, regarding the shadow that is growing on the Others' Overspace. They elected to terminate those Anchors."

"Terminate...a Key?" Wyo said. "How is that even possible?"

"It's not, for us," Lethiah said. "But for the machines, Keys are just another kind of machine. When a machine stops functioning correctly, and becomes dangerous, you destroy it."

"But that doesn't do anything to the ships," Wyo said. "Or does it?"

After a few more moments, several bolides appeared in the sky overhead. Followed by several more. And then, a host of burning daylight meteors appeared, each one more brilliant than the next.

"What happened?" Garsina said, looking up at the spectacular morning fireworks display.

"Whatever the Keys did—when they terminated—it seems they took the destroyers with them. Those are pieces of ships burning up in the atmosphere."

"The Anchors store a *lot* of energy, even when not in use," Lethiah said. "Terminating an Anchor releases that energy."

Wyo stared at the old woman, framed against the backdrop of the arched ribs of her former ark down by the shore. Then he turned back to stare at the pyramid, where untold power still remained. Dangerous power, with disastrous potential? Or, not. Much depended on who used that power, and for what, and why.

For the first time, Golsubril Vex let out a moan—watching the chunks of her ships enter and burn up in Uxmal's upper atmosphere.

Lethiah slowly lowered her arm, and the Key returned to its dormant state.

The Waymaker machines also parted company, allowing Lethiah to step between them as she pleased. Wyo followed her, helping Garsina to her feet, and they came up behind Axabrast, who held the remaining Nautilan soldiers under guard.

"What do we do now?" he asked the lieutenant commander.

Wyo thought about it. If the destroyers—formerly in orbit—were gone, that meant the risk for Captain Loper and his starliners was gone too. But they didn't have any way to notify Captain Loper of this change, nor did they have any way to reach orbit. More seriously, the dangerous nature of Uxmal itself remained. How might their proximity to the pyramid be damaging their bodies? Specifically, testes and ovaries? Lethiah had said she didn't know how long it took, before sterility was permanent. Did Wyo want to live the rest of his life without being able to have kids? For that matter, did Lady Oswight? She—above them all—had a vested interest in continuing the family line.

But they wouldn't know for sure until they'd actually gotten off the surface, and could see a real doctor.

Meanwhile, the kosmarch was still his prisoner. If Nautilan was moving—or had moved additional assets into Uxmal system—he'd have to use her for leverage. Either buying time until Starstate Constellar could rally enough forces to break Nautilan's hold on Uxmal interplanetary space, or brokering some kind of arrangement, with Vex serving as currency. Surely a kosmarch carried high value with Nautilan military planners? They'd think twice about trying to take Uxmal again, as long as they knew Vex was in Constellar's custody.

"I think we need to find out who—if anyone, from Captain Fazal's group—we have left," Wyo said. "Then, we'd better see if Lethiah is willing to let us use her home back at the ark, for both temporary headquarters and a temporary brig. I think we're going to be here for a while. At least until Captain Loper—or Admiral Mikton, or *somebody* else from Starstate Constellar—can send additional ships.

"But I am getting ahead of myself. Mister Axabrast, how good are you at bandaging ribs?"

"As good as I need to be, lad," the old man said, looking at Lady Oswight—whose hands were wrapped around Wyo's supportive arm.

"As good as I need to be."

# EPILOGUE

IT WAS A FULL WEEK BEFORE THE OSWIGHT YACHT RETURNED
to Uxmal space. When she did so, she brought with her a dozen
small frigates, corvettes, and one aerospace carrier ship, which
had all been hastily shunted to Oswight space, once word got out
that Admiral Mikton had gone over the Slipway to secure the
new system. If they had been expecting immediate Nautilan resistance, they found none. Nor did they find any trace of Admiral
Mikton, or her command. They passed through the outer reaches
of Uxmal system, noting the various signs of battle, and leaving
several of the corvettes to begin salvage operations—specifically
looking for the Keys which had been scattered through Uxmal
space like pearls.

Once arrived in orbit around Uxmal proper, they found
three Antagean starliners in good working order, and a grateful
Antagean captain, who'd been driving himself to distraction over
the fact that he had no way to bring any of the people on the
surface back to his ships. Nor had he been able to communicate
with them, despite the fact that the Nautilan destroyers which
had been guarding Uxmal against all comers had disappeared.

The site of the pyramid had been under constant surveillance
since the Antagean ships had returned from their exile in orbit
around the big jovian world near the system's sun. They'd sent
down as much equipment and as many people as they could, using
emergency pods, and the one or two drop modules they could
manage to return to serviceability. But with wireless completely

out, once anyone dropped to the surface, there was no way to know anything. No status report from below.

When three aerospace planes did depart—laden with people and supplies—they carefully flew over the entire pyramid site, noting the scorched crater where the prior Nautilan landing site had been, and chose instead to put down well far of the pyramid itself, on a flat stretch of exposed rock that formed a low cliff overlooking the sea on the far side of the huge, old wreck which dominated the beach opposite the pyramid.

Lieutenant Commander Antagean was there to greet them when they dropped their boarding ramps. As were a small handful of other DSOD personnel, some of them TGO by the looks of their weapons. There was also a crusty old former colour sergeant—pressed back into duty at the lieutenant commander's behest—bossing the enlisted.

Captain Loper, of Antagean Starliners, was the first man down, almost running to greet his boss at the edge of the makeshift landing field.

He hugged Wyodreth—whom he'd known since boyhood—until the lieutenant commander begged off, citing recent injury to his chest, which still hadn't fully healed.

"Damned glad to see you," Captain Loper said enthusiastically.

"Not nearly as glad as I am to see you," Antagean said.

"I'm sorry I didn't come down sooner. Did the stuff we sent—with the people—help?"

"It all helped," Wyo said. "But I think we might have a bigger problem on our hands. It's not safe here, Captain Loper. Not for any human. What's more, the one person we've been relying on to give us answers—about this place—is dying."

"Dying?" Captain Loper said. "Not Lady Oswight!"

"No, not her. But Lady Oswight's been working *with* the dying person around the clock, to try to absorb as much knowledge as she can before the end."

"Who is this person?"

"Somebody older than you and me put together, times a hundred," the lieutenant commander responded. "Would you believe me if I told you she was the lone human survivor we found on this world? And would you believe me if I told you she was from Earth?"

"No," Loper replied.

"Well, there's time yet for you to be convinced, like I was. I just hope Lady Oswight is successful learning what she needs to know."

"What's so important about that?" Loper asked. "We've got time to study this place now. Really dig in, and find out what's what."

"Not nearly as much time as you think," Wyo warned, "and then Lady Oswight may be the only one left who will know how to make the connection."

"Connection to *what?*"

Lieutenant Commander Antagean's arm and finger pointed back to the land—at the slab-sided, sharp-angled, pristine pyramid.

# ACKNOWLEDGMENTS

BOOK TWO SYNDROME. MY MENTOR MIKE RESNICK TALKS ABOUT it. My editors at Baen suffered through it with me. This book began on one military deployment, and has since been finished on yet another. A lot of my struggle stems from the fact I was a short fiction guy before I successfully tackled long work. Retooling for long form has been—and continues to be—a process. I learned a lot while doing *A Star-Wheeled Sky*. I hope my fans from my previous Baen novel—and my continued short fiction output—have enjoyed what I've done here. *Star-Wheeled* contains a lot of ideas packed into a single volume. So many ideas, in fact, I worried endlessly that the ideas might swamp the characters. Similarly, I worried that characters who organically grew over the creation of the story, would become so prominent as to dwarf others. Ultimately, I vacillated most on deciding where to stop. Because there is a lot more "there" there. Having peopled the stage, and set the drama in motion, where does it all go? I hope you will be with me to find out.

Meanwhile, I want to acknowledge friends and family who've been essential since 2015. Larry Correia, Mike Resnick, Mike Kupari, Dave Butler, Kevin J. Anderson, and Sarah A. Hoyt—for being my inspiring and encouraging colleagues beneath the Baen banner. Annie O'Connell-Torgersen, and Olivia Torgersen—the best wife and daughter a Book Two Syndrome sufferer could hope for. Dave Doering, Blake Casselman, and DawnRay Ammon—for always making me feel at home in the Intermountain West genre convention scene. And to Martin L. Shoemaker, who has been my colleague in the pages of *Analog* magazine—a man who somehow knows just the right thing to say, at just the right moment when I need to hear it. Thank you, everybody.